I Know
We Are Better
Than This...

...but you'd never know it by

the worsening culture wars

By B. R. Allen

First edition

Paperback ISBN: 978-1-7342363-0-9

Ebook ISBN: 978-1-7342363-1-6

Table of Contents

Foreword

Let me start this book with an admission of who I am not. I will say up front that I am not a learned scholar. I am not a famous professor with a long list of degrees. I am not a famous politician trying to convince anyone to vote for me. I am not a talking head on a cable news channel trying to hawk my book and purporting to be an expert. I am not an evangelist trying to convert others to a certain way of thinking and believing. I am not a radical with an agenda to radicalize other people. I am not a philosopher intent on explaining esoteric ideas.

No, I am an average guy who was passionate about writing early on in my school years but set that desire aside for several reasons: to have a more predictable career to make enough money to raise a family, to live a happy, peaceful life, and to be a contributing member of society. Recently, I decided to write a book to speak my mind as a concerned American citizen. I have no expectations or aspirations of becoming a famous writer. The purpose of this book is to point out some things that are occurring in our country and our world that we should pause and examine to determine if where we, as a culture, a country, and a global community are heading in the right direction. Perhaps I should have titled the book "What the Hell is Going On?" because there are some puzzling things happening out there.

Some of what is written in this book may reassure readers while some facts may anger readers; some things we will agree upon, while we will agree to disagree on some topics – and that's OK. While some of my thoughts may be considered controversial to some, I have learned that if we venture outside our sphere of influence and comfort zone, we can often understand other viewpoints and grow as a person.

My intent is not to denigrate or offend anyone, but to examine other ways of looking at things. It is healthy to exercise our open-mindedness. Even if I don't change a person's mind about an issue, that's OK by me. My goal is to share various points of view.

There are some things and positions that people are so hardened about that they will never be convinced otherwise, but to be able to look at and consider other viewpoints is a valuable personal asset. To be close-minded, in my view, is a sign of weakness and stubbornness that can be a personal detriment. We must listen and think in order to learn.

One of the beauties of reading is to get us to think and imagine. Reading can entertain us. Reading can make us feel emotions. Reading can take us to another place or time. Reading can challenge us to contemplate other ways to interpret something or look at things differently. It stimulates the brain in a far more productive way than semi-consciously staring at the TV or sitting for hours playing video games.

Much like reading, I find that the writing process challenges me. It forces me to get my thoughts together to explain what I think in a logical fashion so that others are able to understand my perspective – and hopefully find it interesting or thought-provoking.

Sometimes I have a battle in my brain where one thought is countered by another thought, which is countered by yet another thought. The result of this thought process is to examine all possibilities and come to some conclusion in a rational, coherent form that can be put down on paper (or more fittingly, my laptop). Readers can consider the thoughts discussed in this book and come to their own conclusions.

Through any search for knowledge, and before our minds are made up, we must gather information and then examine the veracity of what we find. Skepticism can be a good trait when the goal is to ferret out the facts and find the truth. When we blindly accept something as a fact, we are only deceiving ourselves. When we want to believe something because of an emotional connection, that is a fast track to being misled. Conversely, if we unbiasedly stay the course and follow the facts in our journey to find the truth, the final destination is enlightenment.

I am not seeking an emotional reaction, although some parts of the book will elicit different feelings from different groups of people. As I stated previously, I see some things happening that really need our attention, and these issues, I think, are worthy of examination.

In this book are observations of what I see going on in our communities, our country, and our world. Some of the topics cover political ideology. Some of the subjects cover who we are as a society and where we came from, and why or how we have gotten ourselves in some of the messes we are in. This book is a collection of essays on various issues rather than being a single-topic book.

Introduction

Now a little about me. I grew up in a Baby Boomer Christian home, raised by parents who were some of the finest people anyone could have ever met. I was lucky to have them, as were my two brothers. In high school, college, and into my late twenties, I would characterize myself as center-left in terms of political and social philosophies. My parents were strongly Democrat.

As I entered into marriage, a career, and having a family, my tendencies began leaning more toward the center, and now I consider myself a right-of-center independent conservative. My view of the world evolved, much like a lot of other people's. If our viewpoints don't evolve, then we are probably not willing to listen to or consider other perspectives. Again, in my opinion, close-mindedness is a sign of weakness and stubbornness.

My first introduction to conservatism was when I had to do a school project in my early teens on the election in 1964. I was assigned to write a paper on Barry Goldwater's candidacy and his view of politics. With no exposure to Republicans and conservative thoughts, I was intrigued by some of Goldwater's ideas, but I never thought much more about it through high school and college. I maintained a left-leaning political viewpoint. Liberalism seemed to be cool to me at the time, but there were specific things that were pervasive across liberalism that ran counter my personal beliefs. I had trouble justifying those things and began to realize that many of my foundational principles did not coincide with liberal ideology; however, I stayed the course.

My first presidential vote was cast for Jimmy Carter who I thought was a good and decent man - and I still think so today. I registered as a Democrat, mostly because that's how I was raised. I voted Democrat for a few election cycles, again mostly because that is how I was raised.

When it came time for the election in 1980, out of curiosity, I began listening to some of Ronald Reagan's speeches and was surprised to realize that I agreed with most, if not all, of his political positions. I thought he was on the right track by calling for lower taxes since I was struggling to make ends meet with a wife and family to support.

I agreed with him that we had too many bureaucrats and that a smaller, less intrusive federal government made sense. I liked his position that the government needs to stay out of our lives, and it should be limited in its power over the electorate. He also supported states' rights and the fact that local government was far more effective and efficient than the federal behemoth that was being created in Washington DC., and I agreed with him on that as well.

President Reagan supported a strong military. That made sense to me because of the rise of the Soviet Union, Communism, and the early days of Middle East conflicts as is also evidenced in the Iran hostage crisis. All those threats were concerning to me. I viewed all that as a threat to our freedom and global stability. It seemed to me that the strength of our nation was undeniably critical in maintaining some semblance of peace in the world. In fact, I began to realize that this was ultimately a battle between good and evil. Mr. Reagan characterized it that way. I fully supported him on having a strong military because it was critical for global balance.

When the time came to vote in 1980, I was never more sure of who I would vote for. Mr. Carter was a good man as I have mentioned, but I felt our country desperately needed what Mr. Reagan offered, and that his views were far more closely aligned with my views. Of course, Mr. Reagan was elected, gaining the biggest defeat of an incumbent president in our history. He then went on to win a second term in the largest landslide ever, and I am pretty sure the likes of which will never be matched again.

Mr. Reagan won the battle of bringing down the Soviet Union and freeing hundreds of millions of people without a single missile being launched and not a single shot being fired. This was because of our superior military strength. His strategy was pure genius and it was one of the greatest accomplishments of any president in any country ever. A strong military and six words liberated people from a brutal and oppressive regime: "Mr. Gorbachev, tear down this wall." It's interesting to note that his staff strongly encouraged Mr. Reagan to not use that line; in fact, it had been taken out of the speech. But he had a strong conviction and was compelled to put the power of those words out there for the sake of those that were living under Soviet rule. Those words worked magic and a powerful regime was toppled resulting in hundreds of millions of people being set free over the next few years.

In fact, to further note President Reagan's influence on the entire world, thirty years after the wall fell in 1989, the number of people living in a country with democracy rose from 2.3 billion to 4.1 billion. That means, for the first time, more than half the people on Earth live under democracy in 2019 and the number continues to grow. It all began when President Reagan uttered his famous words.

During President Reagan's tenure, the economy boomed because of the initiative to lower taxes… which he drove. Unemployment was low and people had more money in their pockets – what's not to love about that? President Reagan's conservative policies, some of which were not passed during his two terms, were later adopted. He pushed for a balanced budget amendment, which never happened during his terms, but it set Congress on a course to actually accomplish this feat during the Clinton years. Because of conservative spending principles pushed by Reaganite Newt Gingrich and a willing Congress, the budget was balanced.

President Reagan turned me into a Conservative, and I have never looked back. His values aligned with mine. He pushed family principles. He spoke of higher morality. He spoke of individual responsibility. He spoke of American exceptionalism and patriotism. He did not dwell on the past like so many

4

politicians. He did not look back at things we did wrong - he focused on the future, solving problems, and doing what's right. He was a great communicator, a strong leader, and one of our greatest presidents. In my humble opinion, anyone who does not agree with that is just plain wrong. Results matter more than someone's biased opinion of President Reagan.

With those conservative principles now firmly embedded in my political views, I have never regretted my decision to leave the Democrat Party. I am a conservative, first and foremost. The Republican Party, which leaned more towards conservatism, is how I have generally voted. However, I have had my differences with them, too, which is why I maintain my political party independence.

On social issues, I do have some strong feelings about certain things, but I generally lean towards the philosophy of "you are free to do and think as you want, as long as you don't bring harm on anyone else through your actions, and you stay within the moral framework established by our Constitution and our societal norms." I believe that if we stray too far away from what has made us great, we venture into dangerous territory.

My view is that if people want to put tattoos all over their face and body or pierce their body anywhere and everywhere, they certainly have a right to do that. If a man wants to fall in love with another man, or woman with a woman, I don't care. If individuals don't cause harm to anyone or force anyone else to adopt a certain lifestyle, they can do what they want. However, when people choose to go way beyond societal norms, they risk isolating themselves from other portions of society – that's just how it is. I believe that there are always consequences for behavior, and everyone must be held accountable.

I will examine a variety of subjects such as morality, our country's history, climate change, hate speech, radicalism, social media, technology, feminism, our educational system, prejudice, liberalism, socialism and world issues.

Being able to have freedom and do what we want within the framework of social norms is a major part of what makes our country great. We have had our flaws in the past, but the world would be a different place had these United States not come through in supporting liberty and freedom, not only here, but throughout the rest of the world. We are a strong and unique nation, but there are areas where we need to improve. In my opinion, some of the things we do as a country and the behavior of some portions of the population are beyond acceptable social norms.

We need to turn down the volume and readjust our tone in political and social debate. We will never all agree on everything, but if we listen to each other, show decency and respect for differing opinions, maintain decorum, and understand other viewpoints, we will all be a lot better off. The political chasm that divides our country is inching wider, and it's driven by increased intolerance rather than more tolerance.

We must all accept the fact that we are humans - we are not perfect. I know we have a lot of work to do, and we must correct our course periodically. Because there are some really senseless things going on that should not be happening, we need to address our problems and manage our disagreements more sensibly.

I, like many other people, am worn out from the political chaos and rancor from both sides. We must calm down the rhetoric because shouting and outlandish accusations are totally unproductive to the betterment of our society. We must assess where we are and then raise the bar on our expectations, which is why I titled the book, "*I Know We Are Better Than This.*"

Section 1
This is Our Country

Chapter 1

Faith, Family and Country

Our country was purposely built on a firm foundation which our Founding Fathers constructed for us. Our strength has always been based on three principles: faith, family, and love of our country. That's where they started, and those three values have carried us to greatness.

Prior to the 1960's, it was pervasively clear what morality meant within the borders of our country. Morality was taught in the family. It was taught in our churches. It was taught in the schools. Faith, family and country were the three cornerstones of our culture.

Over the past 50+ years, however, those foundational principles have been impacted by the spread of secularism and liberal ideology. We once had a specific moral framework that we all knew as second nature. Having a religious faith, valuing the family unit, and loving our country were a given – it was "normal." Now, each of those cornerstones is under siege and is being eroded inch by inch.

One of the causes for the rise of secularism is what I will call neo-liberalism. With that, liberalism and the societal turn toward secularism have slowly and surreptitiously unwoven the moral fiber that holds our country together. Yes, that is a bold statement, but in my view, it is readily evident; there is no doubt things changed when neo-liberal thinking sprang up. I was right there in the 60's and 70's, embracing liberalism, supporting free speech and the entire liberal platform, while also being conflicted about where liberal morality was going to take us. That was always in the back of my mind. The morality I was taught, along with most fellow Baby-boomers, was clearly based on religious beliefs which ran counter to liberalism and secularism. Liberalism allowed religion, but it was being deemphasized. The "anything goes" mentality being adopted did not bode well for our future.

Whether one chooses to be a religious person, an agnostic, or an atheist, the fact is the Western World's moral absolutes have been around for thousands of years and emanated from Judeo-Christian beliefs on morality and ethical behavior. There is no doubt that agnostics and atheists can also be moral and ethical, but we have inherited the moral constructs of Judeo-Christian beliefs regarding how we are to live our lives. These moral absolutes have certainly served us well in providing standards for acceptable societal behavior.

Thomas Plante, Ph.D., ABPP, is a professor at Santa Clara University and an adjunct clinical professor of psychiatry at Stanford University. In an article in *Psychology Today*, Mr. Plante stated, "Religious engagement and practices encourages and supports 'clean living.' Research has consistently found that religious people are less likely to engage in criminal behavior, marital infidelity, alcoholism, unprotected sexual activity as well as being more likely to engage in pro social behaviors such as volunteerism and charity. Thus, those who tend to report being spiritual, religious, or both tend to behave themselves pretty well. In a nutshell, people in the church choir usually don't rob banks." He concluded, "… the overall trend suggests that religion does assist and support people in living more ethically."

Religious faith was the first cornerstone on which our country was built. The Founding Fathers had a clear grasp on the ideology based on a belief in God and a reverence for the moral code espoused by religion. Communities were built around the churches. No matter which denomination one belonged to, the common denominator was that the churches were the central gathering places for societal interaction – they provided the moral and spiritual infrastructure that was critical in supporting the newly-born communities in those early days.

What has changed is that in today's world, many people look down on religious faith; especially inside the camp of liberal secularism. There are far too many incidences of bigotry and hatred toward people of faith – no matter what the religion. Anti-Semitism is rearing its ugly head again. Christian churches are being attacked. There is an anti-religion crusade that is under way. Where is this coming from? Why is it happening? I believe the anti-religion sentiment is based in neo-liberal ideology which puts the emphasis on the government to provide moral standards versus the moral codes based in religious beliefs. I will have more to say on that subject later.

Our culture has certainly changed due to secularism and the devaluation of religion. The decline in church attendance in the US has been gaining momentum over the past 50+ years. So why is that? There are several contributing factors. As more and more parents set the church aside because of indifference to religion, their children will be far less likely to adopt religion. Seemingly, unless there is something to counteract that trend, religion will continue to decline with each generation.

It appears our lives have become so stress-filled and so busy that church attendees just don't have time for devoting a Sunday morning to enjoy the social interactions or hear an inspiring sermon. Those that continue to regularly attend church still see the value and feel enriched by the experience, whether it be for the sake of seeing friends or feeding the soul – or both.

When religious affiliation declines, the natural tendency is that a culture will be altered. We are seeing that play out. Due to this decline, the teaching of moral character is not as prevalent as it used to be. As a result, our society is tolerating bad behavior more than it has in the past. The emphasis on honesty and integrity is less important. The whole idea of individual responsibility for conduct is de-emphasized. The rules of what's right or what's wrong aren't reinforced, and there has been a decline in accountability. Those were all cultural centerpieces in days gone by.

Logically, moral character is first and foremost taught within the family, and each individual must be taught the purpose of adhering to society's moral code. If kids don't develop the understanding of morality from the family, they may not get it at all. Lessons used to be learned around the dinner table. Imagine a child that does not go to church or have parents who teach them morality - that is a recipe for disaster. The child is going to have trouble understanding morality and will have difficulty fitting in with society. Ultimately, that child has a much greater chance of turning into an adult that violates the laws because there was no moral foundation established in early childhood. When morality is not taught, it causes society to suffer in terms of victims of crime and taxpayer dollars for incarcerating the criminals. That is one of the very reasons why a strong moral foundation is beneficial to society.

Many people who have turned to secularism have decided the church is less important. Therefore, the rise in secularism is inversely related to the overall decline in the importance of religion.

While this has played out globally, ironically, religion in former Communist countries has seen an increase. That is due to one, or possibly both of these reasons: since religion was banned in Communist countries, perhaps the people missed having religion and spiritualism in their lives; the other reason may be that they realized the importance of religion due to the positive benefits it has on their society.

Another part of the world where religion is on the rise is sub-Saharan Africa (in other words, Africa sans the Middle East). Many of the people in this region have not been exposed to religion outside of tribal beliefs. It appears that they are very hungry for religion, primarily Christianity or Islam. Interestingly, these cultures have always stressed the importance of family and local community loyalty.

Given the rise of secularism within the Western World, one of the contributing factors of the decline in church attendance can be laid at the feet of pastors, priests, and other church leaders. A preacher whose moral character that comes into question can have a negative effect on parishioners. Nobody likes a hypocrite, so some people equate all religious people as either hypocrites or potential hypocrites. Consorting with members of the congregation is generally not a good idea when one is a church leader nor is stealing money acceptable. Financial misdealing among the clergy has certainly soured some people on attending church.

There's also the disgraceful sexual abuse scandal that has sadly befallen the Catholic Church. Unfortunately, human beings make mistakes and those that preach against immorality sometimes participate in immoral acts. They are held to a higher standard, and when they fail, much is made from it.

As Western culture moves away from a morality based on religion, agnosticism and atheism become more pervasive and the moral code changes. One of the worrisome issues with agnosticism and atheism (which are the predominate beliefs in secular liberalism) is that they require a reliance on the government to provide the moral code. That dependency can lead to the government usurping morality dictates, and sometimes, that is a very bad thing.

As stated, when religion and morality are replaced by secularism and amorality, the government takes over the role of setting the standards. The government can write law upon law and try to dictate morality, but that leaves us at the mercy of the government and the whims of those who are in charge. What might be morally wrong can be artificially made right by adopting a law. Remember, adherence to a moral code is a personal choice. Morality cannot be legislated. The desire to lead a moral life comes from the heart, it cannot be dictated – it must be organic.

Ceding power to the government can bring on unintended consequences. For example, a government could make a law that says all brown people are to be shunned and ridiculed, and there is no punishment if a brown person is killed. That would be in obvious violation of personal morality. But if the government makes the rules, the populace must live with them. That is why it's so important for the people to be smart enough and critically observant enough to make sure that the PEOPLE have control over the government, not vice versa.

Abortion is an example of law versus morality. From a sheer human moral perspective, terminating a pregnancy for mere convenience seems to naturally fall under the class of an immoral act that is made right because the law of the land says it's acceptable. Laws can be morally wrong, yet legally right. This is a good example of how liberalism and the reliance on the government to tell us what is right or wrong is a part of the erosion of morality.

Another immoral act perpetrated by government is the slaughter of other human beings just because they think differently, act differently, are a certain ethnicity, or don't agree with what the government wants. Hitler and his government decided the Jews should all be terminated, so his soldiers rounded them up, put them in gas chambers and ended the lives of six million people. The very act of killing humans just because they were Jewish, we all can agree was indeed morally wrong, yet the State said it was acceptable and necessary.

The German people ceded all power to the government to make that immoral decision that was decided by a select few, while most Germans knew, in their heart of hearts, that it was just plain wrong. This is also a good example of putting too much power into the hands of a few people. After all, Nazis made up less than 10% of the population, yet they ruled a mighty and brutal nation.

I asked a German friend of mine if the German people thought that killing 6 million Jews was acceptable, and he told me the vast majority of his countrymen were horrified, but they could not or would not do anything about it because the government (Hitler) was far too powerful. The German people feared retaliation if they spoke out – they would be labeled "Jew lovers" and would be ridiculed and even executed. Again, these things can happen when citizens surrender complete power and moral standards to the State.

Moral codes can be shattered, lives can be destroyed, and freedom is totally lost when the people hand over too much power. There is grave danger in doing this as we have seen glaring examples over and over throughout history. This is why there should always be a separation between moral and ethical standards and the dictates of a government. The citizens should always have control, not the government.

Moral law supersedes government law, and as we have seen from our Founding Fathers, a government based on moral laws will be more reflective of how the electorate wants their government to function. This is in contrast to a government telling the populace what is moral and what is not.

Again, we must understand that religion and morality emanate from within individuals and the citizenry to serve as internal personal guideposts. Government is the external representation of the framework societies require in order to be structured and organized. The citizens dictate the moral standards, while the government enforces the laws derived from those standards.

The second cornerstone is the family, a historically integral part of our culture that has become de-valued. This is evidenced in the number of single-parent homes and children born out of wedlock, while both divorce and cohabitation have become common practice. The decline in the family has had a major impact on our culture.

A growing lack of permanent commitment is eroding the value and joy of a marriage. Marriage to some is an inconvenience because they do not have the fortitude to commit fully and permanently to another person. Marital relationships have become virtually disposable. The norm used to be date, marry, have children, and enjoy the grandchildren. Now, dating and cohabitation have become the norm. The idea of marriage is passé and old-school to many in the younger generations.

Too many young couples date, cohabitate, then break up, and there are no strings attached. When children come along, that complicates matters because raising children and maintaining a workable marriage is a very hard job that is not for the faint of heart – or the lazy. It appears that too many young couples opt for convenience rather than commitment. This is surely not true for all couples, but unfortunately, it has become a troublesome trend. Statistics certainly bear that out.

According to the Pew Research Center, back in the 1950's and 60's when the baby-boomers married and started having children, the family unit was highly valued. That was good for the children, because 73% of kids were born into two-parent households among that age group. In 1980, the number went down to 61%. In 2015, it was down to 46%. Statistics show that children that are raised in two-parent households fare much better than those from single-parent or no parent homes (no-parent homes include children raised by their grandparents).

The size of families has also shown a decline due to couples getting married later in life than back in the 50's and 60's. Couples are having fewer children. One other major factor for a smaller family is the cost of raising a child. The cost of supporting a family has increased dramatically, and spending habits often require two incomes for couples to keep their heads above water. To keep up with the Joneses the cost of supporting a family continues to increase faster than wages. After all, it is required to have the most expensive cell phone. Clothing must have brand names because kids get ridiculed in school if they are not wearing Nike, Under Armor or Adidas. A high-priced SUV is a necessity. Living in a nice, big house is to be expected.

All these niceties that everyone desires cost a lot of money. Stay-at-home moms (or dads) have become a rare breed unless there is a high-income earner. Those families that choose to have a stay-at-home parent tend to struggle financially, and many of them pile up a lot of debt. In 1967, 49% of families had a stay-at-home mom or dad. In 1999, the number had dropped to 23%. There has been a 6% uptick since then, primarily driven by home-schooling. Still, only three of ten families have a stay-at-home parent.

Strangely, even some feminists prefer an old-fashioned family. According to a *New York Times* article by John Tierny from 2006 citing a survey featuring 5,000 couples, "These male providers-in-chief were regarded fondly by even the most feminist-minded women -- the ones who said they believed in dividing duties equally. In theory these wives were egalitarians, but in their own lives they preferred more traditional arrangements."

Another article from the *New York Times* cited a comprehensive survey on what makes a happy and fulfilling marriage. The study is entitled "The Ties That Bind: Is Faith a Global Force for Good or Ill in the Family?" It was released from the Institute for Family Studies and the Wheatley Institution. According to the study, 73 percent of wives who hold conservative gender values and attend religious services regularly with their husbands have high-quality marriages.

The study also revealed something else that makes for a happy marriage. Both secular progressive and religious conservative wives highly prefer a husband who is devoted to the family and actively involved in daily household chores, along with being intimately involved with their children. All of this makes for a happy family, and the biggest benefit is felt by the children.

The primary entity where kids get their cultural and ethical education is in the home – that's where they learn about character, individual responsibility, how to treat our fellow man, and how to behave within society. Kids are an open book and what they are taught early on stays with them for their lifetime. How they are molded also has an impact on society. Children who are raised in a dysfunctional or violent atmosphere have a high degree of criminality and incarceration, which ultimately costs taxpayers a lot of money.

Common courtesy is something else that good parents teach their children. Today's school systems are plagued with rude kids as a result of bad parenting. Unfortunately, the students who suffer most are the kind and mannerly ones. I am personally aware of numerous teachers who have gotten fed up with the disruptions in their classrooms and the lack of any disciplinary actions that are at their disposal. School boards and administrators have completely disarmed teachers from having any recourse if a student misbehaves.

Unfortunately, far too many students address their teachers and principals with expletives and total disrespect. Kids throw temper tantrums these days and know they will not be punished for their inappropriate behavior. There is no accountability. Who controls the classroom is now determined by the students not the teachers.

It truly is a sad state of affairs and blame for out-of-control classrooms falls primarily on administrators and school boards. They are absolutely culpable for what they have allowed their public schools to become. It is disgraceful, and sadly, the kids who want to learn are the ones that suffer the most. However, evidently they are not a priority. Not every school or every classroom is out of control, but the trend is unmistakable. There are many good and dedicated teachers. They are also victims because administrators who are more determined to coddle and pacify students than they are in educating and disciplining them. Unfortunately, the students are the biggest losers.

Parents are also to blame for not teaching their own children respect, common courtesy, and proper behavior in the classroom. In addition, far too many high school kids are there because they must be – not because they want to be.

Changing the trend of little to no discipline in the schools is going to be a gargantuan task, and given today's cultural climate, there's not much hope that things will get better. That is a crime against our children, and we have let it happen.

As a result, home schooling along with charter and private schools are on the rise because parents want their children to succeed in life, and the best way for them to succeed is to have a good education. In far too many localities, public education is a bad joke being played on students – and our society is already paying dearly for it.

When religion and morality decay, coupled with the decline of the family and our educational system, it does not bode well for our society. It's sad but true.

Another sad but true fact is that today there are some portions of our populace that plainly don't like who we are as a country. What is disheartening is that the third cornerstone, love of country, has been under attack. We are a great and prosperous nation that has completely altered the course of world history – for the better, I might add. However, there is a cynicism within the Democrat party and neo-liberalism that has been growing over the last few decades. The Pledge of Allegiance used to be recited with pride and joy. Now, many public schools have abandoned it because it might offend some overly sensitive child – or parent. The National Anthem has been denigrated for being racist and "nationalist." What many people don't realize (because they are so self-absorbed and self-important) is that disrespecting our country is disrespecting ourselves and our neighbors. It is also disrespectful of those that have made the ultimate sacrifice by defending us from evil forces that want to terminate our freedoms and way of life. As a culture, we need to firmly establish the boundaries of what is acceptable behavior and what is not when it comes to our country, its symbols, and its history.

Common sense says that no matter the grievance, the very act of burning the flag, kneeling for the National Anthem, or defacing a monument is just plain ill-mannered. Our founding fathers have given us freedom of speech and expression, and those rights have been maintained by sheer determination, great personal sacrifice, and bravery. We may have the right to do something, but that does not make it right.

Common decency and reverence for our heritage must be priority for us to have a peaceful society. Those who disrespect our country have their right to free speech, but there must be a line that is not crossed. There are a lot more meaningful ways to express our opinions – burning a flag or kneeling during the National Anthem is not one of them. Our culture has devolved into an attitude of "me-first, I'm the most important." Because of this, nothing is sacred, and nothing is sacrosanct. Showing disrespect to anyone or anything should be rejected by society.

If individuals want to spit on a police officer or a soldier who protects them, that's just plain stupidity and crassness. However, we should not be surprised by that behavior given the moral erosion that is becoming all too common. The attitude adopted by these ill-behaved people is that their egocentric right to do something that is normally deemed despicable overrides common decency and respect. They are truly acting selfishly. Having common decency and showing respect goes back to what moral code a person has been taught. If there is none, then such abhorrent behavior can be expected.

We have a great country and great people. We are not perfect, but we are the closest thing to it that our world has ever seen in my humble opinion. What other country has given so much in terms of blood and treasure to strangers in foreign lands? There is none. What other country has raised its people to the heights of prosperity that we have achieved? There is none. What other country has stepped forward when global leadership was needed? There is none.

The negative attitudes some people have are so disingenuous. If those that disparage our country would only stop and think about what freedoms they have and what opportunities are presented to them on a silver platter, they might view things differently. We can always get better as a society, but every US citizen should give thanks every day and show the respect that our country deserves.

As stated earlier, faith, family, and pride in our country were of utmost importance in the last century and all the way back to the founding of our country. The ideals have given us our moral foundation. Those three principles have provided us with an all-important moral compass by which we could find our way as we navigated through the rocky waves in the ocean of history.

It used to be clear as to what was morally right or wrong – there were very few gray areas, which is good because we as humans need a moral framework that is clearly delineated. We need to know the boundaries. Without boundaries, we are more apt to stray from what is good and moral or simply try to justify bad behavior. We can easily become unanchored which leads us to being morally adrift at sea.

When rules are made up as we go along, our society's ship will be at the mercy and whims of which way the wind blows and what direction the currents take us. That creates an inner struggle because not everyone is using the same navigational map. One group wants to go north, while the other group wants to go south. But this group over here wants to go east and that other group over there wants to go west. That leads to swings in one direction and then to another, and then to another, thus creating societal chaos and cultural uncertainty.

Yes, we can't all agree on everything, but without the commitment to everyone heading in the same direction, and without a moral compass, our society will be adrift at sea. This leads to a societal breakdown, resulting in moral confusion and cultural dissention. We cannot let that happen. We must refuse to let our defenses down. We must refuse to relinquish our morality. We must always cling to our faith. We must value the family unit. And we must always love and respect our country.

What's happening today with the erosion of morals, the lack of focus on the family, and denigration of our country is unacceptable. We must all stand our ground and reinforce the cornerstones on which our country was founded. *"I Know We Are Better Than This."*

Chapter 2

Protection From the Government

In a free republic, the power to govern is always derived from the power of the individual rights of the people. Citizens own rights, the government has no rights. The limited power to be governed is provided by the electorate, and for the benefit of the electorate. The singular purpose of the government is to protect individual rights. As Ayn Rand eloquently put it, "The only proper, moral purpose of a government is to protect man's rights, which means: to protect him from physical violence—to protect his right to his own life, to his own liberty, to his own property and to the pursuit of his own happiness." Our republic was not established to control us but to protect us.

Our founding fathers went to untold lengths to protect the citizens of this nation FROM its government. They escaped from a tyrannical monarchy that told them how much in taxes to pay, how to act, what to believe, and what to say. The founding fathers had first-hand experience in witnessing how an all-controlling government could manipulate their lives and the lives of their neighbors.

Those brave souls that decided they wanted a better life and embarked on a journey across the Atlantic Ocean into the unknown knew what they were leaving and what they did NOT want in a government. They knew government was necessary, but they all were seeking one thing – freedom from an oppressive government.

They wanted the freedom to decide their own future. They wanted the freedom to decide how much money would be sufficient to run a government. They wanted the freedom to decide who would lead them. They wanted to be able to speak their opinions without government intervention. They wanted freedom of religion. They understood that inalienable rights and freedom of the individual person is far superior for human well-being than a big government or king running and dictating their lives and destinies. Their goal was to be liberated from oppression.

Let's define liberty. It is "the state of being free within society from oppressive restrictions imposed by authority on one's way of life, behavior, or political views" or "unbounded, unrestricted, and released from constraint." That's the way I want to live; what about you? We don't know what it's like to live under government control, but I suspect that far more than a mere majority would agree that liberty would be preferred.

If we want to maintain our liberty, we must speak up and send a message to our government that we will not tolerate being oppressed. We must let the government know that freedom of speech is essential. We must let lawmakers know in no uncertain terms that we want to live in a moral society. That is not to say that religion must be forced upon the populace – quite the contrary. However, the morality taught to us by religion is a valuable commodity that we can use to our social benefit - even for an agnostic or an atheist. We know what happens when governments take the lead in dictating morality – it very rarely turns out well for the people. Less government means more freedom.

When a free country is founded on a well-defined moral code, history says that country will be a place where peace and prosperity will reign. Perhaps that's what motivated Patrick Henry's famous soliloquy as to whether to fight the British for freedom. British soldiers were offshore, ready to attack and quash any resistance. The colonies sent the demand to the King of England that the colonies be set free and establish their own government. The King said "no" by sending the British fleet to bring the rebellious colonies under control and gain their submission.

The question of what the colonies should do was before the Continental Congress: "Do we fight or submit?" Below is a brief except from Henry's impassioned speech.

> "For my own part, I consider it as nothing less than a question of freedom or slavery; … There is no retreat but in submission and slavery! Our chains are forged! Their clanking may be heard on the plains of Boston! The war is inevitable and let it come! I repeat it, sir, let it come… Is life so dear, or peace so sweet, as to be purchased at the price of chains and slavery? Forbid it, Almighty God! I know not what course others may take; but as for me, give me liberty or give me death!"

It was a moving speech that helped inspire a revolution. I highly recommend reading it in its entirety. We find ourselves in a similar situation today. Perhaps a massive war is not as imminent a threat as it was for the Colonists, but we cannot sit idly by while secularism, socialism, or statism slowly take control and erode our freedoms.

To let liberty slip away would be unconscionable and irresponsible. It would be devastating to our sons, daughters and grandchildren if we were the generation that let it happen. We must stand our ground and defend liberty at all costs. We cannot allow this great country to be further compromised by an amoral, liberty-killing movement. Morality and freedom are the better choices – there is no other acceptable option.

The founding fathers recognized they had a solid moral compass based on their religion. They felt strongly that their religious beliefs were a good place to start in order to create and build a new nation. They realized that the moral code was the foundation, while the law and order provided by the government was the glue that would hold it together.

They knew throughout history, most prior governments were based on either a monarchy whose right to lead was based solely on a family heritage, or a dictatorship that seized power and ruled with fear.

The founding fathers knew neither of these forms of government was the way people should be governed and there had to be a better way. As they sought better ideas, they determined there was no better way to begin than to use their religious mores upon which to build some sort of government. Religious morality established a strong framework.

The first founding principle was outlined in the Declaration of Independence – all people should be free to choose their own life, and their own destiny. The founding fathers' starting point was that ALL people deserved equality. This first basic premise established how the building of a government would start. It was the first plank. They began with the premise that the government should be fabricated around equal treatment for every citizen.

Again, the founding fathers knew that the moral compass of the church was by far the best place to look in assembling a structure and a guiding light upon which the rule of law would be established. Freedom plus morality made for an unprecedented basis upon which a nation would be built.

After equality, the premise of individual freedom was established by Thomas Jefferson in our Declaration of Independence: "We hold these truths to be self-evident, that all men are created equal, that they are endowed by their Creator with certain unalienable rights, that among these are Life, Liberty and the pursuit of happiness. – That to secure these rights, Governments are instituted among Men, deriving their just powers from the consent of the governed…"

There is so much power in those opening declarations. The fundamentals of our nation's foundation were captured in those few words. The founding fathers' vision was clearly laid out. The words of the first sentence are perhaps the most powerful and consequential words ever assembled in the English language.

The influence of the document spread literally around the world. Marquis de Lafayette (a friend of Thomas Jefferson) adopted many of the ideas and language into France's own "Declaration of the Rights of Man and Citizen," using it in laying the foundation for the French Revolution.

Numerous other countries in South America adopted similar language, including Venezuela, Haiti, New Grenada, Argentina, Chile, Costa Rica, El Salvador, Guatemala, Honduras, Mexico, Nicaragua, Peru, Bolivia, Uruguay, Ecuador, Columbia, and Paraguay. Other countries included Czechoslovakia, Hungary, Liberia, and Viet Nam. The words penned by Thomas Jefferson in our Declaration of Independence literally echoed around the world.

Interestingly, John Adams wrote this as part of a letter to his wife, perhaps peering into the future and setting a precedent that still stands today: "I am apt to believe that [Independence Day] will be celebrated, by succeeding Generations, as the great anniversary Festival. It ought to be commemorated, as the Day of Deliverance by solemn Acts of Devotion to God Almighty. It ought to be solemnized with Pomp and Parade, with Shews, Games, Sports, Guns, Bells, Bonfires and Illuminations from one End of this Continent to the other from this Time forward forever more." July 4th is still a revered celebration of our freedom and independence.

The Revolution had begun with the reading and publishing of The Declaration of Independence. Two hundred copies of this historic document were printed and distributed immediately upon gathering the 56 signatures. It was read on street corners in the Colonies. It was printed in newspapers. It was read to a burgeoning army of patriots who began assembling to defend the Declaration. It was the spark that ignited the Revolution. Who could have ever imagined that a small rag-tag bunch of sometimes disorganized, under-funded soldiers could defeat the most powerful army in the world at that time?

It truly was a victory that was won against all odds. That beginning defined us as a nation and is still part of who and what we are today. To discount the bravery and determination of those Revolutionaries is an insult to those early patriots. To denigrate the framework they built with the Declaration of Independence, the Constitution, and the Bill of Rights is disgraceful. Our early founders were brilliant thinkers who forged a pathway that led to freedom and prosperity - based on limited powers granted to a government that was "by the people and for the people." It is awe-inspiring and miraculous to think that this collection of great minds was able to come together and craft a governmental masterpiece that changed the course of human history.

Our inalienable rights are NOT conferred upon us by our government – they are "natural" rights that we are born with – that is an important fact to remember. Our founding fathers laid out clearly that the Constitution and our government was established to protect all citizens from an invasive group of leaders that would take away those inalienable rights. That concept is very important. We empower the government to protect our rights – not take them away.

The founding fathers declared that our rights were unalienable (unable to be taken away from or given away by the possessor) and the government's job is to protect the electorate from any person or law that seeks to violate those rights. These natural rights include the right to think for oneself, the right to life, and the right to self-defense. We don't choose to be free; we are free. We don't choose to have rights; we are born with them.

Freedom is not granted by the government; freedom is to be PROTECTED BY the government. That is an important distinction. Granting freedom or rights means that the government can take it away, whereas the concept of being born with freedom and certain rights means they cannot be taken away – they are unalienable. Governments can make laws to take away or restrict freedoms, but if we believe that freedom is an inherent part of being human, and that we have a right to be free, government cannot take away those basic rights because it is a part of being human.

History has proven that a successful society includes a healthful balance between personal morality and government control. It's a push-pull dynamic that must be equal. When it comes to individuals and the government, the "push" side emanates from the government enforcing what's right and wrong, whereas, the "pull" strategy says that the people are in charge and tells the government what the electorate wants in terms of moral norms. Just like consumers dictating what they want to buy, so should it be when it comes to governance – not the other way around.

When the government has too much power by pushing regulations and laws the people don't want, the people inevitably lose. The "push" portion of this equation must be kept in check. When the government gets too pushy, it always ends up with even more strict control and could lead to authoritarianism or socialism.

The "pull" side includes the power of the people telling the government what they want and how they want to be governed. The people must always maintain and defend that power in controlling the government through democratic elections.

There is an example of how we need to be protected FROM the government that has played out in San Antonio, our nation's seventh largest city. Their city council decided that they were denying an application for Chick-fil-A to open one of its restaurants at their city-owned airport. Chick-fil-A is the third largest fast food franchise in the country and has seen tremendous growth over the last several years because they serve good food at reasonable prices, and all of their employees are the most kind and courteous servers in the fast-food marketplace. Their formula has proven that the public appreciates their food and the friendly treatment by eating at their establishments at a record pace. They must be doing something right, otherwise they would not be rated as the best fast-food restaurant in the business.

I am in and out of airports on a frequent basis, and every time I see a Chick-fil-A location at an airport, the line is always long. I like Chick-fil-A, but I usually don't have the time to stop when I am in an airport. The same is true for their restaurant in my neighborhood – the line for the drive-through lanes are usually ten to fifteen cars deep and the inside line is always long. Sometimes I don't eat there because the wait is too long. Imagine that – they are losing customers because their food is so popular. Every fast food chain would certainly love to have that problem.

As we all know, Chick-fil-A is a privately-held corporation owned by a Christian man who makes no bones about who he is and what he believes. In 2012 Think Progress, a left-wing organization funded by leftist radical billionaire George Soros, went after Chick-fil-A because it's owner donated money to some foundations that promote "family values," which according to Think Progress was anti-LGBTQ. They called for a national boycott that backfired when the American public spoke up with their pocketbooks and their appetites, resulting in a record year for the company. Their growth continues to accelerate despite the fact they are famously closed on Sundays.

Think Progress tried to shame the company for making financial contributions to horribly offensive anti-LGBTQ organizations such as The Salvation Army and Fellowship of Christian Athletes, along with a program for at-risk young men called the Paul Anderson Youth Home. Evidently, Think Progress thinks that somehow offering drug treatment facilities and programs to help troubled teens is anti-LGBTQ. I can't figure out the connection or the objection, but then again, I don't agree with left-wing liberals, and I don't quite understand their type of logic. Or perhaps it's just their bigotry showing.

The San Antonio city council, loaded with liberals and left-wingers, decided to deny Chick-fil-A's application on the grounds that, "San Antonio is a city full of compassion. And we don't have room in our public facilities for a business with a legacy of anti-LBGTQ behavior."

There is absolutely no evidence that Chick-fil-A holds the position of being anti-LGBTQ – it's only hear-say speculation spread by a left-wing propogandist website. Of course, the city council is relying on Think Progress's classification of Chick-fil-A as an anti-LGBTQ company. I'm sure everyone would agree that promoting family values and helping teens that are at-risk is an absolute travesty (sarcasm intended).

Anyone with any common sense realizes that the San Antonio city council is on the wrong side of this issue. They are telling the people of San Antonio, "We know what is best for you and you cannot patronize Chick-fil-A." How stupid is that? The city council has no right to exert this type of control and make value judgments based on their own ideological beliefs and a false narrative pushed by a left-wing propaganda organization. If the people of San Antonio don't want to support Chick-fil-A, it is THEIR choice not the city council's.

San Antonio Councilman Roberto Trevino stated, "With this decision, the City Council reaffirmed the work our city has done to become a champion of equality and inclusion." Hold on. Does anyone see the irony in his statement about equality and inclusion? It appears that we are supposed to believe that by excluding Chick-fil-A, they are exhibiting equality and inclusion. Perhaps I am wrong, but that is a perverse and demented way of showing how inclusive and how interested in equality they are. We are supposed to think that his logic makes sense. It does not. It only brings to the forefront the city council's own prejudice against a company with Christian values that a left-wing organization decided to attack. As stated, it's a completely false narrative – it's an out-and-out lie that Chick-fil-A is anti-LGBTQ.

The precedent set by San Antonio only shows that the emperor and his consorts have no clothes – nor do they have any common sense. Nor do they really value equality and inclusion. Perhaps they need a civics lesson; or better yet, maybe they should read the Constitution.

This is where and why we need protection FROM the government. The San Antonio city council has no business getting involved in dictating what restaurants are located in their airport. They grant licenses to strip joints, massage parlors and adult sex shops that foster misogyny, but they deny a wholesome, wildly popular restaurant's application. It makes perfect sense in the convoluted liberal world of logic, don't we know?

This is a glaring example of left-wing politics overstepping their boundaries and injecting their undeniable **prejudices** into city government over-reach. This type of behavior from any government entity should not be and cannot be tolerated. The voters of San Antonio should send a loud message to the city government. If they don't, they will continue to subject themselves to unfair treatment of businesses and citizens and allow their city council to violate civil rights. If that's what the voters want, then, sadly, they will get what they deserve.

The government should not impose its will on the people; the people must impose their will on the government. Our framework exists only for the benefit of the people, and the will of the people is how we must choose to be governed. Relinquishing our freedoms to the government is societal suicide. By asking the government to take over everything, we are then choosing to become servants to that government. Ceding our freedoms and rights to the government is, in essence, self-inflicted slavery.

If the electorate does not keep the government from slowly infringing on rights and freedoms, they are surrendering their right to claim and defend those rights and freedoms. Thomas Jefferson once stated, "The natural progress of things is for liberty to yield, and government to gain ground." He believed that government was the greatest threat to liberty. And it is.

President Reagan stated, "I hope we once again have reminded people that man is not free unless government is limited. There's a clear cause and effect here that is as neat and predictable as a law of physics: As government expands, liberty contracts." Well said, Mr. Reagan.

Franklin Roosevelt is quoted as saying, "Let us never forget that government is ourselves and not an alien power over us. The ultimate rulers of our democracy are not a president and senators and congressmen and government officials, but the voters of this country."

We must continuously hold everyone who works in government accountable – after all, they get paid with our tax dollars – we are their boss whether they like it or not. When the government or some bureaucrats over-step their boundaries, we need to call them on it. When they are trying to usurp our rights and freedoms, we should recognize that as a big deal, and we should not tolerate it. We do need protection FROM the government.

For those people pushing for socialism, I would say, "Be careful what you ask for." Putting our destiny and ceding all power into the hands of unchecked bureaucrats and government officials is risky at best and disastrous at worst. We've seen it play out over and over in history. More on that in a later chapter.

Fortunately, we have our controls over the government. Our founding fathers had experienced rule by coercion. They knew what it was like to not have freedom. What they did was take what they had observed and learned, and then crafted the framework of a way of governing where the people were in charge and there were protections in place. We are able to enjoy the power of the people because we have been graciously endowed with a moral code to follow, along with documents that brought freedom and liberty to life.

Within the Constitution, our freedoms are clearly and succinctly enumerated to keep us from being controlled and enslaved by our government. It was a very clever and brilliant idea to put the power into the people's hands, enabling them to hold power over the government. Through their keen insight and careful forethought, they purposely limited the power of the government. As stated earlier, that power is granted exclusively at the will of the people.

Unfortunately, we have allowed the government to gain more power than the founding fathers envisioned. Our government has grown into a behemoth that they wanted to prevent from happening. They put their lives on the line for us. They fought and won a battle they had seemingly no hope in winning. But with an unbounded determination, an utterly complete commitment to a vision, a fearless faith, a willingness to sacrifice everything, and sometimes with seemingly supernatural intervention, those great patriots claimed their freedom and then gifted us ours. It is a most precious gift that we must cherish and protect.

Allowing the government to seize more and more control over our lives is dangerous and fraught with great risk that we might actually lose the rights, powers and freedoms provided to us. We must continue to claim our freedoms, and we must remain in control of our own destinies.

Government is not the answer to everything – especially MORE government. This is a fight that our children and their children's children are counting on us to win. It is a constant battle to keep the government under OUR control. We cannot let all of what every one of our brave patriots who fought too hard and sacrificed too much for us to allow our freedoms to slowly slip through our grasp. We cannot continue to give in to misguided politicians and bureaucrats whose sole intention is to control us – we must be diligent, because "*I Know We Are Better Than This.*"

Chapter 3

Truth and Justice Is the American Way

There is one basic principle that holds together our justice system – even our country – and that is we are innocent until proven guilty. Our justice system is based on finding the truth. There are necessary components that make up a fair and impartial administration of justice - evidence and corroboration. These are tools used to protect the innocent or convict the guilty. Without them, there is no justice. Sadly, we have had too many incidences recently where innocent people were presumed guilty and convicted by the media and politicians with an agenda.

Think back to the three Duke Lacrosse players that were accused of raping a young black stripper, who incidentally had a criminal record and later served time for murdering her boyfriend. For the media, it was a perfect storm – black girl raped by three white students. They could not wait to pounce on this story with a full-frontal assault. They went apoplectic because it was a racist hate crime perpetrated by privileged white boys. Virtually everyone in the mainstream media and sound-bite-seeking politicians jumped to the conclusion they were guilty. They were publicly tried and convicted by the media and numerous politicians before any evidence was brought forth. The accusation was sufficient for a guilty verdict according to these numbskull talking heads. There was no need for evidence – if the girl claimed it was true, that was good enough for them.

Politicians used the purported incident to score political points and lecture us about racism and how bad and privileged white people are. The vitriol and rancor went on for days and then months. There was one minor problem - evidence showed the boys were totally innocent.

The collateral damage was that the Duke Lacrosse head coach was forced to resign, and the university cancelled the rest of the season. The Duke president had also jumped to a conclusion and publicly said that the boys were guilty. Thirteen months after the ordeal began, it came to an end when a new prosecutor dropped all charges, and the original prosecutor in the case ended up being disbarred for "dishonesty, fraud, deceit, misrepresentation and conspiring to withhold exculpatory evidence."

The dishonest prosecutor, Mike Nifong, just happened to be running for re-election and won his race while the investigation was being conducted. He received national media attention and was hailed as a bulldog that would extract justice from those privileged white boys and their families.

One of his office employees who was working for Nifong during this time said, "I knew in my heart that day that all of this was a lie." The ex-staffer, Jackie Brown, was dismayed and soon resigned. She stated, "I said to him, do you have any idea what you're doing?" He said, 'Yeah but it's worth a million bucks in advertisements!'" Sadly, there are people like Nifong out there that are a disgrace to the justice system and humanity as a whole.

But the damage was done. Three young men had to go through Hell and will live with this ugly incident for the rest of their lives. A coach got fired, a season got cancelled, and the enormous attorneys' costs incurred by the three families buried them in debt.

No charges were ever brought against their accuser for filing a false police report. Nobody in the mainstream media and no public official ever apologized to the students. One can only assume their attitude was that the falsely accused boys were merely collateral damage for a higher cause. It was more important to rant and rave and throw invectives around about white privilege than it was to tap the brakes, let the justice system handle things, and seek the truth. It's a sad commentary on so many fronts.

Then there's the *Rolling Stone* rape article at the University of North Carolina-Charlottesville. This was another case where the alleged perpetrators were judged by the jury of the media to be guilty. Too many discrepancies in the "victim's" story cropped up and no charges were ever filed. Again, the leap to conclusion was fast and furious by the media, and *Rolling Stone* eventually settled the defamation case brought by the three young men who were falsely accused.

The incident was completely fabricated and false, yet once again, *Rolling Stone* and the mainstream media rolled with the story (pun intended) and seized the opportunity to bash innocent students. Again, no one in the media or political world ever publicly acknowledged they were wrong, and even *Rolling Stone* had to be shamed into admitting they were wrong to publish the story without corroboration. It was poor journalism, and they rightfully paid for their sins – but it still left scars on the falsely-accused victims.

When an accuser makes an accusation, he or she must bring the charges and provide evidence or corroboration. Our justice system mandates that there must be evidence or corroboration by witnesses in order for someone to be proven guilty. The presumption of innocence is where our justice system starts. Without that fundamental principle, we would have a chaotic system of people accusing others without any evidence and guilty verdicts being handed out like candy to innocent people. This presumption of innocence until proven guilty is absolutely critical for our society.

Think back to the Salem Witch Trials in 1689. Twenty innocent people lost their lives and 200 were accused of witchcraft. The trials were a mockery of justice, based solely on hearsay evidence by a chosen few "witnesses". Everyone agrees that whole ordeal was a travesty with tragic consequences for innocent people.

In the Duke and *Rolling Stone* incidences, jumping to conclusions was an outgrowth of a prejudicial attitude that showed its ugly face. The media and public figures spewed their hatred strictly due to a prejudiced dislike for young white teens. How can any other conclusions be drawn? It was intentional and it had a clear purpose.

Conviction of people strictly because of the color of their skin is more akin to vigilantism than it is justice. Vigilantism is defined this way: "Taking the law into one's own hands and attempting to effect justice according to one's own understanding of right and wrong; action taken by a voluntary association of persons who organize themselves for the purpose of protecting a common interest." The common interest in the cases mentioned above was young boys with white privilege, and the vigilantes pounced.

I think everyone has been in the situation of being wrongly accused of something. It's highly problematic if we are not allowed to fight against what we think is a salacious lie against us, and we must cower to what others think and lay down to accept our fate (despite the fact they may be false charges). Obviously, that runs counter to our fundamental right of self-defense and innocence until proven guilty.

If a mob says "guilty," no matter the facts, and we are forced into accepting mob rule, then we do not have justice; we have vigilantism. In the incidences mentioned earlier, the media was guilty of vigilantism just like the politicians who echoed the lies. If that is the type of justice system someone wants to live in, there are lots of countries where justice is served by a mob, a dictator, or a theocracy. Personally, I prefer our country's administration of justice with the "innocent until proven guilty" foundation stipulated in our constitution. That is how humans yearn to be treated. It is the right way, and the ONLY way unfettered justice can be achieved.

The Bret Kavanaugh hearings are another good example of false accusations. Here we had a man accused by a woman of sexual assault some 30 years prior to when the accusation came out. His accuser, Dr. Christine Blasey Ford, famously testified that the assault happened, yet through investigations by an army of FBI agents, there was no evidence and no corroboration - even from Dr. Ford's friend who was with her that night. No witnesses came forward except for a few nut-jobs who were eventually proven to be liars, delusional, or both.

To hang a non-corroborated accusation on this man for the rest of his life is prejudicial and just plain wrong, no matter your political persuasion. If Dr. Ford's accusation could not be corroborated by witnesses or evidence, then the matter should be settled in EVERYONE's mind, and we should move on and leave the man and his family alone. That is how things should work. That is how WE would want to be treated if we were falsely accused. That is how a civil society should behave.

To continue to hold a grudge even though he was proven innocent is also just plain wrong. There will be those on the Left that will never accept anything other than Mr. Kavanaugh was guilty. I would say to those people, "Put yourself in the accused person's shoes – how would you like to be treated through this whole process? How would you like to live with GUILTY held over your head despite no evidence or witness corroboration?" I sincerely doubt people in their right mind would want that, and for him to be treated as such displays an unforgiving heart that is consumed by hatred and divisiveness rather than love and empathy. It reminds me of an old Joe South song called "Walk a Mile in My Shoes."

If I could be you and you could be me for just one hour
If we could find a way to get inside each other's mind
If you could see you through my eyes instead of your ego
I believe you'd be surprised to see that you'd been blind
Walk a mile in my shoes, walk a mile in my shoes
Yeah, before you abuse, criticize and accuse, walk a mile in my shoes

When prejudice and presumption of guilt cannot be overcome in the instances discussed here, then the motivation becomes vindictiveness – not justice and truth. Is that how we want our country to behave? Sadly, I do not believe the Left will ever let the Justice Kavanaugh issue die, and our country will be worse off than before this saga began. In my view, it boils down to one point - there was only one motivation that Democrats had throughout the hearings – keep ANY conservative off the Supreme Court – and do it at all costs, leaving no stone unturned, and no tactic left unused.

I firmly believe Justice Kavanaugh is a very good man and one of THE most qualified Supreme Court nominees in decades. His resume dwarfs all the most recent nominees that have been confirmed. This was a politically motivated fight, plain and simple. What the Dems did in holding onto Dr. Ford's accusation for several months and then announcing it at the last minute was a politically calculated move, despite all the rhetoric to the contrary. To me, it's blatantly obvious. Anyone that believes otherwise, in my view, is mistaken.

This whole thing could have been handled privately months prior to the Senate confirmation hearings, and we wouldn't have had to watch the public circus. However, that is exactly what the Democrats wanted – a big circus that would do the Showman proud.

Dr. Ford asked Diane Feinstein to keep her accusation private; she did not want to go through a big public airing, but Senator Feinstein and the Dems had a higher calling – weaponize a false accusation for political purposes. I'm sorry, but that is abhorrent behavior that we the people should not tolerate. Dr. Ford was not a victim of rape by Justice Kavanaugh – she was a victim of betrayal by a group of politicians that had an agenda. Dr. Ford was used as a tool. For this betrayal, Dr. Ford had to suffer through the public spectacle that she did not sign up for and, according to her, she never wanted. She was collateral damage. Despite the excuses given by Democrat politicians, their actions spoke more loudly than their words, and their political agenda was far more important than common decency and respect – not only for Mr. Kavanaugh, but for Dr. Ford as well. Character matters, and what was displayed in this whole ordeal was a total absence of character on the part of the Democrats. It's sad, but true.

Both people would have been able to maintain their privacy and still get to the bottom of the stories without all the hoopla. However, the Dems felt it was better, more expedient, and more impactful to use it as a political weapon strategically deployed at a calculated time with the one motivation of delaying and/or derailing Mr. Kavanaugh's nomination. All too often, we make judgments that fit our ideology versus what is right, fair, and true. When prejudice blinds our judgment, then justice and fairness is completely lost.

We can't convict people just because we don't like them and what they believe about the constitution. We cannot fairly judge someone when prejudice takes over. Fairness and impartiality must prevail before a conclusion can be justly drawn. If prejudice plays a primary role in forming an opinion while seeking justice, then there can be no justice at all.

We should not cheer for which side "won" – we should cheer for truth and justice to be served and administered in a fair and impartial way that is free from any prejudice whatsoever. And whatever is found to be the truth, it should be accepted without continued prejudice. The definition of prejudice is: "The act or state of holding unreasonable preconceived judgments or convictions. Injury or damage resulting from some judgment or action of another in disregard of one's rights. An adverse opinion or leaning formed without just grounds or before sufficient knowledge."

My greatest fear for our country is for us to devolve into a place where someone can ruin a life with no evidence or corroboration. When mere accusation can destroy a life, where is the justice in that? There is none. We simply must not and cannot allow that to happen. True justice can only reside in a place where the presumption of innocence exists. Justice will find its own pathway when evidence and corroboration are used as guideposts. Only then can truth and justice be found.

In our justice system, we cannot resort to vigilantism and public hangings that are executed by the media or public figures whose only motivation is to score political or ideological points. Lady Justice would be sorely disappointed in those actions, and we should be too. *"I Know We Are Better Than This."*

Chapter 4

The Greatest Generation

The Greatest Generation was taught and lived certain values, and those values enabled them to rise above all the challenges thrown at them. They responded and they overcame. We Baby Boomers were early witnesses to the fruits of their labor with a growing economy and peace after World War II.

The Cleavers in the show *Leave it to Beaver* reflected much of the culture of the USA at the time. Not everyone enjoyed never-ending peace and harmony in their families as depicted in the show, but overall, it was a pretty true representation of "the good life". Not everyone bought into this idyllic life when the mid-60's rolled around. There was an undercurrent of discontent that was causing social tensions, including civil rights and the war in Viet Nam, while secularism was gaining strength.

The Hippie movement was touting free love, peace, harmony, and freedom of speech. Protests broke out led by college kids who were attacking "The Man". Mostly, they were not satisfied with how things were going. Riots broke out over black civil rights and the war in Viet Nam. Sit-ins were all the rage. Things got pretty dicey in the good ol' USA. It was one of those character-building times in our history. After all the dust settled and we worked through all our inner strife, we entered a new era where we got back on track. A good helping of reality set in when the Hippies had to start getting jobs in order to survive.

Hippies were more closely associated with the liberal democrats, certainly not those money-hungry businessmen called Republicans or Conservatives. The free love, free spirit, dope-smoking world of Hippieism had infiltrated the Democrat party. I played my small part in the movement by growing long hair, dressing in psychedelic garb, singing at coffee shops, and acting cool.

The Hippie movement did have an impact on where our country was headed, and some of those impacts were not good. Historically, our culture focused on the family and the importance of the family unit that featured Mom, Dad and the kids with the grandparents supporting from the background. That was the norm prior to the 60's and 70's. Every family strove to work out internal struggles. When dissention or a problem occurred inside the family unit, the goal was to work it out, forgive, and then move on. We were FAMILY, and families stick together – that is just what we did – there really was no other choice.

As seemingly tumultuous as the 60's and 70's were, let's imagine the turmoil our country faced during the Great Depression. There were lines of people blocks long waiting to get a bowl of soup and some bread. It was shocking to think that our country was so devastated that people were starving to death. New jobs were nonexistent. Money was very hard to come by. Basic life necessities were scarce. It was tough times, the extent of which we had not seen before in our country and have not seen since. The Great Recession in the Obama years pales in scope when compared to the Great Depression. Times were really hard. Millions of people were on the brink merely trying to survive.

It was a long slog for our country to emerge from the catastrophic climate created by the Great Depression. It took perseverance. It took hard work. It took a long time to recover. However, recover we did. Tough times and how we respond to them define our character. Some people show strength when things don't go their way, while others wilt under the added pressure and give up hope.

Let's journey back to the end of World War I. Our country had just staved off a takeover of many countries by evil forces. Our country was weary from the war. We were shackled with the hangover of the war which required spending a large portion of our country's wealth and the loss of precious lives to defend our freedom and that of hundreds of millions of other people around the world. It was the right thing to do, but it was painfully costly in terms of our collective wealth and devastating in terms of the loss of human capital.

Let me offer some statistics that put into perspective the devastation WWI wrought. Worldwide, it is estimated that twenty million people were killed, and twenty-one million others were wounded. Those numbers include both soldiers and civilians. Just pause for a moment and ponder those numbers and think of all the people and families who suffered.

The estimated total monetary cost of the war is estimated to be as high as $213 billion globally. The USA lost 116,000 soldiers, and another 204,000 were wounded – a total of 320,000 casualties. Looking at the monetary costs for the USA, the total was $27 billion. Our total annual GDP hovered around $700 billion during that time. The world's only hope was the benevolence of the USA, and we came through when we were desperately needed.

Evil had to be dealt with and obviously the cost was enormous, but worth it. Imagine what the world would be like today had the Allied forces not defeated the malevolent governments.

After WWI, it took roughly a decade for the USA and the rest of the world to recover to a level that looked sustainable. Many members of the Greatest Generation were either born during or shortly after the war, as well as during the recovery period prior to the Great Depression. Many were teen-agers or small children on that infamous "Black Thursday" of October 24, 1929. Imagine being born into a world where unemployment went from 3% to 25%. Top that off with wages plummeting 42% for those jobs that were available. Talk about hard times. The prospects were extremely bleak for these newcomers born into the world during the Great Depression and WWI. Mere survival was a gargantuan task for most families with the odds of enjoying a good life being very slim.

In 1932, Franklin D. Roosevelt was elected president and quickly instigated the New Deal which slowed the depression, but full recovery had not yet been achieved in the USA. In 1933, most of Europe was still mired in the global depression, and Germans were so desperate to put an end to their misery, they elected a new leader who promised prosperity. His name was Adolf Hitler.

During the subsequent six years, recovery in the USA muddled along and turmoil continued to accelerate in Europe until that fateful day September 1, 1939 when Germany invaded Poland. On the Asian front, the war actually began in 1937 when Japan invaded China. The fight between good and evil began here in the USA on December 7, 1941 when Japan bombed Pearl Harbor, and the global fight was on. Soon after that heinous event, World War II was in full swing.

Our country entered the war for two reasons; we were attacked by a hostile nation, and we saw the devastation being wrought on many European nations. Trying to overcome the evil that was being perpetrated on hundreds of millions of people was the moral and right thing to do. Those soldiers were far more noble than most of us will ever be – myself included.

President Franklin Roosevelt, in an address to the nation on radio during the invasion of Normandy on D-Day offered this poignant prayer:

"Almighty God: our sons, pride of our Nation, this day have set upon a mighty endeavor, a struggle to preserve our Republic, our religion, and our civilization, and to set free a suffering humanity.

Lead them straight and true; give strength to their arms, stoutness to their hearts, steadfastness in their faith.

They will need Thy blessings. Their road will be long and hard. For the enemy is strong. He may hurl back our forces. Success may not come with rushing speed, but we shall return again and again; and we know that by Thy grace, and by the righteousness of our cause, our sons will triumph.

They will be sore tried, by night and by day without rest - until the victory is won. The darkness will be rent by noise and flame. Men's souls will be shaken with the violences of war. For these men are lately drawn from the ways of peace. They fight not for the lust of conquest. They fight to end conquest. They fight to liberate. They fight to let justice arise, and tolerance and good will among all Thy people. They yearn but for the end of battle, for their return to the haven of home. Some will never return. Embrace these, Father, and receive them, thy heroic servants, into Thy kingdom."

Thirty different countries eventually joined the war, some by choice, and others by invasion. The Greatest Generation here in the USA had just lived through the Great Depression, and as young adults, they were now faced with trying to win a global conflict that would become the deadliest and most costly war that mankind had ever faced. Thomas Paine said, "Those who expect to reap the blessings of freedom must, like men, undergo the fatigue of supporting it."

The odds were stacked against all the countries in Europe and Asia – the wave of evil seemed insurmountable, but the Greatest Generation here in the USA and in Europe responded with abandon. The only hope for the Europeans and Asians was the USA. The Germans were exacting devastation on physical property along with mass destruction of human capital that had never been seen before, with Japan doing the same. The level of evil trying to overtake the world was unsurpassed historically. Japan was wreaking havoc in Asia, killing an estimated 10 to 14 million people, and the Germans were responsible for killing another estimated 10 to 12 million.

When our country entered the war, hope of overcoming the evils of war spread across Europe and Asia. Cities in Europe rejoiced when American troops began liberating cities in France and Italy after D-Day. It's pretty safe to say that had the USA not intervened when it did, the world would be a much different place. Those heroic American soldiers laid down their lives for the people on two separate continents. What other country in our world history would have done that?

Our government led the rest of the world in throwing all resources available to counteract the heinous wave that was rushing over millions of people in foreign lands. What greater gift is there than for strangers in another country coming to the rescue, sacrificing their own blood and money in order to stave off evil? There is none.

On the 75th anniversary of D-Day and during a memorial service, Queen Elizabeth had these gracious comments about America's Greatest Generation: "The heroism, courage and sacrifice of those that lost their lives will never be forgotten. It is with humility and pleasure, on behalf of the entire country – indeed the whole free world - that I say to you all, thank you."

The Greatest Generation knew what they had to do and they went out, with great sacrifice, and conquered wicked and ruthless dictators, bringing peace to a world that was on the brink of succumbing to evil forces. Every European and every Asian, even every person on the planet that is free today owes their freedom to the most benevolent country our planet has ever seen, and they owe their debt of gratitude to the Greatest Generation the world has ever known.

Let us not focus only on the soldiers that braved the front lines because there were workers back home contributing to the overall effort by producing food, clothing, machinery, and munitions to support those on the front lines. There were doctors and nurses working hard to save the lives of the wounded and dedicating their talents in assisting soldiers as they recovered from injuries sustained in battle. And then there were the families of those soldiers that also made the ultimate sacrifice. Mothers and Fathers lost their sons and daughters. Brothers and sisters lost their siblings. Sons and daughters lost their parents. Friends lost friends. It was a time of great sacrifice.

Here was this generation birthed into a world that was suffering dearly from the Great Depression. They overcame that hurdle. Then along came WWII, the horrific global conflict that cost more than $1 trillion worldwide (about $14 trillion in today's dollars) and an estimated 100 million lives. For the next 70 years, peace and prosperity dominated the world. Yes, there have been local conflicts in countries such as Korea, Viet Nam, the Middle East, and we should never overlook the bravery and sacrifice of those soldiers that fought those wars. Everyone owes them a huge debt of gratitude as well.

Far too many were lost in those conflicts, and many of those brave soldiers that survived are still haunted by the bitter ugliness of war. As painful and as devastating as those wars were, they paled in comparison to the destruction and loss of life in the two World Wars. And yes, there have also been economic ups and downs after WWII, but nothing on the scale of the Great Depression.

The Greatest Generation endured unthinkable sacrifice and hardships, yet they ushered in a golden age of global peace and prosperity. This group of amazing people like my own father who served his country and provided a good life for me, my mother, and my brothers is fading off into the sunset year after year. We have lost most of them, but we must NEVER forget the sacrifices they made, the tribulations they endured, the evil that they conquered, and the precious gifts of freedom and prosperity they gave us. Our appreciation and admiration should last forever. Our world was far beyond fortunate to have been blessed by the selfless contributions of this generation that reached every corner of the globe and affected the lives of virtually every person on the planet.

Thomas Paine said it best:

"THESE are the times that try men's souls. The summer soldier and the sunshine patriot will, in this crisis, shrink from the service of their country; but he that stands by it now, deserves the love and thanks of man and woman. Tyranny, like hell, is not easily conquered; yet we have this consolation with us, that the harder the conflict, the more glorious the triumph. What we obtain too cheap, we esteem too lightly: it is dearness only that gives everything its value. Heaven knows how to put a proper price upon its goods; and it would be strange indeed if so celestial an article as FREEDOM should not be highly rated"

To forget about the untold millions of American heroes or devalue what they accomplished is an utter insult to humanity itself. We, along with billions of other people around the world should always hold all soldiers in reverence and highest regard that have fought to protect the world from evil. They deserve our recognition, they deserve everyone's respect, and most of all, they deserve our utmost gratitude. This is why we deservedly call them "The Greatest Generation".

Those citizens in our country that disrespect the flag and denigrate soldiers that proudly serve or have served our country have probably never stopped to think about what it has taken to provide them their freedom of free speech. I'm sure they have never stopped to consider that without the contributions of our military, their lives would be far different.

Never in the history of the world has a nation been so powerful as the USA, yet that power is not abused. We could have easily stayed in Europe after WWI and WWII and taken over most countries, and the same is true in Asia. Instead, we spent a lot of our own money and resources in helping rebuild those nations. I liken it to a bully who beats up numerous victims, but then a strong-willed person comes along who has benevolence and good intentions on their side and kicks the bully's butt. And when the fight is over, the victor leans down to help the bully to his feet, and then tends to the bully's wounds.

As the only true superpower, we could take over Canada, Mexico, Cuba, and all of Central America in a few days. We could completely dominate the Western Hemisphere if we wanted to. However, we choose not to wield the power we possess because we are good and benevolent nation.

The cost of freedom in our country started with the sacrifices the colonists made and extends all the way into today. Most of these modern-day spoiled brats that don't get it are hopelessly mired in ingratitude; they don't understand the respect that is due, and they have grown up NOT being taught one thing – freedom isn't free. Far too many are completely oblivious and take their freedoms for granted.

People with a derogatory attitude toward the military are clueless, ungrateful and just plain stupid in my humble opinion. If they fully comprehended what it takes to be free, they would not be taking it for granted. They would show respect to those that deserve it, and they would thank God every day for the freedoms they enjoy. If we forget about the sacrifices, if we forget about the price of freedom, we stand a good chance of losing our freedoms through complacency, apathy, and ignorance.

Unfortunately, a disturbing attitude has seeped into our schools and educators. Too many of our children are being taught that the military is a bunch of mean, angry people that go around killing poor, innocent people. The military has been disparaged far too long by educators who really should know better. After all, the military is WHY they are free. If our children don't comprehend the full magnitude of what our ancestors have done for us, then God help us when it comes time for them to defend our freedoms. Are we going to raise a generation that doesn't realize the true cost of freedom and honor the past? If so, we are doing our children a huge disservice. They are not learning to value freedom; therefore, they will not truly understand and appreciate what they have – until someday it's gone.

Freedom truly is precious - it takes hard work and sacrifice to defend. Our rights are not just handed to us; they are earned by the blood of those who have sacrificed and those who died. They are earned by the fathers, mothers, sisters, brothers, sons and daughters who made the ultimate sacrifice. We cannot take them for granted. We must appreciate them, cherish them, and honor those that made it all possible.

The Greatest Generation set an example for the whole world. We must never forget them and when we are idly sitting by enjoying the freedoms we share, we should say a prayer of thanks in honor of every soldier that has ever fought to protect us.

To denigrate and cheapen their sacrifice by burning a flag or disrespecting our National Anthem is unacceptable. It's sad but true, but I think we are raising a whole generation of youngsters who don't know what it's like to sacrifice and fully comprehend what it takes to live free. Complacency has set in, and we have allowed it to happen. Far too many people take our freedom lightly and don't fully appreciate what they have. *"I Know We Are Better Than This."*

And One More Thing…

The generation immediately following the Greatest Generation also deserves some special recognition. These are the earliest of the Baby Boomers born in the mid 1940's through the early 1950's. Full disclosure – that was the era I was born.

The Viet Nam war was never declared as a war even though it lasted twenty years and involved roughly 2.7 million soldiers who served in Southeast Asia according to Veterans Administration statistics. Some 58,000 soldiers lost their lives, and 153,000 were wounded – including my brother. This was a battle against Communism, which at the time was the biggest threat to the USA and the rest of the world.

The hangover from World War II was still present and our country, nor any of the other countries were fully healed when Communism began to infiltrate countries outside of Russia and China. Throughout Southeast Asia, we saw the spread of communism which spawned the Korean and the Viet Nam wars. Our country was war-weary into the late 60's and on into the early 70's. Our leadership at the time felt compelled to fight these wars because Communist regimes were slaughtering their own people at an alarming rate.

Here are some reliable estimates, although because these regimes were so ruthless and controlled the flow of information, we will never know the true carnage.

Korea – 1.2 million deaths from executions, concentration camps, and 500,000 starvations

Cambodia – 2.2 million (24% of the population).

Viet Nam – 3.8 million deaths due to politicide and mass murder

With all this genocide, democide and politicide going on, our country could not sit idly by and watch millions upon millions of people be slaughtered, tortured, and starved to death. It was a benevolent thing to try and do, but unfortunately, what it would have taken to end all the deaths would have been another all-out assault on Southeast Asia. Our country was not in the mood for that, yet our leaders decided that Korea and Viet Nam were worthy of our efforts in an attempt to alleviate the horror of what was taking place.

Saving at least half of Korea was successful, but the challenge of Viet Nam was more than what our country was willing to take on to complete the task of liberating Viet Nam. Our soldiers were sent there to fight the battles to prevent Communist takeover. They served bravely and nobly. They responded heroically to the call of duty.

Here's a quote from John Sorenson, former president of the Viet Nam Helicopters Pilot Association: "…I submit that the men and women who served in the Viet Nam War are the Greatest Generation of our Generation [Baby Boomers]. We lined up when others didn't. We took an oath where others didn't. We served when others didn't. Then we were despised and ridiculed when others weren't. We stuck together and supported each other when others didn't. We are without any doubt the 'Greatest Generation of Our Generation.'" Well said Mr. Sorenson.

The 60's and 70's were a strange time in our country that was challenging on many fronts, from the controversy over the Viet Nam War to racial division. The youth of America were lost and confused (including myself), and college campuses went from a place of learning to becoming a cultural battleground.

When the veterans returned from the Viet Nam War, the country was in bad shape, and as we all know, these brave and noble veterans were unceremoniously greeted with disdain and contempt. It should never have happened that way. There were no parades of celebration. These soldiers, along with having to deal with the horrors of war, had to deal with hostilities in their own country for which they served. The way they were treated was despicable, undeserving, and disrespectful. It was a dark day for our country, not to mention a dark day for those who put their lives on the line for us and the lives of strangers thousands of miles away.

Another forgotten and under-appreciated group that was dishonored was the wives, mothers, fathers, sisters, and brothers that lost a loved one or had to deal with the recovery and on-going problems that the after-effects of the Viet Nam war brought. All those family members paid their own price, and to many, the cost was dear. Sadly, they still live with it today. We honor the soldiers that have served, and deservedly so. Unfortunately, we forget to honor the unsung heroes who had to deal with the consequences of the aftermath of war. I have often thought we should have the day after Veterans Day as the Unsung Heroes Day. The families of soldiers deserve their own recognition because of the sacrifices they made. They deserve to be honored because they served our nation in a different way, and their lives were irrevocably altered.

There is no more noble thing to do than to be willing to sacrifice one's life for others, and our Viet Nam veterans were robbed of the acclaim they deserved. They followed orders. They risked their lives – many lost their lives. They still live with the pain of war and nightmares that followed, and we, as a country, dishonored not only them, but their families as well. It obviously was not a popular war, but every one of those soldiers and their families deserve our full honor, our respect, and our unending gratitude for their nobility and service to EVERY one of us that lives free today. I agree with Mr. Sorenson; they are the Greatest Generation of Our Generation. I will humbly say, "Thank you to every Viet Nam veteran for your service, thank you to the families for their service, and I humbly apologize to you on behalf of our country. We failed you, and for that, we are very sorry." *"I Know We Are Better Than This."*

Section 2

Our Culture

Chapter 5

The Importance of Individualism

A successful, free society is reliant upon the individual. Personal accomplishment and ingenuity build and strengthen a society, as opposed to the oppression within collectivism which intentionally robs a society of individualism.

There are two things for sure - we are all human, and we are all very different. Our fingerprints are not the same, our DNA is different. We are all individuals. Yes, there are plenty of commonalities between us, but we are all unique persons with certain talents and strengths. We are all alike, but we are not the same.

According to the *Oxford Dictionary*, individualism is defined as: "A social theory favoring freedom of action for individuals over collective or state control." *The Free Dictionary* says: "Belief in the primary importance of the **individual** and in the virtues of self-reliance and personal independence."

When I think about individualism, I think about three things: achievement, responsibility, and accountability. Hard workers achieve, they take on responsibilities, and they hold themselves accountable

I believe that when most individuals are challenged with the right to choose their destiny, they will fly higher and go farther with their lives versus being controlled by the state or someone else. Things that are acquired by hard work and discipline are far more rewarding than things that are just handed over to us. Perhaps that's based on the fact that when we earn something, it becomes more precious.

Achieving something has far more personal benefits than a hand-out. Sure, we all like free stuff – who doesn't? However, what a person values more highly are taking pride in self-reliance and accomplishment. It gives our lives more meaning – we are proud of ourselves and that makes us better people. Individualism is not self-centeredness, it is self-reliance.

Very few people find life rewarding when they are living off what other people can give them. Sure, there are slackers that love to take advantage of the benevolence of others, but I believe it is built into our DNA to advance ourselves and reach goals. Who doesn't want a better life?

Think about how we feel when we complete a task – even if it's menial, there's still that feeling of accomplishment. That feeling sends a loud message to us; it increases our self-worth and makes us feel so much better about who we are.

Taking personal responsibility pays long-lasting dividends. We need to get back to teaching self-reliance. When we choose to do it ourselves, we build self-esteem, we have a healthier state-of-mind, and we are a more productive member of society.

Our democracy is based on making choices – for example, voting. We vote for certain people to run the government. There are some politicians that strictly run on what they promise to give away. That's usually good for garnering votes from those in a constituency that are seeking free stuff and free benefits, or those people that have adopted the mindset that society must take care of everyone. It is not the government's job to be a babysitter, daycare center, food provider, ATM machine, cell phone provider, and general benefactor.

People who are dependent or think the government (aka, the society) owes them everything will most likely vote for the person that promises the most free stuff. Sadly, that is why some ethnic groups continuously elect the same persons, and all too often, those elected officials never really deliver on those promises. Their promises aren't fulfilled, so they always need another term to finish the job - which they never do. But the gullible, dependent people still cast their ballot on the promise of free stuff, which is why some ethnic groups are continuously mired in and bound to the status quo. In most realities, if you don't deliver on your promises, you should be voted out of office. And if the only issue that matters as a voter is free stuff, then you get the type of politician you deserve, while you never improve your lot in life.

These dependent people can also be convinced by politicians and ultimately develop the attitude that they are entitled to a certain level of subsistence, and then the next step is they adopt the attitude that this level of subsistence is a fundamental right. It is not a right that everyone is taken care of by the government or society. Yes, there are people that could not live without help from other people because of physical disability, mental illness, or some other health reason. However, we as a benevolent society, should be compassionate and assist them, but in order to live a fulfilled life, we humans need more than just a bunch of hand-outs.

Too often, politicians convince their constituency that the only way dependent individuals can maintain their dependency is to elect them. Unfortunately, those politicians are doing a great disservice by not teaching and not expecting their voters to rise above, to achieve independence, to be self-reliant, and to be proud of their accomplishments.

Dependency can be addictive to some people. Breaking away from dependency can be very tough, but it is necessary for individuals to rise above their current plight and set themselves on a course of betterment and achievement.

Thousands of years ago, we roamed free, we set up our own encampments, and either killed or grew our own food. Those who were lazy and reliant on others for their survival did not fare as well as those that worked hard and fended for themselves. It was a matter of natural selection. This is a basic instinct that has been with us forever. Only recently has the idea become more pervasive that if we are lazy and don't want to work that it's OK – society will take care of us. Yes, we need to assist and provide for those that are unable to work, but there are other ways people can contribute to society without physical labor being involved. We do not exist in order to take advantage or live off other people's labors. Again, it is a basic human instinct to work and produce.

We make choices every day, all day long. The sum total of those choices determines how our lives play out – it defines us – we are the actors. Our lives can be a bad comedy, a horror movie, or a super-hero story. It is our choice. We write the script of our own destiny through the choices we make. Some people are good at making the right choices, but some people are really bad at it. Most of us get it, but others refuse.

As a culture, we will be known for the personal choices we have made. I have always held the position that we are responsible for our own choices - my parents taught me that, and I passed it on to my children. We must hold ourselves accountable for who we are and what we do. We do make bad choices – some people more frequently than others. I will never waiver on the personal choice issue – we are responsible and accountable for our own choices.

Yes, there are external influences that can lead us into making a bad choice, but we are still responsible for our own decisions. We all don't grow up in the best neighborhood or the best family, but that is not a barrier to making good choices and it should not be used as an excuse. Taking individual responsibility for our choices always serves us well – it inspires us to make better choices.

There are expectations we all should live up to, no matter our economic plight, our upbringing, or our level of education. The choice between right and wrong is pretty simple to figure out unless you have severe neurological damage or are mentally challenged. Making the right choice is sometimes easy, and sometimes hard, but what we must always remember is choices have consequences.

That's another thing my parents taught me, and I passed it down to my kids. I am pretty sure they got tired of hearing it, but it is such a fundamental principal that every human on the planet should know and fully comprehend. We are responsible for our choices and those choices have consequences. How can it be any simpler?

I sometimes have trouble getting going on a project, but when I complete a project, I feel proud. I recall when I decided to put in two pocket doors in what became my office. The room was originally designed to be a dining room, but we had little need for it, and I more desperately needed a man-cave. I read about pocket doors and viewed videos on how to install them. This endeavor presented various challenges that I had not taken on before, so I wanted to learn about what it was going to take to have a successful installation.

I am not the best carpenter in the world, but I decided I could successfully take on the challenge and dove in. The most critical thing in the installation was making sure everything was square and level. My usual "close enough for government work" carpentry skills were not going to provide satisfactory results – it had to be perfect for the doors to work properly. After I got started, the challenges began to rear their ugly head. I was trimming and measuring over and over, and the large level I was using seemed to become a new extension of my arm – not to mention the seemingly thousands of steps I took climbing up and down the ladder.

There were times when I became frustrated and doubted that my project was going to be successful, but I persevered and ultimately figured things out. Doing this project by myself presented interesting challenges because I possessed only two hands. There were times when I needed that extra hand, but I used whatever ingenuity I could muster to get things done without assistance.

When the project was complete, I will never forget that feeling of accomplishment when the doors were perfectly level and balanced, and it all worked like it was supposed to. I was so proud of myself and what I accomplished on my own, and I was so filled with joy that I just had to do a little happy dance. Mission accomplished. Even years later after I completed the successful project, I sometimes look at the doors and the beautiful trim-work and smile proudly – and I do have to show off my handiwork to those who visit the house. The feeling of achievement stays with me – it lives inside of me, and I will always remember the saga and then culminating in the feeling of elation. Ultimately, the reward was worth it.

If I had hired a contractor to come in and install the doors, which I could have afforded to do, I would have robbed myself of the opportunity to overcome obstacles and do something I had never done before. I took on the individual responsibility, accomplished my goal, and I am continuing to enjoy the fruits of my labor. It's a good feeling. We all need those types of feelings – it's what keeps us engaged in life. It's what keeps our juices flowing. It's what makes life just a little bit better.

As I experienced with the pocket doors, setting individual goals and working hard to achieve them allows us to revel in our successes. But we must take personal responsibility in order to achieve. And when we do accomplish our goals, there is far more meaning and value than if we were handed something for free. Fittingly, free stuff is never valued as much as something you've worked hard to accomplish. We can feel happy to have received something for nothing, but the feeling of elation is not near as high as accomplishing a goal yourself. Free stuff comes and goes, but the feeling of achievement lives in us forever.

With individual responsibility comes accountability – they go hand-in-hand. The definition of accountability is: "An obligation or willingness to accept responsibility or to account for one's actions and behaviors." When something goes wrong, we must own up to it, and conversely, when things go right, we are then allowed to celebrate the accomplishments.

As mentioned earlier, we are not only accountable to ourselves, but also to society as a whole. In order to succeed in life, we all must set standards for ourselves and we must be willing to put in the work to achieve our goals. We must be held accountable at work to keep our jobs. We must be held accountable to our spouse and family. We are accountable for following the laws of the land. However, first and foremost, it all begins with accountability to one's self. When personal accountability is relinquished, that is going against the very nature of being a human.

Every creature has innate instincts that contribute to survivability. These traits are part of our DNA – they can also be a learned behavior – both are part of our building blocks that have made us successful in surviving in this world. They are part of why we have evolved to the highest rung on the ladder in the animal kingdom. Animals depend on themselves for survival and they are accountable to only themselves – with a few exceptions such as ant colonies and other animal "families."

Removing the need for hard work and personal accountability by giving lots of hand-outs actually lessens the value of human worth. This runs counter to what being a human is all about. It steals from our human-ness and devalues the individual. By doing so, it weakens the individual and reduces the chances for surviving (and thriving) in this world. There is a cause and effect. The cause is the removal of the need for personal accountability and the effect is a diminished ability or desire to succeed and be self-sufficient.

We humans should be encouraged to be self-reliant. We must encourage personal accountability; it is a part of who we are. I don't think we want to end up being a bunch of lazy fools who are accountable to no one. If we evolve into that mindset and belief, we will eventually become a species that will become extinct. Removing basic survival instincts, like removing the ability to smell from a dog, or removing the ability to fly from a bird, will eventually lead to extinction.

Making excuses for people to not be self-sufficient or held accountable to themselves means they are being squelched and held down under the thumb of those who want to control them. Leaders who advocate for free stuff are denying the value of self-sufficiency and individualism, while replacing them with dependency and apathy.

Personal accountability in any type of relationship is founded in trust. In being personally accountable, we make a commitment to live up to the expectation of those who hold us accountable. In playing team sports, the team is relying on all teammates to do their job and perform their best. If a teammate does not feel the need to be personally accountable for his or her performance, players notice that and the trust in their teammate is eroded. It can create dissention and cause the entire team to perform at a less than optimum level. Those players that hold personal accountability in high regard generally play better than those that don't really care about the team. A good teammate is accountable to the rest of the team.

In addition, personal accountability inspires players to take ownership of their job. Pride in performance and owning the outcome shows a commitment to the team. Teammates are far more prone to support and encourage a player who shows ownership than a player who does not care about giving his or her best. By being accountable and owning performance, it deepens the trust of the other teammates and makes the entire team better. Imagine how frustrating it would be to play on a team where none of the players really care about how they perform. That is not a winning formula, and the team will most certainly be in disarray and not win any games.

The same is true in a society. If members do not show any regard for being personally accountable, things will not bode well. Those who choose to violate the law lose the trust of a society and are punished for stepping outside the boundaries of good and decent behavior. That's the way it should be.

When we drive a car, we trust that fellow drivers follow the laws. Those drivers that have no regard for following the rules of the road not only violate the trust of everyone else, they endanger all the other drivers and their passengers. Laws are beneficial because they keep us safe and secure, but all members of society have the responsibility to follow the laws, and they are held accountable by police officers.

Another inherent value accountability provides is that it increases focus and challenges us to achieve. We humans perform better when expectations are clearly laid out. Setting goals and holding ourselves accountable pushes us forward – creating the opportunity to achieve. The same is true for a society. A successful one always strives to improve, which is accomplished when all members take their accountability seriously. The result is a better world to live in.

Sociology professors Catherine E. Ross and John Mirowsky wrote the *Handbook of the Sociology of Mental Health*. In it, they describe how some people "attribute the events and conditions of their lives to their own actions, while others believe their lives are shaped by forces external to themselves, like luck, chance, fate or powerful others."

There are blamers, and there are achievers. There are victims, and there are overcomers. We all probably know someone who is always making excuses about everything. Most of us find those people rather annoying. They usually set themselves up for failure because they are not willing to take individual responsibility or be held accountable for their choices. They would rather make excuses than hold themselves accountable.

Unfortunately, we are allowing people to get away with bad behavior with no accountability. We are losing the desire to hold everyone accountable for their choices, and it is detrimental to our society. When we allow some of our citizens to behave badly, we are encouraging their bad behavior by not inducing consequences. Without accountability, there can be no order.

Regrettably, the vast majority of our schools are not teaching individualism that facilitates kids turning into productive members of society. We don't want to hurt the children's feelings by demanding that they take personal responsibility, nor do we hold them accountable. This does not do the kids any favors – in fact, it is detrimental.

We are also witnessing some profoundly bad parenting going on. Back in my younger years, bad behavior was met with consequences in my family and every other family I knew. My parents held me and my brothers fully accountable if we did something wrong. Today, far too many parents do not hold their children accountable. They give Johnny a pat on the head and say, "Try to do better next time, Sweetie." Far too many parents are sending their children off to school bereft of manners and civility. The teachers, administrators, and other students become victims of parents shirking their duty of teaching their children how to behave and show respect. Those irresponsible parents are not taking their responsibility seriously and the child becomes a disruptive, incorrigible pain in the neck. Since corporal punishment has been taken away from schools, perhaps we can administer the paddle to the lousy parents.

We must stress the importance of individualism, we must instill personal responsibility, and we must demand accountability. Allowing kids or even adults to run wild, cause trouble, and become a problem to our society is unacceptable. We cannot abandon these principles, yet we see them running rampant today. Too many parents are not rearing their children properly. Too many educators are pandering to students. Our judicial system allows grown adults who know better to get away with far too much. The pity is that all of society suffers. Surely we can improve - *"I Know We Are Better Than This."*

Chapter 6

Drinking the Kool-Aid

We've all heard the phrase "drinking the Kool-Aid" - having to do with the consumption and an adoption of an ideology.

There is an act that must be carried out in consuming a liquid – swallowing is a choice. One chooses to consume a drink, whether it's milk, juice, beer, vodka, or tequila. Some people sip drinks while others guzzle. Some people love beer, while others think it has a repulsive taste. Some choose to drink scotch, while others think it tastes like drinking peat moss swamp water. Scotch drinkers will say "it's an acquired taste."

When imbibing in a beverage, we make a value judgment and say, "Hey, that tastes very interesting – it didn't taste like what I was told – I kind of like that taste," or "This tastes awful and I don't want to drink it anymore."

Just like putting something into our body by drinking it – no matter if it's Kool-Aid or Scotch, we are choosing to bring it into our body. Similarly, when we begin to believe something, we let it into our being – we actually "consume" a certain point of view – it becomes a part of who we are when we drink the Kool-Aid.

We initially decide if a viewpoint is worth consuming or rejecting. If it tastes good, we keep drinking it – we acquire the taste for it – it becomes agreeable to us. Then, in some extreme instances, some people become addicted to it. At that point, the Kool-Aid has taken over their life – they have been consumed by the Kool-Aid. How ironic is that?

When someone is completely overtaken by the urge to drink a certain beverage such as alcohol, it becomes a psychosis that leads to other health problems. What inherent problems an individual has as it relates to fitting into society are exacerbated by the drinking problem. Many get violent. Many break the law. Many take the lives of others. It becomes detrimental to our societal welfare.

I bring up the drinking of the Kool-Aid issue because we need to be more cognizant and use better judgment of what we are feeding into our belief system. There are times when we get wrapped up in an emotional topic, and we believe things that may not be the truth or may not be helpful to our own well-being. We must always be diligent in deeply thinking about what we accept as truth. Sometimes, we drink the Kool-Aid without stopping and fully considering what we are adopting as a belief. We like the taste and sometimes we become addicted to it.

All too often, we want to believe something so badly that we forget to stop and really consider all sides of the story. We are always better served if we question something and look at all aspects of a subject before we decide to drink the Kool-Aid. Just slamming it down because that's what we and our friends think is right can be detrimental to our health. Some people get so wrapped up in a certain viewpoint they become fully addicted. Extremism then sets in. At that point, it becomes a form of psychosis, just like alcoholism. The severity can range from mild symptoms of delusions, all the way to full extreme radical.

We all surround ourselves with people who believe what we believe. It validates us and our positions, and we help validate our friends' positions. It becomes a happy circle, and that circle can become a whirlpool that can sweep us down the drain.

The point to be made here is to be careful what we believe. We need to always look at a topic or ideology with some skepticism – always question, always come to a reasoned conclusion – not an emotional one. Never let emotion over-rule reason. When we allow that to happen, we become easily manipulated and relinquish our common sense and rationality.

The Kool-Aid we drink should always be distilled by breaking down a viewpoint through level-headedness and filtering it with common sense. We must probe. We must seek truth. Remember, truth is always somewhere in the middle. Only when we make a conscious effort to seek the truth, can we come to a reasoned conclusion.

When people are unwilling to move from one ideological position to another despite facts and evidence that disproves their position, they have then moved from rational to irrational thinking. Again, smart and reasonable people seek the truth. They inquire and analyze, while always looking for verification versus seeking affirmation. There is a big difference between those two terms.

Verification is defined as "the process of establishing the truth, accuracy, or validity of something."

Affirmation is defined as "a confirmation of something that is agreed upon in order to seek emotional support or encouragement."

In my mind, verification assumes a given position and tests the validity of that position by seeking out and examining as much information as possible. A definitive conclusion is saved until all the facts are carefully and intelligently weighed. An inquisitive mind is open to new thoughts or ideas and is not quick to form opinions based on an emotional feeling, speculation, or hearsay evidence.

Seeking the truth is a noble endeavor, and only brave people are willing to lay down their pre-conceived ideas or positions in pursuit of the truth.

Those who are unwilling to open their minds and consider other possibilities are only seeking affirmation. They are imprisoned by their close-mindedness. They are held captive inside their own ideology. This is a self-imposed imprisonment that need not be a life sentence without parole.

All that is necessary for those who espouse the position that what they have decided is immovable and irrevocable is to simply lay down their preconceived prejudices and open their minds to new possibilities. It might even turn into a new adventure that brings peace and comfort to their lives like they have never experienced before. We never know until we try. To perpetuate this idea that "my mind is made up and there is no changing it," erects the self-inflicted walls that create the prison in which these individuals reside.

Close-mindedness is defined as "intolerant of the beliefs and opinions of others; stubbornly unreceptive to new ideas" or "having a *mind* firmly unreceptive to new ideas or arguments."

What this position of close-mindedness does is create internal anger when the position an individual supports is challenged with facts that contradict what he or she believes. "How dare you think that my version of the facts is not the truth" is the most common response when someone dares to disagree. An angry response to being challenged is generally seen as insecurity, uncertainty, weakness, or the lack of a defensible argument.

When a discussion spirals downward into name calling and personal attacks, then one can assume that the offender has a weak position and is not secure enough in his or her own beliefs to carry on a reasoned and intellectually honest discourse. People like that have chosen to get drunk on the Kool-Aid and become self-radicalized, and they have closed their minds to any other viewpoint, no matter the validity of the opposing position. Being close-minded is lazy and usually leads to unhappiness, discontent and distrust of others.

Conversely, having an open mind leads to happiness and contentment because one is not always on the defensive. It frees the mind to seek further information. It increases intellect and stimulates the mind versus the dumbing down and self-sedation that close-mindedness brings upon us.

It's so easy (and lazy) to outright dismiss or be disrespectful when it comes to personal viewpoints. When we are adamantly for or against something, we make it hard on ourselves for having any chance to consider things from a different point of view. It shouldn't be that way, but it is. In reality, we should be more open to viewing things as the other side views them – there might either be some common ground that can be found, or we might even learn something new that shines new light on a different perspective.

It's hard to get us to change our minds, and it's not easy to admit that we were wrong. Some people are more stubborn than others. When someone is so obstinate about something, it often is akin to having been brainwashed. If we hear something over and over, our mind tends to start believing it. The brain is vulnerable to manipulation when repetitive messaging is used. When we want to believe something very badly, it doesn't take much convincing for our brains to be programmed. At that point, our viewpoints become immovably locked in.

In some instances, stubbornness can be helpful, such as determination to succeed, but in other cases, it can be detrimental to one's well-being. This is especially true on emotional subjects such as religion and politics. Too often, heated conversations ensue because a subject can be so passionately charged that reason and sanity take a back seat to screaming, name-calling, and/or a physical confrontation. When this happens, nobody wins. Convincing someone at the height of a fiery argument is a fruitless endeavor. We might as well take our differing opinion, bow out gracefully, and agree to disagree - it's the better part of valor – and it might save a friendship, a marriage, or a family.

As mentioned before, people who are close-mindedly committed to one ideology tend to seek out others with similar views and feed off each other. These groups quite often become susceptible to radicalism and often suffer from intellectual inbreeding, leading to an "us against the world" mentality. They are drinkers of the Kool-Aid. They view themselves as victims of society, they adopt an underdog position, and they typically begin a crusade against societal "normalism" as a result of their extremism. If others disagree with them, their demise is necessary in order to further the cause. They give people one choice – agree or be removed. The sentiment is, "You are either with us or against us." Extremism relies on emotion and irrationality at the expense of reason and rationality.

Some people are more prone to drinking the Kool-Aid than others. These people are vulnerable to being manipulated into doing something that is against their better judgment. Unfortunately, there have been cults such as the Heaven's Gate group led by Marshall Applewhite where 38 people committed suicide, or Jim Jones in "Jonestown" Guyana where 910 people committed suicide by literally drinking the Kool-Aid (which is where the term originated). These and other mass suicides are examples of how a certain group of people put aside their natural instincts and gave in to manipulation through mind control. It truly is sad that some people are so vulnerable that they take their own life – and sometimes their own children's lives.

We have also seen this play out in Islamic extremism – you either convert to Islam or lose your head. We have seen the same thing occur in numerous Communist countries where people were executed for practicing a religion. We've seen this extremism play out through all of history. Those brave souls that make up the opposition to a totalitarian government are summarily extinguished for having the audacity to not drink the Kool-Aid and to disagree with those in power. Not only do the dissidents lose their lives, innocent people are also terminated. Extremism in every form is dangerous and runs counter to how a civil society should behave.

Extremists recruit their members by pointing out that we are all victims of something. Criteria number one is victimhood – in order to be a member, one has to adopt the victim mentality. That ignites a feeling where the victim must strike back and extract revenge.

Oppression is also a recruiting tool. The attitude is, "If you are down-trodden, it's not your fault - it's society's fault and you have the right to tear everything down." In this world of victimhood, everyone is oppressed, and everyone is a victim. The response is that society must be reconstructed, and the oppressors must pay dearly for their transgressions against the victims. Ironically, the oppressed become the oppressors, and the oppressors become the oppressed. When revenge is extracted, the rationalization is that justice is being achieved and the cost to the oppressors is merely collateral damage.

Another personality target for extremists is the strongly passionate person. Motivating these people is an easy task, making them an easy target for conversion to the cause and then radicalized. These are the people that are out front and center when it's time to protest. They are the screamers, the rock throwers, or the murderers.

Another target is people who are holding a grudge against society and are seeking to retaliate. Still another group that is vulnerable to extremism is abusers who are adept at the art of exploitation. This group often uses a tactic referred to as "crybullying." They try to beat their opponents into submission by publicly shaming them or promoting a boycott. The bottom line is, extremists are a small percentage of people, but they can wreak lots of havoc – and they do.

Extremists think their battle is noble and well worth their efforts. By adopting the moral high ground, it makes it easier and a more justifiable excuse for the war. Their attitude is, "I am more moral than you, and you are an immoral ingrate that must be shamed, silenced or terminated."

As a part of a radical group, the mandate is, "You must always be cautious of what to say because if one dare say the wrong thing, you are a heretic and you will be expunged, if not killed. You must also be committed to the group mentality."

Groupthink allows neither dissention nor disagreement – critical thinking is just not tolerated.

When we really think about it, the life of an Antifa extremist, for example, does not seem to be very pleasant. Everything is wrong. They think everybody is screwed up except for themselves. When victimhood is removed, when oppression is eliminated, and when everyone mind-numbingly thinks the same way, what do they end up with? After they kill Big Brother and the ruling class has been dealt with, when capitalism is dead, now what? What's left over is a bunch of angry anarchists that are supposed to bring peace to all. What remains is a group of extremists with nothing left to live for, because they cannot exist without a cause.

In my opinion, having extremists run a country pretty much sounds like a recipe for disaster. It doesn't instill confidence in me. I don't think we need to completely tear down everything and re-build like some anarchists believe. Maybe a little trimming around the edges would be a better alternative than uprooting the entire tree. After all, our country's roots are deep and strong. Unity sounds like a better idea than anarchy.

Historically, unity has allowed us to overcome our differences. We certainly don't all think the same. I must say, some people use that thing called thinking more often than others – it really is a useful thing! What fun would life be if we were a bunch of mind-numbed entities that looked alike, spoke alike, thought alike, and behaved alike? We much prefer the randomness of uniqueness and diversity – it makes life far more interesting. But it also leads to challenges.

The biggest challenge for us is to not let differing beliefs erect a divide. Taking extreme positions is not conducive to societal unity. Cooperation and acceptance seem to be better ideas. We should all accept each other and allow people to believe what they choose to believe. Looking down on people and thinking we are smarter than the other people is undoubtedly a form of prejudice. I recall the old saying, "I'm not prejudiced; I just know what's right." What we all must remember is that what's right for one person may not be right for another. Open-mindedness is an admirable trait that should be practiced by far more people and far more often.

It's OK if we have differences of opinion as long as it doesn't get in the way of having a peaceful and harmonious country.

Our differences are not only built in our DNA, they are also built by the entirety of our life experiences – we all experience life differently, and life is seen through the eyes of each individual beholder. It's really OK if we are all randomly different – think of how boring life would be without it, but we still must be civil and accepting of other viewpoints. It's OK to agree to disagree.

As pointed out, drinking too much Kool-Aid can be hazardous to our health. Unfortunately, there are no warning labels on bottles of ideology. We must be discerning in what we intellectually and emotionally imbibe. We cannot allow hostility, extremism, and divisive attitudes to overtake us. Before we drink any Kool-Aid that leads to self-destruction, it is my hope that we look around and tell ourselves, *"I Know We Are Better Than This."*

Chapter 7

It's Only Words

Words are amazing. They convey thoughts, ideas, emotions, provide color, and allow us to communicate with each other. They can warn us of danger – even save our lives. They can do so many things – including get us in a lot of trouble if we use the wrong word at the wrong time.

People in high places have been taken down after uttering words or expressing sentiments that some people find not only offensive, but hurtful. The list of famous people that have been severely punished for saying some "illegal" words includes politicians, CEO's, famous movie producers, athletes, police officers, and even the common everyday person like you or me. Why is it that something we say can ruin our lives? Do words have that much power? Evidently so in this day and age. When someone uses critical or derogatory words, there is no blood that is spilled, no bones being broken, and no life is lost. Whatever happened to, "Sticks and stones can break my bones, but words can never hurt me"?

A simple question to ask is: shouldn't there be a statute of limitations for stupid things people say? I know there are many people who would agree there certainly should be. Is it really relevant what someone said 30 or 40 years ago? Are we so wrapped up in "gotcha" quotations that we have lost all sensibilities? I think it's out of control. Someone would really have to work hard to convince me otherwise.

Perhaps the sentiment that "we are what we say" comes into play. But should that be the case? After all, it's only words. I will address the topic of hate-speech later, but it can really rile people up. We can all agree that hate-speech is, well yes, it is hateful. But does it fall in the category of a capital offense? Should someone get the equivalent of a social death penalty just for saying hateful things?

How is it that with one word, we can extrapolate how a person truly feels? Saying the wrong word does not in itself make us egregious hatemongers. If we call a black person a (insert forbidden word here), it's a highly offensive word – but isn't it strange that it's only offensive when someone who is not black says it? Seems as though black rappers are able to use that word as freely and as often as they desire, and they are not called a racist. But if white people, brown people, Asian people or any other people other than black rappers use that word, they would be labeled racists.

I do believe that assuming what someone says defines them forever is a bit far-reaching. It does not make sense. As previously stated, a misused word has almost become a capital offense in the minds of many. Is it not strange that we allow one word or one statement to fully define our viewpoint of a person? Are we really able to discern whether a person is a racist if he or she uses the N-word? Or are we able to determine that a person is a misogynist because he had a huge fight with his wife and he said some bad things? It's truly troubling that we as a society allow that to happen. It's just thoughts – it's just words. Methinks we have gone way overboard.

Now if a person shows a pattern of behavior and actions that can lead us to an educated conclusion, then we can safely call someone a racist or misogynist and then give that person the appropriate public shaming he or she deserves. If it's politically expedient for an opponent that uses an accidental inappropriate word against the opposition, why take a wild leap to conclude the opponent is guilty of racism? Does that make him or her a horrible person for a one-time indiscriminate use of the wrong word?

We all say the wrong thing sometimes. We all say stupid things we regret. But again I ask, must we hand down the death sentence? Why can't we just accept an apology and move on? Why make a huge deal out of one word or phrase? It's most likely a politically expedient thing to do in order to denigrate an opponent. Politicians are the absolute worst as we all have witnessed. It's as if we don't have anything more important to do than to rant and rave that someone used the wrong word.

Why is it that we have dozens, maybe hundreds of words that are completely banned from our vocabulary? I remember hearing George Carlin do a whole comedy show around "Seven Words You Can't Use on TV." I won't list them all because they are prohibited. Society says they are not fit to print – or say. Why is that? They are only words and the vast majority of those criticizing the use of foul language are most likely guilty of the same sin. Words are just part of the English language, and last time I checked, those seven words we can't say are actually in the dictionary.

Is it not intriguing how we have come to determine that certain words are forbidden? Sure, a word can hurt someone's feelings, but are we such a sensitive society that we are unable to forgive the use of a forbidden word? Come on, we must admit that it is a little harsh. Don't we overreact? I guess words do have even more power than we think they do – especially if a single word can ruin someone's livelihood or life forever.

We can't take words back after they leave our mouths – or un-post a statement on Twitter or Facebook (as all too many people have learned). Bad words didn't use to get people in trouble as much as they do now. Currently, there are audio recordings, videos, newspapers and the internet. In the olden days, there was only "hear-say". Proof that someone uttered a forbidden word was a lot harder to come by, whereas today, there is no denying it when it is recorded in print or available for listening or viewing.

If one word or phrase literally makes me into something, then I am going to say I'm a millionaire, and then I will be considered a millionaire. Wow, I guess it's that simple. It seems a big stretch that we can judge people and know who and what they are by the use of one word or statement. We are known by our deeds, not by our words. When we think about it, it really is ludicrous to permanently castigate someone for the use of the wrong word. It's a complete overreaction, but that's where we are today in the politically correct universe.

What I am waiting for is someone to publish a book defining what to say and what not to say. And there's even what we can or can't say in a certain context, so that must be included as well.

I came across a word that was unknown to me. The word is cisgender. I looked it up online and found this definition from the website urbandictionary.com: "The opposite of transgendered, someone who is cisgendered has a gender identity that agrees with their societally recognized sex. Many transgender people prefer 'cisgender' to 'biological', 'genetic', or 'real' male or female because of the implications of those words. Using the term 'biological female' or 'genetic female' to describe cisgendered individuals excludes transgendered men, who also fit that description. To call a cisgendered woman a 'real woman' is exclusive of transwomen, who are considered within their communities to be 'real' women, also."

OK. I read that definition six times and still do not have any idea what cisgender means and why it is relevant to me. If we are going to have to learn all the definitions of these words and try to understand all the rules for how to use them, why to use them, and when to use them, I am surely doomed to an anti-political correctness hell. Sorry, it's hard for a grown man to keep up with all that is required in the liberal world of vocabulary. I just can't do it. I must be a decrepit loser. To all the other decrepit losers out there, and I'll throw in all the deplorables too, we better get in step with the liberal brand of political correctness or we will be severely punished and publicly shamed for every verbal indiscretion. The vocabulary police will be hot on our trail if we don't straighten up. We will have to go to the chalkboard and write a thousand times: "I'm a bad person and I will not be politically incorrect ever again."

Millennial and GenX youth are getting a reputation – perhaps deservedly so. Brett Easton Ellis, noted author and political commenter, has labeled them, "Generation Wuss." In his book called *White*, Mr. Ellis said they had issues with "oversensitivity, their sense of entitlement, their insistence they were always right despite sometimes overwhelming proof to the contrary, their joint tendencies of overreaction, and passive-aggressive possibility."

He also spoke about "overprotective, helicopter moms and dads mapping their every move while smothering their kids and not teaching them how to deal with life's hardships ... people might not like you, this person will not love you back, kids are really cruel, work sucks, it's hard to be good at something, your days will be made up of failure and disappointment, you're not talented, people suffer, people grow older, people die."

According to Mr. Ellis, Generation Wuss has devolved into "victim narratives, anxiety, and neediness." Another observation that is also disturbing is the unwillingness and inability to listen and even consider other viewpoints if they are outside of their "wokeness" standards.

And then, as previously mentioned, there is this outcry for some people to have their "safe spaces" where they choose to isolate themselves as a self-protective mechanism. They are afraid someone is going to say the wrong thing that offends their sensibilities or "triggers" them into feeling angry or dismayed. That sounds like more symptoms of Generation Wuss syndrome.

From an article published in the *Los Angeles Times*, Frank Furedi, professor of Kent University in England stated, "Safe space activism stems primarily from the separatist impulses associated with the politics of identity, already rampant on campus. For some individuals, the attraction of a safe space is that it insulates them from not just hostility, but the views of people who are not like them. Students' frequent demand for protection from uncomfortable ideas on campus — such as so-called trigger warnings — is now paralleled by calls to be physically separated too. Groups contend that their well-being depends on living with their own kind." Mr. Furedi continued, "The popularity of identity politics among insecure millennials threatens to fracture campus life to the point that undergraduates are inhabiting separate spaces and leading parallel lives." In other words, the only way these ill-informed, overly sensitive souls can cope with a bad word or differing viewpoints is to withdraw to their safe space.

Who would have thought that original liberalism, which was founded on inclusion and freedom of thought, would devolve into neo-liberalism where differing opinions cause students to run to their safe space to hide? I went to college for learning, open human interaction, and mind expansion, versus indoctrination, isolation, and brainwashing. I think college students should be learning about integration and open-mindedness versus segregation and close-mindedness – and safe spaces!

Would it be too far out there to say many of our youth are growing up to be wimpy, self-centered brats that have no backbone, no respect for other viewpoints, or self-confidence?   In their world, there is no critical thinking allowed, no thought-provoking discussion permitted, and no disagreement tolerated because it might hurt someone's feelings. Our children and students – and even adults - cannot be coddled and protected because when the real world is revealed to them, their likely reaction is to flee to their safe space, curl up in the fetal position, clutch their cell phone, and seek solace in their isolation. Can anyone explain why this is good for our society? I think not, and anyone that thinks so is sadly misguided and mistaken in my opinion.

Yes, words are powerful tools, but they are not weapons of mass destruction as some would have us believe. Our youth deserve more than what we are giving them in terms of life experiences. If we do not challenge them, and if we do not encourage them to expand their minds, we will end up with a bunch of neurotic children who will grow up to be psychotic adults. I hope we can all join in to say, *"I Know We Are Better Than This."*

Chapter 8

Free Speech with Exceptions

If current liberals were truly "liberal" they would embrace, rather than shun free speech. Early liberals, including myself, were so adamant about everyone having the right to free speech that we marched in DEFENSE of it – we demanded everyone's right of freedom of expression. Today's neo-liberals march to PREVENT free speech and shut down opposing views. We have witnessed the prevention of freedom of expression on numerous occasions – mostly the victims were conservatives.

Perhaps I am wrong, but I don't recall any right-wing or conservative groups who are attempting to silence free speech. It seems to me the only group trying to shut down free speech is coming from neo-liberals on the left. Some liberal political leaders are intent on dictating what we can say and how we can say it – we must use the politically correct jargon. They want the ability to step in when they think someone is getting out of line and does not agree with their elitist dogma.

Here is an example from George Orwell's classic book, *1984* that hits too close to home in this discussion of free speech. The official language in Orwell's Oceania (the "state") was called Newspeak. It was the language of politically correct speech taken to extremes. Newspeak was based on Standard English, but all words relating to nonconformist political thinking were banned and removed from the vocabulary. Interestingly, the idea also intended to reduce the size of the vocabulary in order to limit thoughts and ideas. That sounds strangely familiar, does it not? We can't have thought police or word police running around telling everyone what to think and what to say. Our country isn't run that way, yet we are inching closer and closer to Newspeak.

We have seen violent protests on the University of California Berkley campus prohibiting a speech by Milo Yiannopoulos, the British "alt-right" gay journalist and provocateur. Yes, he is controversial, but he does not call for the overthrow of the government. He's not inciting people to riot. He's not threatening the lives of others. He does not promote the destruction of property. If he wants to speak and there are those who want to listen, he has every right to his own opinions, whether people like them or not. If we don't agree with him, we don't have to listen. In my mind, that's pretty simple, and no one should disagree with that if they believe anything about the First Amendment.

Berkley administrators and many others across the country have given in to Antifa and various leftist groups by preventing or cancelling speakers like Ann

Coulter, Ben Shapiro and numerous other conservatives. There is nothing in the First Amendment that says selective administration of free speech is acceptable. It specifically guarantees freedom of expression by prohibiting or restricting the press or the rights of individuals to speak freely. It also guarantees the right of citizens to assemble PEACEABLY and to petition their government, but it does not say we have the right to prevent free speech, commit violence, or destroy property.

Leftists would not agree with much of what Milo says, but is it really necessary to destroy property and shut down his right to self-expression because they disagree with him? There is no free speech when someone starts inciting a violent uprising or threatening physical harm to someone else.

Yiannopoulos is not guilty of anything other than expressing his viewpoints. Yet the "supreme court" of leftists at Berkley thought they had the right to do what they did – shut him down by whatever means necessary. In what universe does that make sense if we say we support freedom of speech? Somehow, I just can't see the logic nor the justification if one of liberalism's founding principles is being violated. It seems as though the protesters who shut down free speech are overruling the First Amendment rights. Is that acceptable to anyone? Should it be? Of course not, but left-wing liberals think it's acceptable.

What happened on the Berkley campus and other universities across the country where leftists were trying to shut down free speech is absolutely against the law. Whether we agree or disagree with someone's point of view, he or she has the right to freedom of expression without violent and destructive protests. No one was making students attend the speech that Milo was giving. Simple logic says that if we don't want to hear his speech, just don't go. There is absolutely no need for what happened on campuses across the country. Free and peaceful societies do not behave like this. They tolerate debate - in fact, they encourage it!

An interesting factor that plays into on-campus free speech is that virtually every university gets funding from both the state and federal governments. Public universities are supported by taxpayer dollars – even private universities get federal funds. One would logically think that with that funding comes some level of responsibility to follow the laws of the land – with no exceptions. Campus administrative staff and faculty members have no right to limit speech – it's against the law and it violates the fundamentals of education. Those higher education institutions that want to limit free speech should be and must be held accountable. After all, colleges and universities are supposed to be the haven for free speech and debate.

Ironically, UC-Berkley spawned the free speech movement back in the mid 1960's. Students protested and demanded that the university administration remove the ban of political activities on their campus and concede the students' academic freedom, along with asserting their right to freedom of speech.

If this type of speech suppression as practiced by various colleges and universities is what some people refer to as "progressive" thinking, it certainly seems more "regressive" than progressive to me. We should be worried if the thought police knock on our door and ask us to hand over our free speech rights and then provides us with a dictionary containing all the words they allow us to speak as in Orwell's *1984*.

Liberalism claims to embrace diversity. Any liberal one talks to and asks if there should be diversity would spend the next 10 minutes talking about how important diversity is to our society. They will say how we need diversity in race, gender, housing, hiring, friends, and on and on. OK – let's accept that premise – diversity is critical. Got it.

It's interesting that today's neo-liberals say they embrace diversity in everything, yet there is one glaring area where they don't embrace complete diversity – that is, freedom of speech. They can claim they are FOR free speech, but their actions speak louder than their words.

Neo-liberals also claim to be big on punishing bullies. Hmmmmm. It seems like they are trying to bully people into staying silent. Their attitude is: "You can only say what I want you to say, or only have the opinion I want you to have." Sounds like out-and-out bullying to me. Am I wrong?

As stated earlier, there are numerous examples of other conservatives who were prevented from speaking on various campuses beyond Milo Yiannopoulos. Conservatives have the same right of free speech as liberals. There can be differences of opinion, but not differences in who gets to have free speech and who doesn't. If that's how it's going to work, we are in trouble. There cannot be a double standard.

Isn't it a bit of a double standard when Madonna disrespected the president and called for blowing up the White House? Isn't that more inflammatory than anything Yiannopoulos has ever said? Of course it is – yet the leftists don't consider Madonna's comments hate speech? Come on, let's get real. Let's hold everybody to the same standard. The standard should be evenly and fairly administered. No excuses, no bending the rules. No turning a deaf ear. And those that want to blow up the Whitehouse, no matter who is president, well, they are just plain crazy – we should all be able to agree on that.

Kathy Young, in an article from *USA Today* had an interesting observation. She stated, "One may argue that right-wing authoritarianism is the bigger threat in America today. But attacks on unpopular speech in the universities can only make that threat worse, by undermining cultural support for freedom of speech and setting a precedent for speech suppression. Progressives who minimize the problem and excuse shout-downs as mere rudeness or challenge do so at their own peril."

Niall Ferguson with the Hoover Institute at Stanford said, "Freedom is rarely killed off by people chanting 'Down with Freedom!' It is killed off by people claiming that the greater good/the general will/the community/the proletariat requires 'examination of the parameters'…of individual liberty. If the criterion for censorship is that nobody's feelings can be hurt, we are finished as a free society. Mark my words, while I can still publish them with impunity: The real tyrants, when they come, will be for diversity (except of opinion) and against hate speech (except their own)."

We are restricted by political correctness that has gotten out of control. It seems like every month there's a new word that we are not supposed to use because it might offend someone. Question: Are we really that thin-skinned? Are we all that insecure? Comedy has essentially been castrated because of political correctness. Can we not poke fun at each other anymore? Have we completely lost our sense of humor? Is it really necessary for someone to run to their safe space if someone tells a joke?

Jerry Seinfeld stated that he is not working college campuses any more for fear of backlash over political correctness. Kris Rock, Larry the Cable Guy, and many others echo the same sentiment.

"I hear that all the time," Seinfeld said. "I don't play colleges, but I hear a lot of people tell me, 'Don't go near colleges. They're so PC.' I'll give you an example: My daughter's 14. My wife says to her, 'Well, you know, in the next couple years, I think maybe you're going to want to be hanging around the city more on the weekends, so you can see boys.' You know what my daughter says? She says, 'That's sexist.'" Seinfeld continued, "They just want to use these words: 'That's racist'; 'That's sexist'; 'That's prejudice.' They don't know what they're talking about."

Kris Rock said, "I stopped playing colleges, and the reason is because they're way too conservative," Rock said in the interview. "Not in their political views — not like they're voting Republican — but in their social views and their willingness not to offend anybody. Kids raised on a culture of 'We're not going to keep score in the game because we don't want anybody to lose.' Or just ignoring race to a fault. You can't say 'the black kid over there.' No, it's 'the guy with the red shoes.' You can't even be offensive on your way to being inoffensive."

From George Carlin: "Political correctness is the newest form of intolerance, and it's especially pernicious because it comes disguised as tolerance. It presents itself as 'fairness' yet attempts to control and restrict language with strict codes and rigid rules." He refers to those who try and control speech as "PC lingo cops." Mr. Carlin continued, "Political correctness is fascism pretending to be manners...you can also call it 'social Marxism.' Political correctness cripples discourse, creates ugly language, and is generally stupid."

Why did I use comedians to reinforce the over-the-top language control? Because we used to be able to laugh at ourselves and our flaws without people getting offended, their feelings hurt, or having to run to their safes space.

Even Bill Maher, the self-avowed guru of progressivism came out against political correctness in a CNN interview with Chris Cuomo. Here's what he said: "And I think a lot of this far left political correctness is a cancer on progressivism. I think when you -- when you talk to Trump supporters, they're not blind to his myriad flaws. But one thing they always say is he's not politically correct. I don't think you can under -overestimate how much people have been choking on political correctness and hate it. There were two studies about this recently, it was in *The New York Times*, front page story a few months ago. It was also in *The Atlantic* about a year ago. The vast majority of liberals in this country hate it. They think political correctness has gone way too far. No one likes to be living on eggshells."

If someone posts a racist or sexist comment on Twitter or Facebook, why can we not just ignore it, say to ourselves, "Well, that person is stupid," and then just move on? Making a big deal of it only makes matters worse and draws more attention to that individual's stupidity. It really is not necessary for everyone to get up in arms about it. It's free speech.

We have become so thin-skinned that any stupid comment causes a major brain hemorrhage for some people. My fear is that we have devolved into a neurotic state of mind and are raising our children to be super-sensitive spoiled brats that will have trouble succeeding in life. Thank God there are still a lot of parents out there that recognize what's going on and will not let that happen to their kids. But there are still a lot of bad parents and educators out there that might mean well by giving a trophy to everybody and giving passing grades to kids who really should be failed. The sad thing is they are saddling their children and their students with what I would diagnose as OSSS - Overly Sensitive Social Syndrome. In order to survive in this world, we need to have some toughness, grit, and self-confidence. We all must understand what failure is; otherwise, we will not know what success looks like.

The term "snowflake" has been coined to describe those that suffer from OSSS. We have "safe places" where they can hide from the real world and pretend that life is perfect and no one is going to say a bad word to them. They are so self-absorbed that they think the world revolves around them and they deserve a life that is free of conflict. Far too many kids have skin that is so thin we could read a newspaper through it – and way too many parents and educators are feeding into this mind-set.

We are an advanced society and technology is a wonderful thing, it also has some culpability in how young people have acquired OSSS. It has made our lives so much easier than those folks in the past that have had to eke out their own sustenance on a daily basis. We have it so much easier than our ancestors when it comes to surviving and thriving in life. Our silver platter is so overflowing that too many have lost the ability to overcome and fend off the trials and tribulations that life throws at us. When all these kids want to do is run to a safe space when life gets tough or someone says something that offends them, we are in a heap of trouble.

We cannot continue to train our children to go run and hide in their safe place if someone says something that they don't agree with. We cannot allow the thought police and the offensive word committee to control what we say. Words don't cause any physical harm – as long as they are not used to incite others to commit violence (like saying we want to blow up the White House). If someone says something stupid or offensive, the best thing to do is to ignore it and walk away. We all need to understand that stupidity is not a crime. Inhibiting free speech is a crime. Freedom of speech is a fundamental right; having a safe space is not.

Who is assigned to be the word police? Is it the media? Is it our bureaucrats? We must draw the line somewhere, and the line should be drawn that free speech is free speech – there are no exceptions except when someone is promoting or inciting violence. We either have it or we don't.

We must defend the right of everyone to have free speech – even when we disagree with what people are saying – they still have the right to say it. If we allow anyone's freedom of expression to be controlled, we are relinquishing that right and are complicit in allowing it to erode. Eventually, it will devolve into Newspeak as in Orwell's *1984*, and we will become mind-numbed robots.

We cannot let OSSS turn into a full-blown psychosis among our youth and even adults, yet it appears that we are moving in that direction. Political correctness is running amuck and free speech is under attack. It's sad but true, and *"I Know We Are Better Than This."*

Chapter 9

Let's Talk About Respect

In many quarters across the country and throughout the world, too many cultures have lost something that is a basic driver for humane treatment of others, and that is RESPECT. A huge part of being a morally driven nation begins with the principle of respecting each other. It must be a rudimentary tenet and is a telling barometer of the morality – and, shall I say, the sanity of a nation.

Let's look at the definition. There are several meanings of the word and when it's used in different contexts, respect has different connotations. What I would like to focus on is in the context of human interaction. Respect, as defined in this sense, is "due regard for the feelings, wishes, rights, or traditions of others," or "to show consideration for; treat courteously or kindly." When individuals respect others, they are showing deference to the "feelings, wishes, rights or traditions" of other people, even when people don't see eye to eye on a subject.

If we start with the premise that everyone is created equal and is worthy of respect, that seems like a humane and logical foundational piece. Given that premise, human interaction can be a meaningful two-way street in which both parties can derive benefit from each other. By just listening, learning can take place. Things can be more easily accomplished while working together. After all, two heads are better than one, and four hands are better than two.

Our human existence relies heavily on positive interaction between people of different backgrounds and cultures. The world is a far better place when we all can get along with each other and treat one another with respect. Without it, things can go terribly wrong and a lot of people can get hurt.

Most everyone believes that one of the cornerstones on which a culture should be built is what Aretha Franklin sang about – RESPECT. Respect for others must emanate from within, but without self-respect, it is difficult to show respect for anyone or anything else. Exhibiting disrespect for others can be indicative of a lack of internal self-respect and self-esteem.

Rev. Jasper Williams, Jr., a famous black pastor who Aretha chose to give her eulogy had some very powerful and poignant words for us all to hear regarding respect and self-respect. In his sermon at Aretha Franklin's funeral, Rev. Williams stated, "Here's the root of what I've been talking about: In order to change America, we must change black America's culture. We must do it through parenting to go forward, it has to be done in the home. What we need to do is create RESPECT among ourselves.

"If you choose to ask me today, do black lives matter? Let me answer like this. No, black lives do not matter, black lives will not matter, black lives ought not matter, black lives should not matter, black lives must not matter until black people start respecting black lives and stop killing ourselves. [Until then] black lives can never matter. I said blacks do not matter, because black lives cannot matter, will not matter, should not matter, must not matter until black people begin to RESPECT their own lives."

Here are more compelling words from Rev. Williams: "Nobody can put values in people. We can't pay the government to give us the values that we ought to live by. Our values have to come from within. And somebody has got to care, and I care enough to say it and do it."

Rev. Williams continued, "Whether you're old school or new school, RESPECT for each other is the key to the road we are on as a race. I feel we ought to respect each other enough to listen…it's going to take all of us, all of us to turn black America around – even those that don't want to – it's going to take that…all I ask is for you to come on board – I help you, you help me. And together we turn our race around. This is a juncture where nobody can do anything for us but us. But until we reach down on the inside of ourselves and touch our soul, and decide that this is enough, to turn this around, until that happens, it doesn't make any difference about how much money the government gives. To me this is not about dollars. This has got to be about an inner calling of the inner man to do what's right about our people.

"Whatever way the home goes, that's the way the world goes. Did you hear me now? As the home goes, so goes the streets. As the streets go, so goes the neighborhood. As the neighborhood goes, so goes the city. As the city goes, so goes the state. As the state goes, so goes the nation. As the nation goes, so goes the world."

Rev. Wright concluded by saying, "…But Aretha, the 'Queen of Soul' told us all we need to have is a little respect…I heard her sing, R-E-S-P-E-C-T. Congress needs to respect each other. The Democrats need to respect Republicans. The Republicans need to respect the Democrats. The liberals need to respect the conservatives. The conservatives need to respect the liberals. The straights need to respect the gays. The gays need to respect the straights…everybody ought to give a little respect. The Queen did what she could [about teaching respect], but it's time we do what WE can."

We have to get real with ourselves in order for change to come. Again, self-respect is a precursor to showing respect for everyone and everything else. Our whole national culture, even the success of our nation, is built on respecting each other. It needs to be taught through good parenting. It needs to be taught in schools. In addition, it needs to be practiced in every personal encounter, whether it's daily interaction with people or politicians discussing controversial topics.

I brought up Rev. Williams' speech for two reasons: first, because of his insight into the importance of showing respect for others, while also valuing self-respect. Second, I used his speech to illustrate how some people disrespectfully reacted to his words.

Both black and white leaders castigated Rev. Williams, but what did he say that was untrue about respecting ourselves and each other? Many media members, celebrities and activists were highly offended by Rev. Williams' words, and they made disrespectful comments which I will not repeat here. He spoke the truth as he sees it, and the only way those that disagreed with him chose to counter his speech was to use disparaging remarks. There are a lot of people that need to learn a lot more about what showing respect really means.

Again, we can have differences and still show respect. What happens when disagreements come up and how they are handled is what separates successful and peaceful societies or cultures from failed civilizations and warring factions. In order for people to get along with each other despite various differences, there must be at least a modicum of respect upon which a relationship can be built.

If teammates do not respect members of their own team, chances are the team will be dysfunctional and won't win many games. If families do not show respect for each other, there will always be in-fighting. If countries refuse to respect their citizens' "feelings, wishes and rights or traditions," then peace will be very difficult to attain and maintain. Civil détente does not happen without due respect between civilians and the country's leaders.

As an aside, two other words that come to mind in relation to respect are decency and civility. Let's examine the definitions.

Decency is "behavior that is good, moral and acceptable in a society" or "conformity to the recognized standard of propriety, good taste, and modesty."

Civility is defined as "showing politeness and courtesy in behavior or speech." It also is characterized as the ability to disagree without disrespect.

All components of our society, whether it's families, schools, neighborhoods, local governments, or our national government, all function well when people value respect, embrace decency, and maintain civility. All of those are essential if people are going to get along with each other. Without them, peace, harmony, and prosperity are virtually impossible to achieve.

Political opponents, and now celebrities, are the biggest offenders of disrespect, indecency and incivility in public discourse today. There is so much rancor, name-calling and insolence occurring in the political world while we common folk are sitting on the sidelines watching. What we think of all this BS is clearly seen in the approval ratings of Congress and the media. Both are in a mad dash to the bottom, and they are both losing ground.

When an approval rating is below Charles Manson and Satan, it should be recognized that there is a problem – and I think we'd all agree the ignominious honor owned by politicians and the media is well deserved. We certainly need to make our feelings known that this type of behavior is totally out of bounds and should not be tolerated. How can a country be run effectively when respect, decency, and civility have been thrown out the window? It can't.

All too often, celebrities only make matters worse when they interject themselves into the fray. What kind of person behaves like Robert de Niro in disrespecting President Trump? On numerous occasions, he has unashamedly called President Trump vile and obscene names, dropping f-bombs on national TV. In my estimation, looking at it from a rational standpoint, many celebrities come across as people who lack any kind of control or decorum and whose hatred and vitriol overpowers common decency and civility. Their behavior and venomous verbal attacks on the President and conservatives should be roundly condemned by everyone. Shouldn't they be held accountable just like everyone else?

This type of thing would never had been tolerated if it were President Obama being verbally attacked. The media's and celebrity's heads would be exploding, and incessant chants of racism, hatred, and disrespect would have been all over the news 24/7. Any Republican or conservative that behaved like these celebrities would have been castigated, tossed into the scrap heap, and then labeled as a psychotic ideologue not worthy of being a part of the human race.

Commenting on Robert di Niro's disrespectful use of the F-word when speaking about President Trump, Donna Brazile, author, former head of the Democrat National Committee, and cable news contributor said, "This potty mouth stuff...I think it's rude, it's offensive...I support the office of the president, regardless of who the occupant is...to have someone use that word in conjunction with the office of the president, hmmmm...I have [a higher] decency standard [than that]."

It might actually be cathartic for the media, celebrities and politicians to start showing respect to the people they disagree with. A good idea might be showing respect by having honest discussions that are devoid of any ideology, then understanding the opposing point of view, and then finding common ground and compromise. That is the moral thing to do. It seems pretty simple...just saying.

It's funny that in sports there are deep rivalries between teams – the Red Sox and Yankees come to mind - but when on the playing field, the players respect each other. Even off the field, we don't see players dropping f-bombs in tirades against their competitors (like many celebrities have done). The players might do it privately, but there is a certain level of public decorum that players are expected to adhere to. If a player did what these celebrities have done, he would be chased from the sport, publicly humiliated by the press, and receive a lifetime ban from Major League Baseball for disrespecting players and the game of baseball.

Besides de Niro, there are literally hundreds of examples of blatant and disgraceful episodes of utter disrespect hurled at President Trump, as well as members of his cabinet and his staff. Even his supporters have been attacked. There are a lot of people who don't like him and he undoubtably can be a caustic figure himself (I have a problem with his behavior sometimes as well), but he is our duly elected president despite what Hillary Clinton or any other Democrat thinks.

The fact is, and it's indisputably true, they just can't accept the fact that they lost the election and are totally committed to not respecting the will of the voters. This is driven because they didn't get their way – they didn't win. It truly is disgraceful.

We try and teach young kids when they play sports to be respectful to their competitors and not to be a sore loser. Mrs. Clinton and innumerable Democrats are certainly not being good examples of good losers – quite the opposite as a matter of fact.

Good losers don't whine and complain about losing. They may be sad and disappointed, but they don't ask for a re-do or want to change the rules because they lost. Nor do they travel across the country making excuses and saying, "I was robbed!" That is the type of behavior one would expect from someone who was not schooled in the art of losing gracefully. Quite honestly, adults should really know better and should behave better. Sore losers offer excuses, while good losers offer a hand of congratulations to the winner. Showing respect is the right and moral thing to do - at least that's what we teach our Little Leaguers to do. It's only common sense that adults should be expected to follow the same rules of respect, decency and civility as we expect from our Little Leaguers. I respectfully say that the mentality of "do as I say, not as I do" is a glaring example of hypocrisy.

When politicians are consumed by antagonism, it shows disrespect to the people they represent. Not too many sane constituents want their congressional representatives to go to Washington DC just to create havoc for the president and the opposing party. Voters send their representatives with the expectation of actually doing something productive.

Why is it that politicians are so disrespectful? Are the tactics of polarization and radicalization executed just to get attention? Maybe they are seeking more Twitter followers? Perhaps it's simply to appease and build endearment to those that are radical supporters?

As much as Democrats personally despise President Trump, the hatred and disrespect that has been shown by their party and followers is appalling and abominable in any rational universe. People who disagree with that statement, need to ask themselves if the shoe were on the other foot, how would they classify that type of behavior? I would bet my house that Democrats would be up in arms if President Obama had been treated the way they have treated President Trump. Again, the mainstream media would be apoplectic – everybody knows that because it's indisputable.

I will add that President Trump could also use a few lessons in how to respectfully treat the opposing party. There is no denying that he is guilty of indecency and incivility as well. Both sides need to get a grip and display better behavior.

There is no rational reason to totally abandon respect, decency and civility no matter how much one disagrees with an opposing party. What happens is that hatred overrides everything, and partisanship along with out-of-control anger takes over. It really is a non-productive thing to do and shows a lack of self-control, not to mention self-respect. Far too many Democrats lost their minds when President Trump came into office and have allowed themselves to be consumed. Such a character flaw emerges and overwhelms common respect, decency and civility. We can disagree about policies and personality, but it is unnecessary and unhealthy to lose control of oneself. That goes for Mr. Trump as well.

In order to be a peaceful and successful society, there must be norms and expectations, and with that comes accountability. Acting out and making a public display of hatred is undoubtably beyond the pale. And implicitly endorsing it by not calling out people for their wayward behavior should be regarded as unacceptable (hello, media?).

I disagreed with just about everything that President Obama stood for, but I would never have done anything like what de Niro and many others have done. To my knowledge, not ONE famous conservative or Republican celebrity disrespected President Obama the way that hundreds, even thousands of Democrats and famous celebrities have attacked President Trump with foul language and vile rhetoric. Disagreement on policy is expected, but disrespect is unacceptable if we truly are a fully civilized society. Shameful behavior should be called out. Do we really want our society to be filled with hatred, disrespect, loss of decency, and incivility? I truly hope not.

It is free speech for people to knock any public official, but we must have standards of behavior. Bad behavior should never be justified no matter who it is or what is involved. Wrong is wrong and bad behavior is bad behavior no matter how anyone tries to spin it or justify it. And if we do try and justify it or spin it, we then become as guilty as the perpetrator by being an accessory to the crime. Celebrities like Robert de Niro and all the other Democrat offenders have never been held accountable publicly for their behavior and they should be. President Trump has been incessantly called out on his behavior by politicians, celebrities and the media, but where is the outrage from Democrats, the media, and celebrities when one of their own gets out of line? There is a big helping of moral relativism clearly on display here – not to mention double standards.

Do the rules change if we are a Democrat or a Liberal? It seems to me that must be the case. It's pretty obvious that no one in the Democrat party has the guts to stand up and call out those that show disrespect, indecency and incivility. By their silence, they are showing what kind of people they are and what they endorse.

In other words, showing respect is a good and moral thing to do. Disrespecting someone is outside the moral code. Treating people with decency is morally correct, while indecency is not. Behaving in a civil manner is on the right side of morality, and incivility is on the wrong side.

We cannot throw respect, decency and civility out the window and expect our society to advance. If that is what we are devolving into, then there's trouble ahead. Whether we are a Conservative, Liberal, Democrat, or Republican, we should be able to agree with that statement. Both sides need to calm down, take a deep breath, show respect, keep decorum, make civility a higher priority than hatred and vitriol, and finally, act like we value being a respectful member in good standing in the human race. *I Know We Are Better Than This.*

Chapter 10

Prejudice and Racism

One of the ugly traits we have as humans is prejudice. We form pre-conceived ideas that are sometimes difficult to give up. We build walls between ourselves and someone who is different. Sometimes the reasons for prejudice are handed down for generations, similar to inheritance, and sometimes the reasons just don't make any practical sense – it's just tradition.

Prejudice can be defined as "an opinion or belief that is not based on reason or experience." Prejudice usually refers to a prejudgment that an individual has adopted. It is an attitude, and prejudice can be manifested in innumerable ways, from race, sex, religion, and all the way to an opposing baseball team.

Bigotry is the result of prejudice. Bigotry is defined as "extreme intolerance (or prejudice) against any creed, belief, or opinion that differs from one's own." Bigots are very devoted to their beliefs, and they think that anyone who holds an opposing viewpoint should be the subject of hatred and intolerance. Prejudice and bigotry have a highly detrimental impact on society. Prejudice is an extreme opinion coupled with a strong devotion to an opinion that can potentially lead to fanaticism and divisiveness.

Where does prejudice come from? Prejudice most often emanates from lack of knowledge, lack of communication, and lack of trust. It comes from the human trait that we must immediately determine on what level we should deal with a new person we meet. That first impression begins to take us down a certain pathway that leads us to analyzing and mentally characterizing something in order to form an opinion. If there is anything we don't like about someone or something, or if anything makes us uncomfortable, we start forming a mental and emotional reaction. At some point on the journey to prejudice, the dislike of something turns into hatred, and the next stop is bias. Beyond bias is the adoption of extremism, and once we are there, we have arrived at our final destination - prejudice.

There is this innate human need to quickly assess and judge people we meet. It's our very nature to form an immediate opinion which can lead the relationship astray. It's a battle we will always have to fight against. We generally assess people when we meet them to seek some sort of comfort since we are encountering an unknown entity. The relationship or encounter begins with impressions that either continue to inhibit mutual understanding or lead to acceptance of each other. We subconsciously probe for commonalities and differences between us.

We ask questions in order to validate our thinking or to lead us to a more comfortable state where we feel connections.

This need to categorize people we encounter is a survival mechanism that stems from a primal force within us. Imagine a caveman encountering another caveman that is a stranger and they cannot communicate. The first thought is likely to be, "Is this person going to be a friend or foe? Does he want to befriend me or eat me?"

Initial prejudice is a protective wall based on survival. Communication tears down those walls. Imagine the difficulty in trying to advance a relationship without the ability to communicate. We are fortunate to have an advantage over the cavemen because we are able to verbally communicate.

From an article published in *Current Directions in Psychological Science*, a journal of the Association for Psychological Science, Arne Roets and Alain Van Hiel at the University of Belgium wrote about characterizing prejudice. According to Roets and Heil, people who are prejudiced have a much stronger need to make quick and firm judgments and decisions in order to reduce ambiguity. Roets says, "Of course, everyone has to make decisions, but some people really hate uncertainty and therefore quickly rely on the most obvious information, often the first information they come across, to reduce it." That's also why prejudiced people favor authorities and social norms which make it easier to come to conclusions. Then, once they've made up their minds, they stick to it. Roets stated, "If you provide information that contradicts their decision, they just ignore it." The wall gets built quickly and prejudice takes over.

Roets also argues that categorization is part of how we deal with things, and it often happens unconsciously. "When we meet someone, we immediately see that person as being male or female, young or old, black or white, without really being aware of this categorization," he says. "Social categories are useful to reduce complexity, but the problem is that we also assign some properties to these categories. This can lead to prejudice and stereotyping."

Some people are more able to easily remove walls, whereas others struggle. Roets and Heil concluded that the fundamental source of prejudice is not from ideology. "Instead, prejudice stems from a deeper psychological need, associated with a particular way of thinking. People who aren't comfortable with ambiguity and want to make quick and firm decisions are also prone to making generalizations about others."

Roets also states, "To reduce prejudice, we first have to acknowledge that it often satisfies some basic need to have quick answers and stable knowledge people rely on to make sense of the world."

Prejudice manifests itself in a variety of ways. For example, in ideology, we often fence ourselves in to our own detriment by not seeking and probing ideas that may make us uncomfortable. Too often, we burden ourselves by being close-minded. Again, it's a defense mechanism. When we encounter a political position that runs counter to what we think, it challenges us. We often bristle up and flatly dismiss another viewpoint because in order to consider another side of an issue, we must remove the walls we built up and admit our prejudices.

Political prejudice occurs when a particular position is summarily rejected before one can fully and intelligently contemplate what the opposing view might be. Many people's initial reaction is to reject the other point of view automatically. However, considering other points of view challenges us. I believe that political bigotry is defined as deafness toward hearing the other side, and blindness toward any type of intellectual enlightenment.

If someone has a closed mind that is unable to weigh valid arguments from both sides, that person is doomed to lead a prejudiced, bigoted life and will always acquiesce to that primal reaction of prejudice.

It's hard work to be non-prejudicial. It seems that close-minded, dismissive people seem to be insecure with a strong need for protecting their viewpoints, often at the expense of rationality and logic. These individuals, unfortunately, are typically more radical in their thinking, while also being more prone to unhappiness.

Jonathan Haidt, a well-known social psychologist from New York University stated in his book *The Righteous Mind*, "We are selfish hypocrites so skilled at putting on a show of virtue that we fool even ourselves…We make judgements rapidly and are dreadful at seeking out evidence that might disconfirm our judgements." Mr. Haidt concludes, "Extreme partisanship may be literally addictive."

One of humankind's flaws is that we are inclined to deny truth even when it is staring us in the face. We often go to great lengths to avoid accepting a fact we don't want to believe. It is sometimes a conscious decision, while other times it occurs subconsciously. Blaise Pascal, a famous mathematician, philosopher and great thinker who lived in the 1600's stated, "People almost invariably arrive at their beliefs not on the basis of proof but on the basis of what they find attractive."

Strangely, educated elites are more prone to prejudicial tendencies than those of us that are not among the more enlightened. This comes from an attitude of self-assurance that because the elites conclude they are more learned, they are quicker to judge and are not as willing to debate and probe new ideas. It seems counterintuitive, but a study entitled, "The Perception Gap" from the research team More in Common claimed that, "The best educated and most politically interested are more likely to vilify their political adversaries than their less educated, less tuned-in peers."

Another interesting conclusion from the study is that "while Republicans' misconceptions of Democrats do not improve with higher levels of education, Democrats' perceptions of Republicans actually gets worse with every additional degree they earn."

Pascal also stated, "We hide and disguise ourselves from ourselves. All our dignity consists in thought…we must strive then to think well; that is the basic principle of morality." My interpretation of what he was thinking is that being open-minded and seeking to understand opposing ideas is moral, while prejudicial thinking and being judgmental is immoral.

Disagreeing with someone's viewpoint is not immoral, but attacking someone because of his or her beliefs is immoral. There is also a big difference between thinking the other side is wrong versus thinking the other side is evil. The latter way of thinking is a form of prejudice too often displayed in the political world. Disagreements should not excite emotions to the point of spewing hatred. That is uncivil and should never be tolerated in public discourse. People who must resort to hatred should be shunned by the rest of society – it's unacceptable behavior and we need to stand up to it. If people cannot debate in a calm, respectful fashion, then the best course is to just stay silent. The sad thing is, if there is hatred and discontent in one's heart, peace and contentment will forever be elusive and can lead to militancy.

This radicalism often leads to confrontations with people that have differing opinions. More often than not, these types of people try to shut down differing opinions through the use of scare tactics, shouting down the opposing viewpoint, or committing violence - all the while using the excuse of "hate-speech" or accusing the opposing side of being stupid and close-minded. The all-to-obvious irony, of course, is that those people trying to inhibit opposing ideas are, in fact, practicing the same prejudice they are protesting against.

A good example of preconceived prejudice occurred on Fox News personality David Webb's radio show. Mr. Webb brought on a call-in guest, Areva Martin, a CNN legal analyst. Mr. Webb was speaking on his radio show about how qualifications are more important than skin color when hiring someone. He spoke of how he worked his way up through various media jobs and has enjoyed success because he worked hard at it. Ms. Martin, who is black, then chimed in, "That's a whole 'nother long conversation about white privilege – the things you have the privilege of doing, that people of color don't have the privilege of." Then an awkward, yet revealing moment happened.

Mr. Webb replied, "How do I have white privilege?" She responded, "David, by virtue of being a white male you have privilege." Webb then cut her off and said, "Areva, I hate to break it to you, you should have been better prepared, but I'm black." Webb continued, "You went immediately to an assumption. You are talking to a black man who started in rock radio in Boston who crossed the paths into hip-hop, rebuilding one of the great black stations in America and went on to work at Fox News, where I'm told apparently blacks aren't supposed to work. But yet you come with this assumption, jumping to white privilege – that's actually insulting." Martin then replied, "It is, and I apologize because my people gave me some wrong information." Hmmmm, sounds like a pretty lame excuse from someone that is supposedly not a racist. She may not have been aware of Webb's color, but HER true colors shone through brightly and undeniably. She was and is, ironically, prejudiced.

The conversation continued. Mr. Webb stated, "But based on my color, you were going to something I was a part of and just to add to it, my background is white, black, Indian, Arawak, Irish, Scottish, I mean it's so diverse, I'm like the UN. And this is the part of driving the narrative around a construct like white privilege."

On a TV show the day after the ugly and highly revealing interchange, Webb said, "She (Areva) immediately defaulted to an attack which is a false narrative. There is no such thing as 'white privilege.' There is only EARNED privilege in life."

Now, we can disagree with Mr. Webb, but no one can disagree with the fact that hard work and discipline are what earns us privilege. Determination to change one's plight is the driving force behind changing one's life. Hard work and fortitude alter the trajectory of a person's economic plight. No one can deny that. And then there will be some that say, "Yeah, but they are (insert an excuse) and that prevents them from being successful." Again, if everyone accepted that way of thinking, nobody would ever get anywhere. More from David Webb, "Our skin is an organ, it doesn't think, it doesn't formulate ideas. It is just a result of your parentage."

Prejudice and ideological bigotry never have a positive outcome. By their very nature, they will always produce a negative result. Too many people have the viewpoint that "It's my way or the highway." The attitude is, "You are not allowed to have an opposing view because I have already determined that the way I think is the way you should think. You are not as good a person as I am simply because you do not agree with me."

That's the message of prejudice, and that is a bigoted, dangerous arrogance that is all too often played out in today's political discourse. Calm, rational debate is a good and productive practice, whereas dismissing or shutting down an opposing position does nothing but generate animosity, hatred, and prejudice. It is also counterproductive to the advancement of our society.

It is our very nature to quickly form our opinions and be contemptuous because it is the fastest and most direct path to being comfortable. It is in our very nature that when we see someone on TV who has a different point of view, we all too often quickly and decisively dismiss it. We all have been guilty of this attitude, and unfortunately, it is all too pervasive in today's public discourse.

It seems as though bigotry is breaking out everywhere – even in the places we are afraid to admit it's happening. The people who loudly shout that they are not bigoted too often turn out to be exactly what they preach against - prejudiced. The irony is painfully obvious and eloquently stated by what Matt Blevin, former Governor of Tennessee said. Let me repeat it: "There are none so intolerant as those that preach tolerance. There are none so quick to judge as those who tell us to be non-judgmental."

Too often, we tend to migrate to TV shows and news broadcasts that espouse the same ideology we hold. After all, it's easier to tell ourselves, "See, that's exactly how I feel – I totally agree with that."

We always like confirmation – it feels good to stay in our comfort zone. It's far more discomforting to listen to an opposing ideology that challenges the positions we have adopted. It's hard for a prejudiced person to listen to an opposing argument and say, "Huh, I never thought about it that way" or, "I never considered that."

Gordon Allport's book entitled *The Nature of Prejudice* is one of the most definitive studies in examining prejudice from both a psychological and sociological viewpoint. The Need for Cognitive Closure (NFCC) is the basis on which Allport's theory of prejudice is built. Two prominent characteristics of prejudicial people are the urgency tendency, which is the inclination to reach closure as quickly as possible, and the permanence tendency, which is the tendency to maintain the prejudice as long as possible. Here are some characteristics from the book that intolerant people tend to have:

- Urge for quick and definite answers
- Like order, especially social order
- Feel more secure when they know the answers
- Latch onto that which is familiar
- Afraid to say "I don't know"
- Better not to hesitate
- Cannot tolerate ambiguity

- Narrow-minded
- Fail to see all relevant sides to a problem

The paper of Roets and Heil cited earlier also stated, "The key to answering this question is in the way that high-NFCC individuals seek to satisfy their need for quick, easy, firm, and stable knowledge about the world. That is, to meet their desire for closure in the social environment, people typically resort to essentialist categorization and authoritarian ideologies, which represent some of the most powerful, proximal determinants of stereotyping and prejudice."

Individuals with high levels of NFCC (or prejudice) tend to migrate toward a strict social order because it provides the most comfort. In addition, a centralized government structure is also preferred, a la communism or socialism. Ironically, exposure to other groups of people and having the freedom to exchange ideas actually **reduces** prejudice.

One study concluded: "...the superior effect of intergroup contact in high-NFCC individuals can be explained by the established notion that intergroup contact diminishes intergroup anxiety, which consequently reduces prejudice. Those who feel most averse and fearful toward the unfamiliar, ambiguous, and unpredictable, are likely to benefit the most from the anxiety-reducing effects of the salient information provided by positive intergroup contact." The conclusion then, is that communication and interaction remove prejudicial barriers, leading to a more harmonious society.

Can it be said that prejudiced people are intellectually lazy? One can say that just might be true. The need for speed in coming to conclusion hinders true intellectual discovery. Scientific experiments that are performed in haste are certain to lead to false assumptions.

If we walk outside into a field, look around and see that the field is flat, then draw the conclusion that the world is therefore flat, that leads to a false assumption. Despite what the flat-earthers think, the Earth is round. Despite the fact that where they are standing in a field is flat does not change the reality that the Earth is round. Drawing a conclusion through one observation usually leads to false assumptions.

Back in primitive times, it was pretty easy to understand that everyone thought the Earth was flat because they were only using one perspective. When the concept that the Earth was round came up, it was considered heresy. The round Earth believers were persecuted for their scientific position. There was intense prejudice against the Round-earthers. The Earth being flat was "settled science" and anyone who believed otherwise was a heretic. Ultimately, more and more scientific proof was brought to the masses and the round-Earthers won the argument. Prejudicial walls were torn down and the way we looked at the Earth was changed forever.

Another manifestation of prejudice that we are all too familiar with is racism. Although we might think racism is fairly new and tied to slavery, it has been prevalent throughout history across the globe. The Jewish people have been perhaps the longest-suffering group in our recorded history, but the prejudice shown towards them is more ethnic than it is racist. In any case, it is prejudice.

We use race categorizations such as Caucasian, Black, Asian, Hispanic, and others. Skin color has been the primary identifier of race, but that can be flawed because of the vast number of inter-racial marriages and their offspring. Race and ethnicity are closely tied together, and the differences are getting blurred. To separate the two, race is tied to physical attributes, primarily skin color, whereas ethnicity is more closely tied to culture and customs. Race is inherited while ethnicity is learned. Prejudice can be inflicted on both racial and ethnic groups.

Racism is defined as, "prejudice, discrimination, or antagonism directed against someone of a different race based on the belief that one's own race is superior." It also can be defined as prejudice based on physical features.

Ayn Rand described racism this way: "Racism is the lowest, most crudely primitive form of collectivism. It is the notion of ascribing moral, social or political significance to a man's genetic lineage—the notion that a man's intellectual and characterological traits are produced and transmitted by his internal body chemistry. Which means, in practice, that a man is to be judged, not by his own character and actions, but by the characters and actions of a collective of ancestors."

As we have witnessed, racism, bigotry and prejudice against black people are real. Unfortunately, some individuals are ill-informed and downright hateful, and they carry out actions intended to hurt black people. Racism, bigotry, and prejudice against white people are also real. Many leftists and the mainstream media rail about how all conservatives are racists, and it is truly ludicrous. However, there are those on the left that actually believe that and have a prejudicial attitude, which is in itself racist.

Take for example MSNBC's Nicole Wallace when speaking about racism. She stated, "This (racism) does not have a parallel on the left…it doesn't [exist]. There isn't a strain of racism on the left." Her point, to try and interpret what she was saying, is that there are no racists on the left. They are pure as the white driven snow (pun intended). The presumptive attitude is that racists can only be conservatives – it is impossible for anyone on the left to be racist. That simply is not true. It's a gross generalization designed to divide people and instigate hatred – and it's also prejudicial.

So, let's look at some of the headlines from various left-leaning publications and see if there is perhaps just a hint of racism against white people in the media.

From a BuzzFeed article headline: "37 Things White People Need to Stop Running in 2018."

From the *National Review*: "Women's March in Mostly White City Canceled for Being too White"

From a *New York Times* editorial: "Can My Children Be Friends with White People?"

I could go on, but hopefully my point is obvious. This type of rhetoric is contentious – no doubt about it. It is racist since it is pointed directly at white people. Hatemongers on the left are just as guilty of racism as those misguided bigots in the KKK. Regrettably, in some circles, it appears to be acceptable for blacks to exhibit racism towards whites, but it is not acceptable for whites to exhibit racism towards blacks. That's where things become contentious.

What if all white people were encouraged to adopt this attitude: "I don't like myself because I am white. I don't like my ancestors because they were evil. I don't like myself because I am mistreated due to my whiteness. I don't like myself because I must always defend myself for being white. I cannot succeed in this world because of my skin color. Therefore, I don't want to be white."

Sorry, but I don't feel that way. I am proud of the person I am and the content of my character – my self-worth has nothing to do with the skin color I happen to wear – it has everything to do with who I am as a person. I am proud that I have no hatred in my heart for blacks, browns, Asians or anybody else. The only people I don't like are hatemongers, anarchists, and holier-than-thou politicians who try and convince me that I am a bad person because I am white. I reject that notion. I reject their attitude towards me. They are wrong. They are the bad, prejudiced people – not me.

Some people have a penchant for making accusations toward other people for the same thing that they accuse others of doing. Could it be that those who cry racist at every turn are so consumed by racism that they become a racist? All too often, they frame the entire country into one big bunch of racist people. They look at the world through such a restrictive point of view that they cannot see anything but a racist world. I've got news for them. They are the ones with the problem – not the rest of the country. They are so preoccupied with reading into every word some sort of racist slant from even the simplest, most innocuous statement. In doing this, they make their own lives miserable. It consumes them.

Their first reaction is to criticize and condemn, and then jump up and down. It's sad but true. All too often, the virtue displayed by some people is to cover up for their own sins.

Contrary to what most on the left believe is that racism comes in ALL colors. To view racism through one myopic lens (whites committing ALL of the racism) is in itself racist. But seemingly, the rules don't apply if we are in a minority group – we are allowed to be racist against white people. In the minds of so many leftists, that is acceptable and justifiable. But I have news for those people – they are wrong to think that way. They are guilty of what they preach against. That is the epitome of hypocrisy and racism.

Let me repeat – racism and prejudice come in ALL colors, and those people that spread this unfounded attitude that racism is everywhere need to lay down their swords and fight another battle – like promoting moral virtue, embracing the value of the core family, and the power of individual determination and achievement. Our society would benefit greatly, and those people might actually start liking themselves and other people while not being consumed by hatred.

Professional race baiters only spew negativity. When something bad happens, they are the first ones on the scene shouting injustice and spreading fear. Has anyone besides me ever noticed that? What they preach is that if we are a victim, we are screwed. Why is that? Is that the only subject they know to talk about? Is that the only way they are capable of looking at things?

Have any of the race baiters ever stopped to think that their message is always beating down the opposite side while also subtly telling their followers that they are losers because of the color of their skin and that they must fight back? Is the only solution to the problem tearing down and berating other people? The only conclusion to draw is that they do it because otherwise they would be out of a job, and they would lose their notoriety. They would not have anything to talk about. How about preaching positivism? What about stressing the importance of individual responsibility? Why not promote family values?

Two of the manifestations of prejudice are discrimination and segregation. We know all too well the result of those actions, and neither of those are acceptable in today's world, yet they still exist. We can't control every mind and all thoughts in our society, but we can hold those accountable that practice discrimination and approve of segregation – no matter their skin color or ethnicity.

I have met thousands and thousands of people throughout my life, and I can honestly say, I have met only one person that I would call a racist, and she was a psychotic nut-job that belonged in a mental ward somewhere.

Bob Woodson, a black leader quoted elsewhere in this book appeared on Tucker Carlson's show, and when asked about racism accusations readily being thrown out today whenever someone disagrees or is critical of a person of color, he stated, "I don't think we need to fight their arguments [about racism] with a counter argument, we must confront them with a counter experience. Black America is among the strongest supporters of America. We fought in every war, and not a single black was ever tried for treason. Also, we as a people fought for the promise of America against the problems of racism. So, we need to go to those communities that all those politicians are talking about and work with and identify grassroots leaders who are black…who use the principles of our founders as the principle means to deliver themselves and redeem themselves from self-destructive behavior, from drugs and alcohol because they are the living witnesses that America is defined by its promise.

"For example, [as a black community], we have built hospitals, insurance companies, hotels. These are the stories of how we have achieved against the odds. We had twenty blacks who were born as slaves who died millionaires. Some of them actually went back into those plantations and purchased them where they were a slave, and even took in the families of the slave masters. So, if blacks were able to achieve these great feats in the presence of racism, raw racism, then they [the same principles] can be used today. So, these same principles are alive [today]…We love this country, we fought for this country. We fought for its promise. We achieved [greatness] in the face of racism, not in the absence of it."

We cannot change history, but we can start with changing ourselves. The world must become more tolerant to differing opinions and beliefs. Racial intolerance has been greatly reduced over the years, and because we are human and imperfect, I don't foresee the world ever being free of racism or prejudice, whether it's white on black, black on white, or brown on black and white.

As a society, we cannot control the thinking of every individual, but what we can control is our own attitudes and behaviors. We can understand how prejudice is formed and how bigotry is acted out, but we must reject prejudice and racism of all kinds and replace it with communication, love, acceptance, and understanding. Pointing fingers, making threats, sewing divisive seeds, and carrying around a prejudicial grudge are all unproductive. We cannot eliminate all prejudice and racism, but we can use self-reflection to work on our own prejudices because "*I Know We Are Better Than This.*"

Chapter 11

Cultural Victimhood

Some people might disagree with what is covered in this chapter, but to become a better society, we must confront issues and problems head on. We can't be afraid to talk about things that make us uncomfortable. Sometimes we must face tough truths in order for us to fully examine our problems and find a solution. I am not attacking anyone or any race or ethnicity. What I am trying to do is to ask questions and seek answers in order to come to some conclusions on how to improve who we are as a country.

There are certainly too many people that truly have been victims – we all have been victims at some point in our lifetime. I have been a victim of robbery. I have been the victim of false accusations. I have been a victim of unfairness. We all have our own stories. We've all experienced hardships and adversity. How we respond to being a victim is the most important thing. We cannot let victimhood become our identity. We cannot let it define us or ruin our lives. It is to our own personal detriment if we choose to go down this route of wearing the mantle of victimhood.

In our community, there are some who still cling to the ugliness of slavery and will not let it go. There is no doubt in my mind that the victims of slavery suffered mightily and the hangover lasted a long time, but there is one thing to consider: The trap in looking back hundreds of years and trying to extract vengeance from those living today who had absolutely nothing to do with past history is unproductive. To hold an innocent person responsible for someone else's behavior that occurred in the distant past is like punishing grandchildren for their grandfather's behavior. How is that justified? Simply put, it should not be that way. When we really think about it, blaming generations of people that are far removed from historical wrongdoings just does not make sense in any form or fashion. It's history, and the only history I am responsible for is my own. I am accountable for my behavior, not my great, great, great, great, great grandfather's.

So, is it necessary to extract revenge from a certain portion of society? An ethnic group? How exactly is that accomplished and what does it specifically achieve? Carrying around a vengeful heart is wasted energy that is often manifested in hatred and violence. It is divisive and detrimental to the cohesion of our country.

When people adopt the attitude that they are victims of society because of their race, ethnicity, cultural background, gender, or whatever, it puts them in a situation where the natural human response is to seek vengeance or reparations.

Vengeance is an unproductive activity which may make the victims feel good because they "put it to the man," or "I really taught them not to mess with me." Getting vengeance may create a temporary feeling of accomplishment. Did it remedy the original problem? Most likely not. Did it advance the cause? Most likely not. Did it bring harm to someone else? Probably so. Was that harm justified because of the past? Probably not. Did it change the past? No, that's not possible. After the possible euphoria, a victim is still left with an empty feeling that it felt good, but what did it accomplish beyond the euphoria?

If a wrong is brought against someone for a misdeed, we hold that person responsible – we don't go to the family and friends who had nothing to do with the crime and hold them responsible. Only drug cartels and the mafia do that. Is that how we want to behave? An example: why must an entire ethnic group (white people) be punished for something they deplore (racism and slavery) that occurred more than a hundred years ago? And to extract vengeance on that group is unjustifiable when simple logic is used. Again, I am not responsible for my ancestor's behavior – I am responsible for myself and no one else. End of story.

In the first 200+ years of our country's history, slaves were undoubtably victims. Many were literally treated as animals and property. It was wrong, inhumane, and inexcusable. These slaves were victimized by mostly white owners that made considerable amounts of money while their slaves suffered greatly.

There are also some interesting things about early American slavery. Were white people responsible for the majority of slave ownership? Yes, they were. But what most people don't know is that there were a lot of blacks who owned slaves. The census of 1830 lists 3,775 free black people who owned a total of 12,760 slaves. William Ellison, a very wealthy black landowner in South Carolina, owned 63 slaves according to the 1860 census. Are the descendants of these black slave owners responsible for their ancestors' sins as well?

At a congressional committee hearing on the subject of reparations, Coleman Hughes, a black columnist for the website Quillette.com had some very interesting comments that were not received well by Democrats and racial activists on the left who support reparations. Here are Mr. Cohen's powerful and provocative comments in their entirety.

"Thank you, Chairman Cohen, ranking member Johnson, and members of the committee. It's an honor to testify on a topic as important as this one. Nothing I'm about to say is meant to minimize the horror and brutality of slavery and Jim Crow. Racism is a bloody stain on this country's history. I consider our failure to pay reparations directly to freed slaves after the Civil War to be one of the greatest injustices ever perpetrated by the U.S.

government. But I worry that our desire to fix the past compromises our ability to fix the present.

"Think about what we're doing today. We're spending our time debating a bill that mentions slavery 25 times but incarceration only once, in an era with zero black slaves but nearly a million black prisoners—a bill that doesn't mention homicide once, at a time when the Center for Disease Control reports homicide as the number one cause of death for young black men.

"I'm not saying that acknowledging history doesn't matter. It does. I'm saying that there's a difference between acknowledging history and allowing history to distract us from the problems we face today. In 2008, the House of Representatives formally apologized for slavery and Jim Crow. In 2009, the Senate did the same. I'm not against apologies. But black people don't need another apology. We need a less punitive criminal justice system. We need safer neighborhoods and better schools. We need affordable health care. And none of these things can be achieved through reparations for slavery.

"Nearly everyone close to me told me not to come today. They said that even though I've only ever voted for Democrats, I'd be perceived as a Republican and therefore hated by half the country. Other people told me that distancing myself from Republicans would end up alienating the other half of the country. And the sad truth is that they were both right. That's how suspicious we've become of one another. That's how divided we are as a nation.

"If we were to pay reparations today, we would only divide the country further, making it harder to build the political coalitions required to solve the problems facing black people today; we would insult many black Americans by putting a price on the suffering of their ancestors; and we would turn the relationship between black Americans and white Americans from a coalition into a transaction—from a union between citizens into a lawsuit between plaintiffs and defendants.

"What we should do is pay reparations to black Americans who actually grew up under Jim Crow and were directly harmed by racist policies like redlining—people like my grandparents. But paying reparations to all descendants of slaves is a mistake. Take me for example. I was born three decades after Jim Crow ended into a privileged household in the suburbs. I attended an Ivy League school. I grew up with programs designed to uplift black people—from Affirmative Action in education to diversity and inclusion programs in the labor market. Yet I'm also descended from slaves who worked on Thomas Jefferson's Monticello plantation.

"So, reparations for slavery would allocate federal resources to me and not to an American with the wrong ancestry—even if that person is living paycheck to paycheck and working multiple jobs to support a family. You might call that justice. I call it justice for the dead at the price of justice for the living. The question is not what America owes me by virtue of my ancestry; the question is what all Americans owe each other by virtue of being citizens of the same nation. And the obligation of citizenship is not transactional. It can't be paid off. It's not contingent on your ancestry. And it never expires. Reparations for slavery would keep us stuck in the past and distracted from the present; it would solve none of the major problems facing black Americans today; it would waste resources on people like me who don't need them, and most importantly, it would make our obligation to our fellow Americans, which should be ongoing and unconditional, into a lawsuit that can be settled once and forgotten forever. For all these reasons, bill H.R. 40 is a moral and political mistake. Thank you."

Burgess Owens, an outstanding NFL player had these comments at the congressional hearing: "I do not believe in reparations because what reparation does is it points to a certain race, a certain color and it points to them as evil...reparations also turns black people into beggars."

He also went after the Democrat party stating, "I used to be a Democrat until I did my history and found out the misery that that party brought to my race. I do believe in restitution. Let's point to the party that was part of slavery, KKK, Jim Crow, that has killed over 40 percent of our black babies [through abortion], 20 million of them. [In the] State of California, 75 percent of our black boys can't pass standard reading and writing tests - a Democratic state. Let's pay reparation. Let's pay restitution. How about the Democratic Party pay for all the misery brought to my race?"

One of the main takeaways from the congressional hearings regarding reparations was the behavior of the chairman Stephen Cohen of Tennessee, a left-slanting Democrat and a proponent of reparations. He showed disrespect towards several witnesses who he disagreed with. He couldn't help letting his partisanship show when after Coleman Hughes completed his testimony, there was a snide statement made that was uncalled-for and unprofessional. And not to mention disrespectful. Mr. Cohen essentially dismissed Mr. Hughes' comments by saying, "He was presumptive, but he has the right to speak." Why couldn't Mr. Cohen just leave it at "Thank you, Mr. Hughes"? That's what anyone with any common courtesy and professionalism would have done.

Following Mr. Owens' comments, Mr. Cohen did not say a word – not even "thank you." He basically ignored Mr. Owens and moved on. It was rude, disrespectful, and showed Mr. Cohen's insolence.

Reparations for slaves have been bantered about for 100+ years, and they have resurfaced recently. This subject is brought up by liberal politicians for one simple reason – they want to continue to maintain the loyalty of black voters. In my opinion, no people in their right mind think that reparations have any hope of practical application – it should be viewed for exactly what it is – political rhetoric intended to gain more votes.

The truth of that statement lies in the fact that NONE of these politicians that call for reparations have laid out a clear and discernable plan that stipulates exactly how they are going to accomplish these reparations. If they were truly serious about the subject, they would tell us exactly how reparations were to be administered. Instead, all they spew is hollow soundbites that are devoid of any meaningful substance.

One politician throws the subject out there and then like-minded candidates simply start agreeing and hopping on that bandwagon. They rush to say, "Yes, we do need reparations," hoping that black voters and guilt-laden white voters will agree and cast their ballot for those candidates. Shallow-thinking voters then jump on the bandwagon without really thinking through the whole idea of reparations, in not only its impracticality, but also the modern-day justification for it. Their decision to support the reparations idea is based on two things – emotion and guilt, and they both wrap into each other. That is not to mention the fact that many politicians shamefully use the victimhood of slavery to their political advantage in order to gain more votes.

The emotion aspect is played out through the thinking that the oppression that black slaves suffered during the 1600's through the 1800's was horrendous – and it was. Again, slavery was (and still is) evil – it's a vile and repulsive way to treat people. However, liberation and equal rights ended that ugly period in not only our country, but our leadership in ending slavery everywhere has had a global impact.

Slavery is an emotional subject, and it is a topic that politicians can resurrect to get potential voters emotionally engaged. However, our country offers opportunities for everyone if they merely choose to take advantage of the greatness our educational system and economy offers. All it takes is a choice, a commitment, determination, and hard work.

The guilt side of the equation is pretty obvious. Many white people still carry around the feeling that their "whiteness" means they are to bear the responsibility of the enslavement of black people from 200, 300 or 400 years ago. There shouldn't be guilt. What there should be is a commitment that each one of us should live our lives providing opportunity and support for EVERYONE, no matter race or ethnicity. Feeling guilty for something we had nothing to do with is focusing our energies in the wrong direction. Dwelling on it is fruitless. White people who feel like they must punish themselves and think they must live in a perpetual apology mode should put to rest their guilt and move on to more productive things. All of us should be willing to free the black community from victimhood and help them thrive in our communities.

Appearing on Tucker Carlson's Fox news program, Bob Woodson had some interesting comments. He is a black leader who established the renowned Center for Neighborhood Enterprise (later renamed the Woodson Center) which helps revitalize urban neighborhoods and works to reduce youth violence. In response to a question regarding reparations, Mr. Woodson commented, "I think it's fool's gold. It demeans both whites and blacks. To Black America, you can [somehow] monetize oppression. Also, what it does is send a message to Black America that somehow, your destiny is determined by what white people do – what white people give you, and not what you are able to do for yourself. It undermines Black America."

He continued, "I just think it's virtue-signaling for white candidates, or for some white guilty people … It's very crippling to the nation, very crippling … These people on television and the candidates pander to the black community and assume that they don't have to speak to the legitimate needs on Black America, for jobs, for better health care, for neighborhoods that are not being gentrified. But instead, they can just pander and walk through the civil rights door. It is pandering, it is insulting to Black America."

A prominent Democrat politician expressed that he did not feel responsible for the sins of his father or grandfather. He went on to say this from the Senate floor: "I do not buy the concept, popular in the 60's which said, 'we have suppressed the black man for 300 years and the white man is now far ahead in the race for everything our society offers, we must now give the black man a head start, or even hold the white man back to even the race. I don't buy that."

He also stated, "[There is a] cadre of young people, tens of thousands of them, born out of wedlock without parents, without supervision, without any structure, without any conscience. We should focus on them now, not out of a liberal instinct for love, brother and humanity, although I think that's a good instinct, but for simple pragmatic reasons, if we don't, they will, or a portion of them will become the predators fifteen years from now, and Madam President, we have predators on our streets." That was said in a speech on the Senate floor by the one and only Joe Biden when he began his career in the Senate.

Whether it is whites owning blacks, blacks owning blacks, or anyone owning anyone, slavery is absolutely despicable. But we are 150 years removed from slaves (no matter what color of skin). Yes, it took us right at 100 years to pass the Civil Rights Act which outlawed any type of discrimination. Since then, great progress has been made in terms of equality and opportunity. The result is a country that honors the rights of everyone equally. Are we perfect? No. Are we further down the road than we were 50 years ago? Undeniably. Equal opportunity is far better than it was. Those who choose to work hard, play by the rules, and set their sights on achievement and individual responsibility are rewarded – that's how people thrive in our free society.

Ayn Rand stated, "Poverty, ignorance, illness and other problems of that kind are not metaphysical emergencies. By the metaphysical nature of man and of existence, man has to maintain his life by his own effort; the values he needs—such as wealth or knowledge—are not given to him automatically, as a gift of nature, but have to be discovered and achieved by his own thinking and work."

The culture in which our youth are raised is critical. If a good work ethic and personal responsibility are taught, the chances for a person leading a productive and fulfilled life are far greater than if a child is the victim of poor parenting.

There are literally millions of success stories of under-privileged kids overcoming adversity - some are well-known, while most are unknown. Stories of triumph against all the odds are countless. Sadly, there are more stories of individuals that settled for victimhood and lived their lives blaming others and feeling sorry for themselves. Why can't we celebrate the victors who have overcome versus focusing on and encouraging victimhood? If we do not challenge ourselves and our children to break out of victimhood and aspire to higher goals, then we set them up to be less than mediocre, and failure to become productive members of society is pre-ordained.

Albert Einstein had an interesting quote that is pertinent: "Everybody is a genius. But if you judge a fish by its ability to climb a tree, it will spend its whole life believing that it is stupid." If people choose not to aspire to improving themselves and their plight, that's their choice, and if we continue to label them as victims, they will never rise to their full potential. In doing so, we will sentence them to a less than productive life. It's human nature. We cannot reinforce bad behavior and expect anyone to break the chains and alter the cycle. And it is a cultural cycle.

People who decide they are victims of society and do nothing on their own to improve their lot in life are actually admitting that they are inferior – they are different – they are separating themselves from the norms of society and then they want to say it is society's fault. It is actually admitting they are defeated and the only recourse they have is strike back to get even with society and exercise their victimhood. They believe the scales should be weighted in their favor and they must blame someone else while not owning up to their own inadequacies brought on by their choices. We must teach aspiration, not dependency. It will pay dividends to not only the individual, it will benefit our entire society.

I ask what is accomplished within victimhood? Does adopting the role of victim solve any problems? Does it right any wrong? The answer is no, and no – the wrong cannot be righted – it can only be observed and can be used as a learning experience to not let it happen in the future. Then we rise above it and move on to make better lives for ourselves.

Pouting, wallowing, and miring ourselves in victimhood never accomplishes anything. Instead of looking at the vast opportunities life brings us, no matter our plight, neighborhood, ethnicity, family upbringing or education, asserting ourselves as a victim is a cop-out that gets us nowhere. Making excuses for ourselves is admitting we can't succeed. Overcoming our obstacles is the greatest antidote in freeing ourselves from the bondage of victimhood.

Living the life of victimhood is lazy and the easy way out. Putting limits and restrictions on ourselves is self-defeating. It is like a sprinter that has chosen to carry an extra 100-pound suitcase in a 100-meter race. He knows he can't compete with those runners that have no baggage to carry. He knows he could never win; therefore, he has already lost the race before it even started. Getting rid of the extra baggage will allow him to compete. It's a choice to be a victim and be burdened with that baggage. Life ain't fair sometimes, but admitting we've already lost the race leads us to think we need an excuse for losing when we haven't even started the race. It's a lot easier to claim victimhood than it is to run the race.

Granted, many children suffer from the decisions their parents or even grandparents have made. That is not fair to the child, but that is not to say that these children cannot overcome the faults and bad choices of their families.

Our country provides us with the ability to be ourselves and rise above the victimhood attitude. Freedom provides us with opportunity. Freedom also provides us with a choice. Isn't freedom what everybody wants? We are not bound with any chains when we are born. The only chains we wear are those we put on ourselves. But we must want release from being a victim before we can claim that freedom. Those of us who decide to achieve must embrace that freedom with all our soul. We must declare our freedom and remove the barriers and challenges that we all encounter – it is absolutely necessary in order for us to overcome and achieve.

We must embrace freedom and be willing enough to fight against those who want to take it away. Otherwise we allow ourselves to put our own chains on and submit to oppression brought upon us by a force that wants to enslave us. Victimhood is a state of mind that erects a barrier to overcoming. Determination to rise above an insurmountable circumstance is worth far more – just ask those that have put aside being a victim and achieved greatness. That is the only revenge against anyone or anything that is worth extracting.

Carrying around the mantle of victimhood becomes a heavy weight to bear and only breeds additional hatred. Many people relish living in victimhood because it gives them an identity. Most likely they were not a good student, a good parent, a good role model, or a good person in general. Having a burden to bear gives them meaning and an excuse. One would think that this type of person would be far better served if they would relinquish the chains of victimhood and claim a life that is free of bondage and self-doubt. Aspiring to overcome obstacles and enjoying the fruits of one's labor is where true meaning in life can be found.

Our political leaders need to promote individual responsibility and the freedom to achieve more than they currently do. We need to teach our children the value of freedom and the fact that opportunity is available to everyone. Focusing on victimhood is an antithetical attitude that leads no one to the promised land of opportunity and achievement.

Those people who preach victimhood and vengeance are leading their congregations or followers down a pathway to misery and failure. Is that what they really want or is that the only way these so-called "leaders" can maintain their self-importance? The constant chant of, "You're a victim and it's their fault" is completely counterproductive to helping anybody rise above. All it does is promote cultural victimhood that spreads to others who claim they are victims, and that is then passed down to other generations.

Politicians or "community leaders" who spend their time encouraging victimhood and inciting anger, jealousy, and hatred are stifling, destructive, and do no good for anyone. They might win a few votes or help raise money for their foundations or political campaigns, but they contribute nothing to advancing anyone's well-being. It truly is sad that there are people out there who exploit victimhood, but that's exactly what many leaders are doing. If they keep their constituency shackled in the bondage of victimhood, they are doing their followers a great disservice. However, once their followers are freed from the bondage of victimhood, the leaders lose their power over them. It is exploitation that only benefits the race mongers – not the people they claim to "serve." Unfortunately, there are far too many race shysters who only preach victimhood, and they all should be called out for what they are. It seems to me that we all should agree with that statement because *"I Know We Are Better Than This."*

Chapter 12

Moral Relativism vs. Absolutism

A structure is far more stable when built on solid rock versus sand. The same is true for the morals of a society. When starting with strong absolutes, people have a clear understanding for what is expected of them. An "everything's relative" morality creates confusion that can lead to unhinged and unchecked behavior which is not healthy for a society.

Moral absolutism is centered around a strict moral code based on universal principles such as natural laws and conscience in order to protect human welfare. Religions establish moral absolutes and governments set the rules. Moral codes and laws are necessary to differentiate between right and wrong while providing clear definitions of a society's behavioral norms and principles.

Moral relativism is conversely based on a more "common" standard where there are no strict rules. Fundamentally, relativism is based on ethical variables where there are no clear-cut principles – just whatever norms are established by the culture at the time. Simply stated, morality is relative and malleable – there are no absolutes in moral relativism.

An interesting phenomenon occurs when societies battle over absolutism and relativism. When the inertia of the disagreement of what's moral, and the gap between the two sides grows, societal danger can ensue. When the tension grows between those who hold to certain moral absolutes and those who believe in moral relativism, small societal skirmishes can begin to occur. Moral disparities between groups can lead to differences in interpreting what's right and what's wrong, and then they can escalate from vocal disagreements to violence.

Although many people have different practices of morality, such as various religious beliefs, they can still share a common morality. Abortion is a good example where there are distinct sides – those who believe it is morally wrong, and those who believe it is acceptable. From the pro-abortion group, it is justified through moral relativism. From the pro-life side, their belief is that it is against moral absolutes.

In some societies, killing a family member that disgraced the family is justified and acceptable. In some parts of the world, this type of murder is not only tolerated, it is a necessity to "maintain family honor." Let's stop and think about that. The cold-blooded murder of a family member who made a mistake (deliberate or not) is fine in some cultures. In our country, it is obviously against the law and violates our moral standards. Endorsing this type of murderous behavior seems to violate the very soul of humanity – I doubt Mother Nature thinks too kindly about murdering anybody. The family reputation becomes more important than the life of an individual. "Honor killing" is a selfish and vengeful act of inhumanity. A moral relativistic ethical code allows for these types of cruel deeds to be "normalized." Our human common sense should dictate otherwise.

The danger of moral relativism is that we humans need right and wrong and good and evil to be plainly defined. We function better as a society when moral standards are held in high esteem and we all follow the rules. Absolutes are not a bad thing - they actually allow a society to function at a higher level because people understand what type of behavior is acceptable and what is not.

Moral relativism is not specific, and it can fluidly change from day to day and year to year. It is selective and prejudiced in enforcement of the law. Those in power can set certain standards, but those standards can change at their whim. In fact, there are no absolute standards in moral relativism.

In our history books, we see how moral relativism allowed for the extermination of the six million Jews under Hitler's regime. It was a morally relative assault on a group of people, and it became an acceptable practice that those in power were able to pull off. A segment of the German populace was convinced that extinguishing Jewish lives was a necessary action for the nation. I never have figured out where all that hatred came from. Most citizens knew, however, that slaughtering millions of people because they were a certain ethnicity was morally wrong. Nevertheless, because of moral relativism, it was deemed appropriate in the minds of enough people. The natural moral absolute that killing is wrong was violated and six million people paid the price for Hitler's moral relativism.

Moral relativism can also play out in a judicial system. What's wrong for Harry can be OK for Joe because of certain circumstances. Unfortunately, we see this play out for many politicians. Way too often, politicians get away with a lot more than we average Joes could get away with. Why? It's purely because of their position in society. We should never tolerate it, but we do.

Unfortunately, we see justice being applied unevenly because of moral relativism. Justice is the application of the law of the land and it should be equally administered. When everything is relative, nothing is definitive.

Moral absolutism, whether we agree with the standards or not, at least provides a stable, understandable code of ethics that has a firm foundation. Moral relativism is a slippery slope. I look at it this way – for those that seek moral relativism, be careful what we ask for because it may come back to haunt us. A fluid justice system leads directly to injustice for some and undue punishment for others. True justice cannot be served in moral relativism. That leads to no justice at all. Equal justice adjudicates all persons equally, regardless of personal circumstances, ethnicity, gender, political affiliations, or cultural differences.

For example, assault is not right sometimes and wrong sometimes – it's just plain wrong. Hopefully, we can all agree on that. Defending and dismissing a crime by making excuses does not right the wrong that was committed, nor does it bring any solace to the victim. If the law is broken, there must be consequences. There are certainly degrees of severity of crimes and punishment, but if there is no punishment, there is no accountability. We are personally responsible for our own behavior. Our laws dictate that we are to live up to the moral standards that are stipulated, and everyone should be equally held accountable.

Some people might argue that it's not that simple and that some excuses for bad behavior are acceptable. I say no they are not! There is no excuse for bad behavior. There may be reasons why wrong choices are made, but that does not alleviate any responsibility or culpability. Wrong is wrong in any language and in any culture.

Another societal requirement that goes along with our choices is accountability. We are first and foremost accountable to ourselves, but we are also accountable to society. It is a requirement that we hold each other accountable. That's why we have a legal system. Our country has laws that we are expected to abide by that are dictated by us – we have come to agree on certain standards. The assumption is that if we are going to inhabit our country, we should follow the laws. We determine what is acceptable and what abhorrent behavior is. There is a price to pay for breaking those laws – in other words, we are responsible and accountable for our own behavior, and there are consequences for bad behavior. While moral absolutism infers accountability, moral relativism removes responsibility and consequences.

It is essential to teach children these basic principles to have a peaceful and productive society. When going by the rules, life is easier and far less complicated. It also benefits our entire society because we don't have to spend time, energy, and resources chasing after people who just don't make the right choices. A good, moral citizenry benefits everyone, and each individual is a benefit to society – it's a win-win proposition. If only it were that easy, right?

Admittedly, we are all human, and we are flawed and fallible which throws a monkey wrench into what ideally would be a society that ran like a well-tuned engine. Instead, we currently live in a culture where we have lowered our expectations and reduced the importance of personal responsibility. That has led to an overall decline in morality, and sadly, far too many people find that acceptable. That presents a problem for us going forward if we don't veer back toward adhering to more strict moral standards.

The "anything goes" and "I don't want to judge you" attitude is pervasive in moral relativism, and it stems from the 60's and 70's culture and progressive liberalism. Ultimately, it can be a real danger to an orderly and peaceful society. Moral neutrality means there is no definitive moral code at all – there is no right, and there is no wrong. Again, everything is relative.

We all know that recognizing and admitting we have a problem is the first step in recovery. It would greatly benefit our country if we made a concerted effort to change our behavior and aspire to be better individuals with high moral character – that's where it must start. We can change things, but it is going to require a re-education starting with young children. It's going to necessitate raising our standards and expectations and teaching responsibility and accountability. Making a fundamental change is not going to be easy. It's a choice we will make. Either we continue on our current path of ethical decline, or we make some changes and move away from moral relativism. By making a course correction, that will alter the trajectory of our country from a moral perspective. My hope is that more people will see what's happening and decide to do something about it.

Granted, we can't be total moral absolutists. A mass murderer can get the death penalty, while a parking ticket will get a small fine. There is some level of relativism on the crime scale because it is reasonable. There is a happy medium that allows for a reasonable moral code yet holds people accountable. Our justice system is built around weighting crimes and the associated punishment.

If freedom and equality are for everybody, then it makes logical sense that the same justice should be dispensed to everyone equally – there should be no special dispensation because of race, ethnicity, gender, or any other personal attribute. It gets to be a mess when justice is administered based on certain criteria or circumstances – that's moral relativism, and by its very nature it shows favoritism to special individuals and groups.

For example, we don't have laws that say someone can commit a crime against someone else and it's morally acceptable because the criminal was a homeless person or a poor kid from the ghetto. It can't work that way. Equal justice under the law means everyone is judged the same. Our laws are a reflection of our moral standards, and our justice system is what makes people accountable to follow the moral code.

Something is either morally right or morally wrong; that is the basis for moral absolutism. Moral relativism says something may be right or it may be wrong;

judgment is contingent upon other factors. Right and wrong do not depend on anything – they are what they are, and they stand on their own.

It seems pretty obvious that liberal Democrats seek to mete out justice unequally. Sanctuary city mayors have ordered their police to let illegal aliens who have committed a federal offense go free, while in the same jail sits a legal citizen who committed a lesser federal offense. There is no question that justice is not equally administered in those cities. How can there be any justification for having a double standard? Logic would dictate that there should never be a double standard. However, logic is sometimes missing in the world of progressive liberalism.

Why on God's green earth are illegal aliens not held accountable while citizens are? It makes absolutely no sense at all – it is bastardizing the rule of law, and there is no reasonable excuse or rationality for it. Defying the law, especially for police officers and mayors who take an oath to uphold the law is disgraceful, and it is moral relativism at work. Two criminals, one who is an illegal alien and one who is a citizen, are held to different standards. Burt Prelusky, a famous Hollywood critic stated, "If Liberals didn't have double standards, they wouldn't have any standards at all.

James Howard Kunstler, a noted author and social critic, commented on our current societal condition by saying, "This is exactly what you get in a culture where anything goes and nothing matters. Extract all the meaning and purpose for being here on earth and erase as many boundaries as you can from custom and behavior, and watch what happens…"

We humans need clearly delineated behavioral boundaries. When strong absolutes are present, people have a clear understanding of what is expected of them. An "everything's relative" morality leads to an uneven, unequal application of justice and leads to societal confusion. Our country cannot successfully operate without moral absolutes. Moral relativism brings nothing beneficial to a society.

Within our country today, moral relativism is becoming more and more rampant, with the line between what's morally right and wrong getting wider and wider. We cannot let our morals deteriorate; the outcome will be detrimental to our society. We must maintain and defend moral absolutism; we cannot let moral relativism take over. We should all agree with that because "*I Know We Are Better Than This.*"

Chapter 13

The War on Men

Just after the turn of the century, 1920 to be exact, women rightfully were allowed to vote. Why it took so long is ridiculous by our current standards, but that was a different time and place in history from where we are today, no doubt about it.

Women should always have been considered equal to men; no one would argue that – well, except for those men who either don't have a wife or they are psychotic. But think about it. For hundreds of thousands of years, men were the breadwinners – they were the providers for the family unit. That is such a noble thing to do and that was the expected role for men. For all those years, men had their place in society as did women.

Women certainly weren't staying home in the cave eating bon-bons and sipping tea all day – they had their roles as well. Responsibilities of who did what in the family unit – and even in the villages - were clear and were readily accepted by each gender.

Now there are some females who want to change men's roles and their place in society. Many so-called feminists are not satisfied with women being equal to men – they want the female gender to be dominant to make up for thousands of years of oppression. Many of these feminists have out-and-out declared a spite-filled war on men.

Christina Hoff Sommers, American Enterprise Institute, stated, "Basically, we are treating masculinity as a pathology in need of a cure. It's as though the average male needs to be re-engineered or be re-socialized according to specifications from a certain group of females."

The functions set forth for each gender were logical back in a more primitive time. Men were more physically endowed with a frame and a muscle structure that better lent itself to hunting, doing hard physical labor, and providing sustenance. They were also more capable of defending the family from animal or human attacks.

Women were not weak and helpless by any means – far from it since they had to be pretty tough to survive back then. They raised the kids, prepared the meals and kept the cave clean and tidy. In many cultures, the women were the farmers tending the crops as well. The roles were clear, and it seemed to work out well for a few hundred thousand years. We survived pretty well with that societal structure and gender roles in place.

Let's leap forward to the modern era in the US, specifically to WWII when men were called upon to join the military to defend our democracy and put an end to European and Japanese dictators. Women's role in modern society changed during and after the war. In order to support the war effort, women had to work in factories and perform tasks that they were previously not expected to perform – and they came through and contributed to our society in new ways, helping our country defeat evil.

When soldiers returned and life started to get back to normal, the role of women had been permanently altered. They were now equipped with skills developed from working in the factories or service jobs. In the post-war era, for essentially the first time, men were working with women in the same workforce. After the war, the Baby Boomer era was ushered in, and prosperity was everywhere, but gender definitions and roles were being redefined.

In the late 40's, 50's, and on into the 60's, the labor pool grew much larger, and women filled in the gaps where needed. More women were employed. That second income allowed families to enjoy more luxuries like televisions, new cars, refrigerators, and washing machines. This buying spree continued to such a point that in order for a family to thrive, a second income was vital. The role of women moved from homemaker to income producer. Men were still the primary source for income, but the wife's income helped subsidize a more upscale lifestyle, and that became the norm rather than the exception.

Then in the late 60's, a movement arose for the emancipation of women. At this point in history, the battle of the sexes was on. Women were no longer going to be oppressed, and a semi-militant faction grew. Bras were burned, sexual freedom was touted, protests took place, women's rights groups formed, and the women's liberation revolution was in full swing. There were many positives that came out of the feminist movement and much was accomplished over the next 40 years in terms of leveling the playing field for women. However, in some instances, the field became slanted more towards women at the expense of men. Some will object to that point, but it was true because quotas for hiring were adopted. Quotas for college admission were in place. The workforce, historically dominated by men, saw a continued increase in female employment. The two-income family was fully solidified as a requirement in order to enjoy the many conveniences of a nice home, two cars, more electrical appliances and funding to send kids to college.

I, like most rational men, fully support equality for women, but through this whole process, some unintended consequences have crept in.

The women's movement veered in the direction toward an anti-men crusade in some circles. Men were being demonized, labeled as sexists, and ridiculed for simply being of the male gender. Yes, there were and are some bad, sexist males, but this radical push gained traction among more and more women to such an extent that all men were segmented into one group – all were demons. That sentiment still lives today in some quarters. A new term was invented that described most men as low-lifes, and "toxic masculinity" was born.

According to radical feminists, masculinity is poisonous to our society, and men were encouraged to cure themselves of this debilitating disease by renouncing the fact that they were of the male gender and that they should behave more like women. Radical feminists used a very broad stroke in painting all men as evil and toxic, and that attitude gained more traction than one would think it merited. Some feminists would say, "All men are bad, and they get what they deserve." Needless to say, that is a very radical, bigoted thing to say because not ALL men are ogres and anti-women.

One of the unintended consequences that has emerged holds a bit of irony. Radical feminists led the charge for the female gender to be sexually liberated. In a Town Hall article, Laura Hollis summarized the unintended consequence this way: "Not all men are monsters. And morality *shapes* culture. But that conclusion is deeply unpopular with large segments of the American population, especially on the left. The 'anything goes' ethos of the 60's sexual revolution -- and the abandonment of individual restraint and traditional sexual morality -- has only empowered the Harvey Weinsteins of the world."

Sexual norms were altered by feminism and a cultural change occurred. The point is, the sexual revolution ushered in a new thinking about sex that had a subconscious effect on both men and women. Ms. Hollis also pointed out: "While heterosexual and 'cisgendered' men endure a barrage of criticism and suspicion, the media fawns over men who wear makeup, dress like women, and cut off their genitals. The symbolism here is profoundly disturbing." Hollis concludes, "There have always been men who exploited their power over women (or children, or other men). But this is *not* characteristic of all men, and saying so is a terrible slur. The solution *is* morality -- a return to sexual restraint, and personal and professional decorum. What we need are more men who are trained to be gentlemen, not boys who have been indoctrinated to be feminine."

As pointed out by Ms. Hollis, a result of the feminist movement was that women became more sexually active and felt more empowered to freely choose their sexual partners, resulting in a reduction of moral standards – not only by women, but it had an effect on men as well. Along with this, the importance of the family has been overlooked and de-emphasized by the feminist movement.

Mona Charen, author and contributor to National Review, shared some of her thoughts on feminism in an interview with National Public Radio. She stated,

"Obviously, the gains of feminism are obvious, and all reasonable people agree women should be full legal, moral, ethical and every other way equals of men, and women should earn the same and so on and so forth. But where I believe feminism took a couple of very disastrous wrong turns was in rejecting the family as antithetical to women's interests and in endorsing the sexual revolution, which turned out to be less than satisfactory for women, and actually, we're now seeing has very, very baleful consequences for men as well.

"So, I join others in calling myself, I suppose, an equity feminist, believing in full equality between the sexes, but I don't necessarily agree that we are the same. We're not. We have important differences. And many of the choices that women freely make tend to get attributed to lingering prejudice - glass ceilings, leaky pipelines and that sort of thing - whereas I think women make choices about prioritizing their families that ought to be upheld and honored and not denigrated."

Ms. Charen shared her thoughts on the plight of the male gender in saying, "It's really important for people at the lower end of the socio-economic spectrum - for them even more than people at the upper end - to have those intact families that are the cradle of good habits, good character, good upbringing. And for boys in particular, we are now [seeing] the social science is showing us that boys who are raised in single-parent families suffer even more than girls. They are less likely to be employed, less likely to go to college, less likely to have ties to their communities and more likely to have drug and alcohol problems than their sisters who grew up in the same kinds of environments."

Suzanne Venker has an interesting take on feminism and what it has done to the psyche of men. This is from her book, *The War on Men*: "In the span of a few short decades, the [feminist] movement managed to demote its men from respected providers and protectors of the family to superfluous buffoons. To a large segment of the population, the idea that men can be victims at all is preposterous. Everyone knows there's more work to be done for women to achieve so-called equality. Everyone knows the patriarchy is alive and well. But Americans have been had. Feminism isn't about equal rights, nor is it about providing women with choices."

She continued, "I don't care how pretty feminists package their agenda - the mission is clear: Feminism is a war on men. It's time to say what no one else will: the sexual revolution was a disaster. Modern men have no respect for modern women and vice versa. Marriage has turned into a competition rather than a partnership. Dating is defunct and any reference to gender differences is met with skepticism or outright derision. Post-feminist America thinks males and females are virtually identical. We've become genderless. To end the war on men, women must stop clamoring for something we already have - and have had for quite some time: equality. They must adopt the mantra 'equal, but different'. Men and women have been equally blessed with amazing and unique qualities that each brings to the table. Isn't it time we stopped fussing about who brought what and just enjoy the feast?" Many feminists vehemently disagree with Venker, but her point is well communicated and insightful.

Also from Venker in an article for the Daily Beast: "The so-called rise of women has not threatened men," she wrote. "It has pissed them off. It has also undermined their ability to become self-sufficient in the hopes of someday supporting a family. Men want to love women, not compete with them. They want to provide for and protect their families—it's in their DNA. But modern women won't let them."

She continues: "Women should understand that they absolutely can be strong and independent and be married, but that being feminine and vulnerable and taking on that more traditional role as being dependent on a man and letting him have some say in the matter is not wasting that empowerment. They [women] are confusing what empowerment means. They think it's about money and prestige, but there is a tremendous amount of empowerment in surrendering in the home and letting the man in your life be what he wants to be, which is to protect you and care for you and provide for you."

Care and protection seem to be an honorable trait, but somehow those attributes have been skewed in a totally different direction by feminism. As stated earlier, this whole attack on men, ironically, is causing a wide array of unintended consequences that are backfiring on women. Looking at it from a macro perspective, the changes brought on by feminism are having not only a negative effect on men, they are harming women, harming our culture, and creating dissention between the genders.

Perhaps what began as a good idea has somehow found itself in a position where the thought of "be careful what you ask for" has raised suspicions on what has been accomplished. After all, I do not know of any man who thinks women should be treated as anything other than equal to men. Sure, there are nut-jobs out there, but all in all, men want women to be their partners as they care for them and live a fulfilled existence – happy wife, happy life. No, sorry feminists, that was not a sexist comment – it's the truth. Men, as a whole, truly want a partnership – not a contentious, adversarial relationship.

The public often tires of the "end of the world, every woman is being mistreated" mentality – it wears on the nerves of most people, including many women, over an extended period of time. Many women, if given the choice, would prefer a happy, loving marriage to a man over a life alone in a dysfunctional feminist's world where the hens have kicked the roosters off the roost.

The vast majority of women don't look at male-female relationships through the eyes of a radical feminist. This group of women gets tired of hearing the same old mantra, especially when evidence proves that our country in particular has responded accordingly by giving women equal rights.

As a whole, men have changed their behavior toward women. Yes, there will always be idiots out there, but the vast majority of men are not ogres and abusers. As a society, we no doubt still need to be vigilant in protecting the rights of everyone, but perhaps it's time for feminists to give it a rest and let us move on to other issues. Does it accomplish anything productive to continuously criticize men and pummel them into submission?

After a while, it's only human nature to want to strike back. When a boxer is cornered in the ring and his opponent is beating his brains out, natural instinct is to either run or fight back. Our society has heard the call of the feminist movement and has responded. The world for women is not perfect, but neither is it for men. Respect for women has been restored in virtually every circle. However, there is a pocket of radical feminists who have become men-haters, and they still hold influence in some circles that keeps the extreme feminist ideology alive. If some women choose to become that, so be it. I am reminded once again that "you can please some of the people some of the time, some of the people all of the time, but you can't please all the people all the time."

A woman can choose to raise a family with a man she loves and enjoy the benefits of traditional marriage or not – it's her choice. Many feminists have failed in their attempt to have an extended male-female relationship or be married, and they blame it all on men and their "toxic masculinity". It's the husband's fault that he cannot adapt to the expectations set forth by feminist attitudes and behaviors. Many of them become antagonistic toward men and then wonder why they can't get along with the opposite sex.

Our society cannot continue down the road of the de-masculinization of men. We rely on the traits men bring to the party – they are integral to our survival as a species. We cannot throw the baby out with the bathwater and expect our society to move forward. "Be a man" or "man-up" do not have to be removed from our vocabulary. Male and female DNA are different whether we are prepared to accept that or not, and anyone who wants to eliminate gender roles that have been with us since time immemorial is messing with Mother Nature – not to mention abandoning common sense. Remember, it's not nice to fool Mother Nature - there are consequences. In my opinion, we don't need to kill off the male gender as some radicals purport. A gender-neutral culture is the ideal for feminists, but in practice, it is not practical nor is it reasonable – it's an extreme viewpoint that needs to be addressed as such.

Feminists were horrified with both Hollis and Venker's viewpoints mentioned above. To speak such things is feminine heresy. Frankly, I see their comments as speaking truthfully and putting forth cogent observations. However, to many feminists, the truth hurts so much that they must attack the messengers and label them as heretics, not deserving to be called women. That's a sad commentary for the state in which we find the feminist movement

What is most troubling is that it appears that we are now at a place where men have been devalued and their roles in society have been turned upside down. If any of us has a son, a husband, or both, we should be worried about where things are headed when it comes to the overall health and well-being of the male gender. There is a lot of evidence to consider and trends to observe that shed light on what's going on. It's worth examining and drawing a conclusion. Some of the statistics listed below are shocking and worthy of taking pause to realize what's happening to the male gender.

As mentioned earlier, throughout all of history, there has always been pressure on males to be the breadwinners and be the provider for family needs. Males have always had specific functions to fill within our society. Generally speaking, today's males, as a whole, seem to be struggling to fulfill their roles and responsibilities. Most men are living up to societal standards, but there's a growing segment that is worrisome – enough that it seems as though a trend is being set. The beating up and dumbing down of masculinity, along with the health status of the overall male population, is having an effect that is clearly born out through statistics.

The suicide rate among men is frighteningly high. According to the CDC, the suicide rate among males is four times higher than their gender counterparts, and white males are far more likely to commit suicide than any other ethnic group. The CDC also found that males are the only category where more than 50% of suicides are committed by men with no history of mental illness.

When we combine the fact that life expectancy has been on a steady increase while male suicides are escalating faster than historic norms, it becomes an issue that deserves our collective attention. The escalation mapping of male suicides overlaying the time period of the 70's until today shows that something is going on within the male gender. The trend line should be discouraging to us. This phenomenon can be characterized as a silent epidemic that is doing considerable damage to the male gender.

Another stunning bit of statistics from statista.com reinforces the fact that suicide is a major problem among the male gender. The suicide rates per capita (100,000) in the year 2000 were 17.7 for men and 4.1 for women. Carry that forward to 2016, the rates were 24.1 for men and 6.0 for women. The percentage increase was greater among women, representing two additional suicides per 100,000 people, but the increase for men represented an increase of 6.4 suicides per 100,000. Both statistics are sad to read.

Alcoholism is also a major contributing factor in the overall mental health of men. There are more men with alcohol problems than women by a nearly two to one margin. According to a study by the National Institute on Alcohol Use and Abuse, for the age group of 18+ years, 8.4 million males in the US and 4.3 million women suffer from Alcohol Use Disorder (AUD). Again, the trend arrow is pointing in the wrong direction.

It's sad to say, but drug abuse is also taking a major toll on the male gender. In New Hampshire, one of the states with the worst opioid addiction problem, men make up 73% of all abusers. In Massachusetts, it's even worse at 76%. Opioid addiction in males between the ages of 20 to 40 has now reached a catastrophic level. Here are the startling numbers according to the CDC: 70,237 deaths in 2017 from a drug overdose, with males making up two-thirds of the deaths (46,552). Imagine an NFL stadium packed with 70,237 fans. That's how many people died in the US in 2017 from opioids and two-thirds were men. Back in 1999, there were 16,849 drug overdoses. That's more than a 300% increase in 18 years. We can all agree that women do have a drug problem, but men have a far bigger problem.

The whole opioid crisis is worthy of its own book. Opioids have become more deadly than car accidents. It's a problem that does not get the attention it deserves.

Here are some more statistics gathered from various sources supporting the premise that men are on a downward cycle.

Education:
- More girls graduate from high school than boys
- In 1966, 61% of college graduates were male, 39% were female. In 2018, those percentages completely flip-flopped to 39% male and 61% female
- Women now earn 60% of all associate degrees, 57% of all college degrees, 60% of all master's degrees, and 52% of all doctorate degrees
- In 2007, for every 100 black males receiving a college degree, there were 230 black women who got their degrees.
- Among Hispanics, for every 100 men who got a college degree, 211 women got a degree
- 70% of all master's degrees among blacks went to women
- 2 million more women are in college than men
- Women receive privately funded college scholarships 4 times more often than men

- More women go on to obtain a graduate degree than men, and women are earning more doctoral degrees than men
- IQ tests show women scoring consistently better than men

Jobs and Economics:
- More young men are now more likely to live with their parents than are women
- Single women buy a home at a rate two times higher than single men
- Between 1979 and 2010, male high school graduates saw their real hourly wages drop 20%, while during the same period female wages rose
- When comparing wages in the same jobs, there is no wage gap. In fact, according to census data, single women living in metropolitan area now earn 8% more than men
- One study showed there were more women in management positions than men
- In 2018, 17% of men 25 to 64 years old are unemployed in their prime earning years

Health Issues:
- The average male will die 5 years sooner than a woman
- There are 42% more deaths caused by cancer in males vs. females
- 70% of all men are overweight, while 59% of women are overweight
- One in 5 boys is diagnosed with ADD, compared to 1 in 11 girls
- Sperm counts are down 70% since the 70's
- Testosterone levels in men have declined dramatically, 1% per year since 1987 (scientists don't know why)
- Since 1987, the average 40-year-old male has shown a 30% decline in testosterone levels
- Lower testosterone levels lead to weight gain, depression, suicide, decreased cognitive abilities and addiction

It is a false assumption that there is a major gap between what men are compensated in the workplace and what women are paid. According to statistics from 2010, the "wage gap" was about 19%. But what that statistic does not take into account is that men choose to take on physically demanding jobs that pay more, while women tend to seek out jobs that are more comfortable and pay less. Men often choose to take higher paying jobs that require lots of travel and long working hours, while women tend to prefer jobs with set hours that don't require travel.

It is not a cardinal sin, nor does it go against feminist orthodoxy to admit that women have come a long way in the workforce and in society as a whole. Progress has been made and it should be recognized and appreciated. Have we reached perfection? No. The scales have been generally leveled in the business world. Does it make good sense to tilt the scales toward women to make up for past generational inequities? Logically, it does not make sense. We are seeing the results in what's happening to the male gender.

The new phrase "toxic masculinity," as mentioned earlier, has come into being out of a necessity for the leftists to categorize behaviors that they deem inappropriate. They are the judge, jury and executioner. They assume that it is their right (or duty) to point out the deficiencies of the male gender. So I ask, if there is toxic masculinity, is there "toxic femininity"? Surely there must be, and from all the aforementioned statistics, it seems as though we are experiencing it.

How would feminists react to the male gender complaining and railing on how women exhibit behaviors that males consider toxic? To admit that females are not perfect would weaken their position and they would have to then admit that women, like men, are an imperfect gender.

Feminism sets a high standard for males, and the question is will they hold themselves accountable for the past and future sins of the female gender. To do that, they would have to agree we both have a problem, and that working together in a mature, meaningful manner is a far cry better than continuous battles between the sexes. Frankly, it's unproductive and does neither gender any good.

The trends are ominous, and ignoring the decline in men's education, employment and health does not bode well for our species. Each gender is dependent upon the other - we can't live without each other. We should not be at war with each other.

There's a fundamental fallacy that if we hold back boys and give girls more opportunities, girls will catch up to boys and everything will be hunky-dory. The question becomes, at what point do we flick the switch and say, "OK, girls are now equal to or better than boys and we can stop showing girls preferential treatment?" By that time, we may have done way too much damage to the male gender that it sets back our species and could even jeopardize our own survival. That may sound crazy and impossible, but it certainly bears consideration.

Bottom line: females are enjoying more success and faring better, while males are in decline. As a general trend backed up by a lot of salient data, females are thriving while males are failing.

Anyone with a husband or a son should see this as an ominous warning. A parent who has a daughter and wants her to have a happy marriage and family and have a good man should also be highly concerned. It's obvious something is going on among the male gender.

Women can be a major contributing factor in turning things around, unless of course they merely prefer to antagonize and jeopardize their intertwined relationship with the opposite sex. First, we must admit there's definitely something happening – that point seems to be pretty evident. Second, we must understand what's really causing the decline and de-masculinization of the male gender. Third, call a truce in the battle of the sexes, and fourth, take corrective action – and it better be soon! *"I Know We Are Better Than This."*

Section 3
Today's Liberalism

Chapter 14

About Liberalism...

Most likely, liberals will be uncomfortable with this chapter, but that's OK –
perhaps it's a good thing, because it might generate some honest assessment as
to where current liberal ideology is today versus what liberalism stood for a mere
ten or twenty years ago. True old-school liberals would not agree with where
things are today in terms of social behavior and attitudes toward freedoms.

The word liberal shares the same root word (liber) as in liberty. The Latin
root actually means "free."

Dr. Milton Freidman is a Nobel Prize winner, Presidential Medal of Freedom
winner, author, and all-around brilliant man. In his book called *Milton Friedman
on Freedom,* he spoke of the fundamentals of liberalism. Here's what he said:
"Liberalism, as it developed in the seventeenth and eighteenth centuries and
flowered in the nineteenth, puts major emphasis on the freedom of individuals to
control their own destinies. Individualism is its creed; collectivism and tyranny
its enemy. The state exists to protect individuals from coercion by other
individuals or groups and to widen the range within which individuals can exercise
their freedom..."

Dr. Friedman continued, "In politics, liberalism expressed itself as a reaction
against authoritarian regimes. Liberals favored limiting the rights of hereditary
rulers, establishing democratic parliamentary institutions, extending the franchise,
and guaranteeing civil rights.

"...In any issue involving a choice between centralization or decentralization
of political responsibility, the nineteenth-century liberal will resolve any doubt in
favor of strengthening the importance of local governments at the expense of the
central government; for, to him, the main desideratum [meaning something that
is wanted or needed] is to strengthen the defenses against arbitrary government
and to protect individual freedom as much as possible; the twentieth-century
liberal will resolve the same doubt in favor of increasing the power of the central
government at the expense of local government; for, to him, the main

desideratum is to strengthen the power of the government to do 'good for' the people."

Does twenty-first century liberalism even have a remote likeness to the tenets outlined my Dr. Freidman? No, it does not seem like it.

Part of the roots of "neo-liberalism" can be traced back to a left-wing philosopher named Herbert Marcuse. In his essay entitled "Repressive Tolerance," Marcuse openly advocated for eliminating free speech for conservatives, along with preventing them from exercising their freedom of assembly. In his essay, he supported "the practice of discriminating tolerance in an inverse direction, as a means of shifting the balance between Right and Left by restraining the liberty of the Right..." Does that even have any remote likeness to old-school liberalism? Of course, it does not. It is more of a display of self-righteous indignation, which is defined as "an excessive awareness of one's own virtuousness and a feeling that one person is morally superior to another."

As an avowed Marxist, Marcuse was also an advocate of totalitarianism, and he greatly influenced the new left radicals that cropped up in the late 60's and early 70's. Marcuse supported shutting down free speech when it was expedient in order to assure an opposing viewpoint was silenced. I suppose he just decided to redact that part of the Constitution that guarantees the right of free speech and expression. Again, that doesn't sound like what true liberalism is supposed to be all about.

The advocates of Macuse's teachings spawned today's neo-liberalism which wants to limit speech if someone takes a contrarian stance. Today's neo-liberal is in favor of collectivism, not individualism. Today's liberal wants a large, centralized government that exerts control over the masses. All those basic tenets of today's neo-liberalism are the polar opposite of old-school liberalism. So much so, in fact, the "liberal" label does not even fit any more – the resemblance is far more akin to socialism and communism than it is to original liberalism and democracy.

Strangely, old-school liberalism sounds far more like today's conservatism. Somewhere along the way, modern liberalism has been co-opted and perverted to such a point that it has morphed into something entirely different than original liberalism. My guess is that the vast majority of people who call themselves liberals may not even realize what liberalism was originally all about. It's strange but true that in today's political climate, old-school liberals would most likely be card-carrying members of the Tea Party which supports free speech, limited government, fewer taxes, and individual rights.

Conservatives have outnumbered liberals since Gallup's baseline measurement in 1992, but the gap has narrowed from 19 percentage points to nine points in recent years. Interestingly, the number of states where liberals outnumber conservatives has dropped more than 30 percent in recent years, with just six now in the liberal majority category: Massachusetts, Hawaii, Vermont, Washington, New York, and New Hampshire.

Also of interest is that in California, a seemingly bastion of liberalism, the Gallup poll showed an even split of 29% for both liberals and 29% conservatives, with the highest density of liberals concentrated in the San Francisco Bay Area and the Los Angeles basin. Nationally, the largest segment of those claiming to be liberals is concentrated heavily on the east and west coasts and major metropolitan areas. In Middle America, often referred to as "flyover country," voters still tend to lean heavily toward conservatism.

We all are aware that the vast majority of entertainment personalities have adopted neo-liberalism as their go-to ideology. Most of them sit in their ivory towers attending cocktail parties and rubbing elbows with like-minded neo-liberal politicians and industry cronies. They are the elites who look down their noses at common folks – especially conservatives.

A fitting description for this group is "limousine liberals," and they loudly pontificate and try to make everyone think they are sanctified. Most of them wear an arrogance toward the common man that drips with a holier-than-thou attitude. They live in gated mansions and fly around in their private jets. Most of them would never dream of getting their hands dirty – they just want to make people think they are supremely noble as they advocate for social justice, racial equality, and rail against white privilege.

Limousine liberals wear their moral superiority on their sleeves and tell us how much more moral they are than we are. I've got news for them, "If you were truly morally better, you wouldn't have the need to rub your superiority in the faces of us deplorables. Flaunting, bragging and pretending you know what everybody should think is not becoming to someone who is morally superior." And here's a message for the Hollywood liberals who think they are morally superior: "You are not, so get over it."

Ironically, most of these snobby celebrities and politicians are white people who enjoy tremendous privilege because of their fame. And they would rather keep all their money than use their wealth to help solve social problems. Those things sound strikingly similar to the monarchies of the past, do they not? The limousine liberals need a little less talk and a lot more action in putting their money and their ideology where their mouth is. The good news for them is that they can go on social media and convince people they are virtuous, and they don't actually have to do anything – they can just tweet. Or they can go on TV and shame us all into submission.

Spiked.com columnist Andrew Doyle on his satirical and somewhat infamous "Woke" Twitter character Tatiana McGrath wrote, "The obsession with victimhood from predominantly bourgeois political commentators is something I have always found inherently funny. It's a phenomenon that has been amplified to a great extent by social media. This extremely vocal minority of activists enjoy pontificating to the masses from their online lectern, berating those who fall short of their moral expectations, and endlessly trawling through old tweets in the hope of discovering a misjudged phrase or sentiment that could justify a campaign of public shaming. In their eyes, there is no possibility of redemption. The most vicious remarks you'll find on social media come from the racist far right and woke intersectionalists[on the left]. They are two heads of the same chimera."

He continued, "It makes sense, then, to think of the social-justice movement as a kind of cult. Its members are generally decent people with good intentions. They have an unshakeable certainty that their worldview is correct. They feel the need to proselytize and convert as many of the fallen as possible. And even though they are capable of the most horrendous dehumanizing behavior, they think they are the good guys." I say they are not. They sit on their high horse and spew platitudes but never can figure out how to solve problems as is evidenced on several fronts.

One of those interesting fronts that is fascinating is the abject failure of so many Democrat state and local governments, from governors all the way down to city councils, mayors and school boards. While they are running for office, they state confidently they know how to solve problems and get things done to improve the lives of citizens. They are morally superior; therefore, they know what is right for everyone.

The growth of the Democrat party in the inner city has led to large metropolitan areas converting the populace to neo-liberalism. Some localities vote 80 to 90% Democrat. The results have been less than stellar as most people would have to admit. The examples of societal degradation and even breakdown are seen on the streets of San Francisco where residents must step over human feces and hypodermic needles as they walk on the sidewalks of what once was one of the most beautiful cities in the world. Los Angeles is not any better – maybe even worse due to the size difference in population.

Consider what has happened in Chicago, Baltimore, Detroit and other major cities where there are murder rates higher than even third-world cities. Sadly, it's unsafe to walk down the streets in far too many major USA cities. And then there's our largest city, New York, which will eventually crumble under the weight of its own dereliction and dysfunction because of neo-liberal leadership if the residents of NYC don't figure out what's really going on.

The good people in these cities are suffering because of the leadership (or lack thereof) of the Democrat party and neo-liberalism. They have developed a voting monopoly and the results are costly to the populace of these cities and states. The results speak for themselves. Is there some other reason why there's perpetual chaos, high crime rates, burdensome taxes, and miserable living conditions? Who else is to blame but the leadership of those cities? What do all the major cities have in common? The answer is undeniably obvious, and the track record speaks for itself, does it not? It is not a stretch to say there are no shining examples of successful cities run by Democrats. Virtually all Democrat-run cities are a hot mess. It's undeniable.

Another question to ponder is when will it get any better? How long do Democrats and neo-liberals have to be in power to solve the horrendous problems facing our big cities? We dare not ask WHEN it will end, because there IS no end in sight. When the problems are greater than the solutions they are able to offer, it's time to seek a different answer. What's the definition of insanity again? And why do people keep voting for incompetence? It truly is a mystery because it makes absolutely no sense at all.

Modern-day liberalism also has the largest and loudest megaphone by way of the complicity of the mainstream media. In addition, academic institutions are espousing and teaching neo-liberalism as outlined in the chapter of this book called, "Liberal Academia".

It is actually surprising that moderates and conservatives still make up the majority of our populace. However, that is ever-so-slightly being altered, because if neo-liberals control the educational system and control a society's mass communication vehicles, one can somewhat safely assume that eventually some people within the masses will become indoctrinated. That is the goal of neo-liberalism. The strategy is to stifle free thought, control what everyone thinks, control what we hear, and begin the programming at an early age.

Is it just me, or does that sound a lot like what happened in Germany starting in 1936? It also sounds a lot like what happened in Russia prior to WW2. It sounds a lot like what happened in China after WW2 (and continues to this day). Government control of societal thoughts and beliefs through the media and the educational system is what all those examples had in common.

Ultimately, I do not believe that the masses want to be controlled. If people believe that all people should be free, how can they support the type of societal control and manipulation that has occurred throughout history? Based on what is happening today, it threatens our country, and far too many people don't even know it.

When one sector of a populace says, "I know how you should feel, I know how you should think, I know what you should believe, and I know what you should say," that looks a lot like communism, totalitarianism, authoritarianism, or socialism. Is that what we want as a country? Would we, as a free people, accept being treated like that? I certainly hope not.

Control of the masses is what current neo-liberals, otherwise known as progressives or leftists, want. They can disguise it all they want with bleeding-heart rhetoric and happy-sounding speech about equality and social justice, but the ultimate goal is to exert more control over our lives. Disagreement or questioning of the leftist viewpoint is not allowed. Evidently, they just don't understand or cannot comprehend the dangers in groupthink. We humans are all different, and we should be allowed to think as we wish, speak what's on our mind, and we should enjoy the freedoms we have.

According to neo-liberals and leftists, anyone who disagrees with them is just plain wrong and the first reaction is to attack the heretic that holds a different viewpoint. Let's give neo-liberals credit – they have a strong conviction for what they believe. That conviction is strong enough to order boycotts through social media for companies that do not toe the line and espouse their ideology. That conviction is also strong enough to shout down people who disagree with neo-liberal ideology which can also lead to violence when believers are radicalized and incited by demagogues.

The newly coined phrase, "cancel culture," describes how neo-liberal "woke" individuals have adopted a holier-than-thou attitude, and their first reaction to someone they disapprove of or disagree with is to attack. The "wokers" are quick to judge, slow to consider all the facts, they adopt a mob mentality, and they use social media shaming, bullying, and boycotting as their weapons of choice. Evidence, logic, and reason are unnecessary in their minds. The other sad part of the woke mentality is that they relish the opportunity to attack and they get enjoyment out of their "cancelling" someone. In the aftermath, they feel vindicated and righteous, and they get a high from their actions.

Former president, Barack Obama, had some interesting thoughts and advice for the woke group of students at colleges and universities. "This idea of purity and you're never compromised and you're always politically 'woke' and all that stuff - you should get over that quickly. The world is messy; there are ambiguities. People who do really good stuff have flaws. People who you are fighting may love their kids and share certain things with you.

"One danger I see, particularly on college campuses ... I do get a sense sometimes now among certain young people, and this is accelerated by social media, there is this sense sometimes of: 'The way of me making change is to be as judgmental as possible about other people … like, if I tweet or hashtag about how you didn't do something right or used the wrong verb, then I can sit back and feel pretty good about myself, cause, 'Man, you see how woke I was, I called you out.' That's not activism – that's not bringing about change. If all you're doing is casting stones, you're not going to get very far."

Cancel culture conduct in the woke community is more akin to a toddler's behavior than an adult. It is also indicative of an overly sensitive, self-absorbed person who is not capable of dealing with the realities of life and the imperfections of the world they live in.

The cancel culture employed by neo-liberals intends to shut down free speech, which runs counter to original liberalism. The neo-liberals among the current Democrat party say they want free speech, but in actuality, they want controlled free speech. Freedom and control are at the opposite ends of the spectrum. The "freedom" they espouse that comes with thought control and speech control is not freedom at all. It is, in itself, speech and thought bigotry.

Yes, in far too many instances, it has happened, still happens, and will continue to happen unless the masses recognize what's going on and refuse that type of control. We must reject it, and I am hopeful that more people will realize the trap that is being set.

Disagreement should be OK, while silencing others must not be. There is also a big difference between thinking the other side is wrong versus thinking the other side is bad or evil. Disagreements should not incite emotional reactions to the point of spewing hatred. That is uncivil and should never be tolerated in public discourse. If people must resort to hatred and name-calling, they should be shunned by the rest of society – it's unacceptable behavior and we need to stand up to it. If they cannot debate in a calm, rational and respectful fashion, and if they cannot tolerate freedom of expression, then the best course for them is to just stay silent.

Imagine a college debate team whose only strategy is to denigrate their competition by calling them names and accusing them of racism, misogyny, and all sorts of slanderous things. Do you think the judges would think that is acceptable? Of course not – that team would be disqualified. The only takeaway the judges would have is that those team members were poor sportsmen and the absence of valid arguments merely showed the weakness of their positions - not to mention the fact they were vile human beings.

No matter how much today's neo-liberals try to convince conservatives that we are bigots, racists, and horrible people, conservatives know we are not bad people. These mischaracterizations are shameful; they have no place in any political or social discourse - and guess what – liberals that lob hate-filled grenades at conservatives are actually practicing their own type of bigotry and racism. Who in the end comes off as being the horrible, hate-filled person? The irony is unmistakable. Conservatives know who they are and what they believe, and the constant onslaught from the left has become tiresome. Disagreement with someone is one thing. Denigration because of differences is a whole other story.

One other thing about many neo-liberals and leftists is that it seems as though they are always complaining about something – they are always mad, and they seem unhappy about everything. In order to be a neo-liberal, must people abandon positivity completely? Surely there are things in which they can find happiness.

Neo-liberals and right-wing supremacists for that matter are looking for their peace and contentment in the wrong place, and when people live and breathe negativism, they become consumed by that negativity – it feeds on itself. They seek out media outlets and associate with friends that affirm their nihilism, narcissism, and pessimism. Eventually, they end up being a victim of their own self-hatred. If there is always animosity, envy, victimhood, and vengeance in their hearts, they will never find peace and contentment. It's time for all radicals to recognize this. In other famous words, "Don't worry, be happy."

Leftists incessantly attack conservative talk show hosts such as Rush Limbaugh, Mark Levin, Sean Hannity, Tucker Carlson, Laura Ingraham, and numerous others. Media Matters, a left-wing website that purports to be a watchdog for media, is nothing more than a group of attack dogs whose sole mission is to denigrate and silence any and every conservative talk show host. Why should Media Matters even care what conservative talk show hosts say? What does it matter? How does it affect them? Who gave them their marching orders, and what right do they have to try and silence and/or launch personal attacks aimed at destroying someone? It's vindictive and hateful. Do they really need that to feed their own narcissism? There is no rational justification for these behaviors. I don't think it is overstated to say that these vengeful acts are an indignity and a slap in the face of humanity.

Strangely, Media Matters is a "non-profit" website that is exempt from taxation, yet the IRS rules on non-profits clearly stipulate that non-profits are not supposed to engage in these types of activities or politics. But that really doesn't matter because according to leftists, the ends (silencing conservative voices) justify the means (constant ridicule and personal attacks). The hatred and rancor that spews from the writers (or should we just label them as they are – assassins for the left) is repulsive and obscene. It is extremism that has moved to obsession.

The fact that all the hosts on Fox News and other conservative media folks have to employ heavy security as they come and go to work, along with requiring 24-hour security in their homes is appalling. Why can't leftists just leave them alone? What exactly compels them to attack conservatives?

Disagreement is not a reason to harass and protest at a person's house. It is downright despicable behavior. It should be characterized as fascism, and leaders on the left should speak up and condemn these types of actions. If it were happening to one of their own, they would be screaming to high Heaven.

Where was anyone in the mainstream media or the Democrat party coming to his defense when protesters showed up at Tucker Carlson's house and were harassing his family, disturbing the neighborhood, trespassing on his property, and making death threats to his children? No one in the mainstream media said a word in defense of Mr. Carlson's right to free speech and safety in his own house, and their silence spoke loudly about what kind of journalists, let alone what kind of human beings they really are.

Let's see, has anyone ever heard a neo-liberal come out and say, "Enough is enough – leave these people alone?" Of course not, and by not condemning these radicals, Democrat leaders and fellow media members are complicit. Left-wing media and politicians have become bereft of common civility, and no political leader or journalist has the guts or the decency to tell these radicals to cease and desist. Perhaps they are afraid the radical ire might be turned on them if they dared to stand up for decorum. That is a pretty lousy excuse and shows the true colors of these individuals.

This is also a sad commentary on the current state of affairs within the Democrat party. Hatred, incivility, criminal trespass, property destruction - is that what neo-liberalism is all about? Last time I checked, liberalism was supposed to stand for peaceful coexistence, freedom of speech and equal treatment for all. Somewhere along the way, liberalism has veered off into the ditch. JFK would be horrified. FDR would be dismayed. LBJ would be shocked.

While the Liberals and Democrats devolve into the party of intolerance and incivility, it is evident that conservatism has taken up the mantle of tolerance and civility.

Hark back to the Tea Party protests that occurred early on in the Obama years. The enormous gathering on the Mall in Washington DC and other areas of the country were peaceful, and they actually picked up after themselves when the gathering ended. There were no riots. There was no violence or property destruction. There were no marches in the street with the sole intent of stopping traffic. There were no marches designed to prevent businesses from conducting their business.

Contrast that with the protests of the Occupy movement where numerous protests around the country turned into looting and violence, and businesses had to shut down. Traffic was stopped for hours in many major cities, disrupting commerce and inconveniencing millions of people. It also took several days and untold millions of taxpayer dollars to clean up the messes these protestors left behind. Is that a true representation of modern-day liberalism? If not, then why was there no condemnation for this type of behavior from politicians and the mainstream media? One can only assume that they were not only sympathetic to the Occupy protestors, but they also showed their support through their silence.

Any well-meaning, law abiding American would abhor the behavior exhibited not only by the Occupy group, but also the Antifa protestors that advocated and carried out violence against people and property in Portland, Oregon and in other cities around the country. If those protesters are an accurate representation of today's liberalism, true old-school liberals should run away as fast as they can from this bastardized ideology. And while they are running away, they should condemn such incivility. Yet they have not, and by their lack of action, they are implicitly endorsing it.

Most mainstream media members were actually calling the Occupy and Antifa movements as the left-wing equivalent of the Tea Party. From any unbiased observer, the two were diametrically opposite, not only in ideology, but also in tactics and methods in trying to get their points across.

The only violence instigated at the Tea Party rallies was brought on by Antifa and other radical left-wing rabble-rousers whose only purpose for being there was to incite violence and cause trouble. Tea Party members did not respond in kind.

The rules for attending a Tea Party event were clearly stated: "No fighting, no littering, no violence, be peaceful and never let a single thing be said about us being disruptive and breaking the law."

The same cannot be said for the Occupy and Antifa movements. After an extensive search for the number of arrests at Occupy protests, I found a website that was sympathetic to the movement and they had tracked more than 4,000 arrests – and that's just the Occupy protests.

In searching for the arrest numbers for Tea Party rallies, I found ten people were arrested for refusing to leave the Congressional building in DC, and a skirmish in Michigan where a single arrest was made for disturbing the peace. Let's look at the score: 4,000 to 11 – and again, that doesn't include the arrests of Antifa members in numerous cities across the country.

No reports of property damage were reported at Tea Party rallies, while damage as a result of the Occupy movement (including property destruction and clean-up costs) numbered in the tens of millions of taxpayer dollars. Instead of that money being spent on inner city education or drug rehabilitation, it was absolutely wasted on cleaning up a bunch of irresponsible, disrespectful people's mess.

Portland is a prime example of how NOT to handle lawlessness when riots broke out in November of 2016. The mayor and other city officials made the decision to allow hooligans to commit anarchy – plain and simple. The same thing occurred in Baltimore and Oakland where the mayors ordered the police to leave the rioters alone and "let them get it out of their system."

For the leaders to sit around and watch businesses in their city be trashed by a bunch of thugs was absolutely horrific. Perhaps those city leaders would have felt differently if it were their businesses being vandalized, but then again, maybe they wouldn't care.

Come on now, anybody with any common sense and common decency would have stepped in and become the adult in the room and said, "This is a temper tantrum that goes beyond the pale of what's is acceptable social behavior, and it won't be tolerated in our city."

The mayors and all the city officials that allowed the rioting and looting might as well have been down there on the streets participating in the pure and unadulterated lawlessness. They were accomplices by not having the courage to stand up to anarchy. Small businesses were hit hard financially – they are the ones that paid the price for city officials turning their heads away and pretending nothing was happening.

The entire citizenry of those cities should have been livid that their fellow citizens were being hurt and victimized. Neo-liberals love victims – so where was the outrage when people and businesses were victimized? Few words are strong enough to use to describe the inaction by those leaders, but shameful, disgraceful, and cowardice come to mind.

David Mamet, an award-winning author, producer and director [and former liberal] stated "the essence of Leftist thought" is a "devolution from reason to 'belief' in an effort to stave off a feeling of powerlessness. And if government is Good, it is a logical elaboration that **more** government power is Better. But the opposite is apparent, both to anyone who has ever had to deal with Government and, I think, to any dispassionate observer."

Mr. Mamet one day realized there were two worlds "where everything was magically wrong and must be immediately corrected at any cost; and the other— the world in which I actually functioned day to day—was made up of people, most of whom were reasonably trying to maximize their comfort by getting along with each other (in the workplace, the marketplace, the jury room, on the freeway, even at the school-board meeting)." Mamet came to realize that he preferred the second world over the first one. Neo-liberalism didn't work for him anymore.

For those who are neo-liberals, perhaps it's time to stop and really look at what is going on. If they are truly for free speech, freedom of expression, the power of individual responsibility, and less government control, then their ideology is far more like conservatism than neo-liberalism. They are only fooling themselves into believing that restraint of speech, limiting critical thinking, collectivism, and more government intervention into our lives is beneficial to the betterment of themselves, their families, and our society.

Our government needs to stay out of our business and let us live free. The foremost job of government officials is to protect their citizens and their property – that is job one and a central tenet of old-school liberalism. The vacuous absence of leadership in the cities mentioned earlier is monumental and indicative of where we will be going if we allow current-day neo-liberalism and radical leftists to take over our country. If that's what we must look forward to, then, as Bob Dylan said, "A Hard Rain's A-Gonna Fall." *"I Know We Are Better Than This."*

Chapter 15

Dissecting Diversity and Multiculturalism

For more than 20 years, many Democrats, Liberals and Leftists have been all caught up in the push for diversity. People are shamed if we don't agree that diversity is the most important thing in the world – outside of climate change, of course. They have pushed the narrative that "diversity makes us stronger" and have demanded that we all buy into this premise.

Ironically, another way to put their "diversity is our strength" slogan is "the less we have in common, the stronger we are." Huh? How does that make any sense?

Diversity, in and of itself, contributes nothing to building unity. The root word is derived from the same Latin word as "different," "divisive," "divergent," and "divorced." Another translation of *diversus*, is "hostile." Do any of those words have anything to do with unity? Of course not. So why would Democrats adopt that as their slogan? Maybe the reason is to let every minority know that the Democrats support diversity at all costs.

Democrats really should not try and coerce everyone into accepting their form of diversity – it really needs to be organic, natural and not forced. If it is forced, that can lead to further division and marginalization.

Forced diversity, as in Affirmative Action, leads to exclusion and unfairness because making sure that an institution is diverse overrules fairness and achievement. There is debate about the fairness and effectiveness of Affirmative Action, but it has caused some unintended consequences that are detrimental to a certain portion of the population.

The roots of Affirmative Action date back to President Kennedy's Executive Order 10925 in 1961 regarding government contractors. The order said, "The contractor will take **affirmative action** to ensure that applicants are employed, and that employees are treated during employment without regard to their race, creed, color, or national origin."

Since then, Affirmative Action has evolved and is covered under several proclamations, court orders, and voluntary programs. In hiring and advancement, special rights are rendered to ethnic minorities, women, and those who are disabled. It applies to businesses and educational institutions as well as government contractors and agencies. The purpose of AA is falsely interpreted to atone for past discrimination and achieve more diversity. That was not the intent of Kennedy's proclamation. It was about equal treatment, not a tool to achieve diversity.

The constitutional principle of equality is the primary legal position from which Affirmative Action emanates. The interpretation says that all persons with equal abilities must be given equal opportunities. The key words are "all people".

The word diversity started taking hold during the 80's and 90's. One of the reasons it began is that there was a focus by the government to force certain standards of how many of this race, how many of this ethnic group, and how many of each gender must be admitted to a university or hired by a corporation or governmental agency. A certain percentage was required in order to meet a quota.

Perhaps it would be better characterized if it were called what it is – rationing. Keep in mind, it was forced and not organic. In the corporate world, diversity became a buzzword and led to hiring regulations dictated by the government as well as in response to social pressure.

The meaning and impact of the word diversity has seemingly been diluted because of over-use and it has lost its punch because of its forced and negative connotation. All these government programs and corporate rules regarding diversity create friction. Who gets hired or admitted to a prestigious university should be based on merit, not ethnicity or gender. The best candidate for a job is the one who should be hired. Quotas are nothing more than social engineering.

Colleges and universities must meet certain "allocations," and to achieve them, someone must win, and someone must lose. It's not about achievement, it's about pleasing board members, bureaucrats, and administrators so they can claim, "Yes, we are a diverse institution."

Let's look at the differences between what is a much more palatable word, and that is "inclusive." Inclusion, by definition, is designed or intended to accommodate diversity with no regard to differences, including age, income, race, or any other category. It is the act of embracing an attitude that has no caveats, no qualifiers, and no exceptions in terms of accepting people for who they are and what they are. The picture that comes to mind is that of open arms, willing to accept, and warmly greeted with no prejudices or qualifications.

On the other hand, exclusion, by definition, is to restrict or segregate based on some specific criteria. It can include rejecting or showing prejudice toward someone based on age, income, race, or any other category. In order to exclude, it requires a classification or categorization, and that is followed by an act of rejection that is based on certain criteria. Neo-liberals have spiraled down into an obsessive urge to say, "This group gets this, that group gets that, and the others get nothing." Minorities are favored for the mere fact that they fall into a certain category. Women are in the favored category based on their gender. Verna Myers, who runs a diversity consulting firm in Baltimore, states it eloquently: "Diversity is being invited to the party. Inclusion is being asked to dance."

There have been innumerable social programs attempting to make sure that past societal sins are reversed. Some have worked, but most have come up far short of expectations.

Don't get me wrong, there have been injustices perpetrated on people based on ethnicity or gender, but society cannot be ruled by who gets what and who gets left out. The ideal is that all people are equal, and all people have the same opportunity to lead a successful, productive life. Our Constitution guarantees equal treatment.

We truly should stop and think about the message that is sent to minorities and women that they are not good enough to compete on a level playing field, so it's imperative to give them an advantage. We have the mistaken instinct to try and make up for past transgressions by taking away from one group and giving more to another group. This pay-back tactic has played out in plain sight in an effort to achieve diversity just for diversity's sake.

Individual achievement is rewarded in our society, whether we are a professional athlete, great guitar player, great scientist, great businessperson, or great at any one thing. Our society is set up to recognize outstanding performance, no matter the color of our skin or cultural heritage. I personally could not think of an endeavor where outstanding performance is not rewarded. Achievement is color-blind, and there's no need to favor one group over another. When we give an advantage to certain competitors and disadvantage to others, it cheapens the accomplishments of everyone. Is a winner really a winner when he or she won because someone else had a disadvantage? In the true sense of fairness and equality, it is obviously not the case.

Today's neo-liberals claim they value inclusion, but strangely enough, it doesn't appear to be that way. Neo-liberalism supports dividing people into groups based on one's ethnic or gender category as further discussed in the chapter about identity politics. A value judgment is then made about who gets what.

Here's an example of how this works: there are a certain number of college applicants that can attend the college of their choice, while another group cannot. As stated before, by putting admission levels at certain required percentages or quotas of minorities or gender, other groups like white males will be excluded simply by the color of their skin and their gender.

The justification for this is that white males have had more than their fair share of college opportunity, so in order to counterbalance this, those that are not white males will get preferential treatment. So, what is the purpose of this? Is it because society just doesn't like white males? Is it because we want to make up for past sins of our society because of our guilt? If so, the unintended (or perhaps intended) consequence is that one class of college applicants or job applicants get preferential treatment at the expense of another group. That, in its essence, is justified exclusion.

The excuse may be that it's OK to be exclusionary as long it's aimed at a certain ethnic background and gender that is considered "privileged." To me, that runs completely counter to the whole concept of inclusion, which neo-liberals are so adamant about. I thought ALL people should be treated equally. It gets right down to it – we are either inclusionary or we are exclusionary. We can't have it both ways. The rules should be the same for everybody – that's fair, that's equitable.

Logic would dictate that excluding one group at the expense of the other is an attempt at social engineering. A white male student from a family in poverty who has risen to the top of his class by hard work can be excluded from a college scholarship simply because of the color of his skin. Is it equitable that another student with a lower GPA gets accepted simply because of the color of his or her skin? I struggle to accept that rationalization. Fundamentally, it should not matter what color of skin one has – it should matter what we have achieved.

The unintended consequence in this case is that the poor white male student is punished because of his ethnicity and gender. Where is the equity in that? Where is any logic to that? Where is fairness? The poor white student certainly was not born into privilege, yet he was punished for simply being white.

What if the poor white male student throws in the towel and returns to his poor status and gives up on his dream of getting a college education and having a successful, productive life? Is that OK? And who has the right to deny him his equal rights? Who is going to tell that student he cannot attend college because he's white and male, even though he achieved?

Quotas and admission percentages are antithetical to how a good and equal society ought to behave. The intent of this admissions strategy is to disadvantage white males. It then seems obvious to conclude that this poor white student is being punished for historical things that did not involve him. He did not promote slavery. He was not a member of the KKK. He never discriminated against women. Yet he is being held accountable for the sins of others. Perhaps I am mistaken, but that doesn't sound fair and equitable – it actually sounds like, dare I say it, racism aimed at white males. What else could it be?

It makes one wonder if racism is supported and encouraged under certain circumstances. It seems rather obvious that is the case. The attitude of many neo-liberals is that white males deserve to be discriminated against because of their "white privilege." By definition, that can only be called one thing – it is the practice of racism. In order to escape the shame of practicing racism, perhaps neo-liberals would simply call it "justifiable racism." No matter the justification, it is racism by definition.

Allow me to repeat what Ayn Rand had to say on the subject: "Racism is the lowest, most crudely primitive form of collectivism. It is the notion of ascribing moral, social or political significance to a man's genetic lineage—the notion that a man's intellectual and characterological traits are produced and transmitted by his internal body chemistry. Which means, in practice, that a man is to be judged, not by his own character and actions, but by the characters and actions of a collective of ancestors."

She also stated, "My philosophy, in essence, is the concept of man as a heroic being, with his own happiness as the moral purpose of his life, with productive achievement as his noblest activity, and reason as his only absolute." It is built into our DNA to achieve. Achievement should be rewarded without regard to any individual trait.

Many neo-liberals are OK with all this social engineering. The attitude is that, yes, there must be casualties that the majority must endure because their ancestors made grave mistakes in how certain groups of people were treated. A poor white student's crushed dream of a better life is merely collateral damage and necessary to make up for societal missteps from 200+ years ago. Frankly, I cannot buy into that. And it's not because I am a white male – it has everything to do with fairness and equality for ALL as is guaranteed in the Constitution.

I do not understand the moral justification for favoring one person over another. I do not see where there's any logic in that. What exactly has been accomplished other than assuaging guilt feelings for anyone who happens to be in the majority? I'd much rather put our focus on the fact that we are all human and eliminate colors, ethnicities, and classifications. If we believe we are ALL equal, then we ALL should act like it. No exclusions and no excuses – only inclusion - and no apology or special dispensation is needed for being a certain race or gender.

Let me counter forced diversity with this argument: "E pluribis unum" means "From many, one," or another translation is "Out of many, one." We are a diverse nation by nature, but that does not make us strong – it is unity that makes us strong. It is everyone pulling together in the same direction. It is togetherness and inclusion. We do not need to classify everything and everybody or meet diversity quotas to be a fair society that treats everyone equally. In forcing diversity for diversity's sake, we will become a nation that is divided into certain groups such as whites, blacks, browns, Asians, geeks, athletes, men, women, adults, children, and on and on.

We really shouldn't be saying this group gets this many points while that group gets fewer. That's not treating everyone equally – that's saying this group is more equal than that group. More and equal are words that don't belong together. Equal is equal – there must not be any ifs, ands, buts, excuses, or rationalizations for not treating people equally just for the sole purpose of achieving diversity.

When we allow diversity to take precedence above accomplishment, exclusion comes into play. A complete focus on diversity above all else ultimately leads to exclusion, which is antithetical to unity. "We will be united as one at the exclusion of another" does not sound like a slogan that promotes unity.

One of our most esteemed universities, Harvard, admittedly manipulates its admission procedures to insure diversity balance across the campus. Let's examine this to see if, by employing a "diversity first" admissions process, Harvard is either inclusionary or exclusionary. Remember, if the goal of diversity is to be "inclusive", does the Harvard process achieve this goal?

Harvard receives millions of dollars in funding every year from the Feds with the agreement that the school will follow the laws of the government and not discriminate based on "race, color, or national origin in any program or activity," as stipulated in the Civil Rights Act. Harvard, however, admits that it voluntarily uses race as a factor in deciding who gets in and who does not. The justification used is that the use of race in the admissions process is "necessary to its pursuit of the educational benefits of diversity." That's their justification - diversity above equality, and diversity over achievement.

So now, according to Harvard, diversity is more important than providing equal opportunity in getting into their university. Some applicants get preferential treatment to the detriment of others. But wait a minute. That runs counter to what is stipulated in the Civil Rights Act – no discrimination of any kind is allowed. The result is that Harvard's diversity policy overrules equal opportunity for everyone. However, that's acceptable in their minds because the need for diversity is more important than equal civil rights. I disagree with that.

Competition is fierce in trying to get admitted into Harvard. It can be a life-altering event. The admissions board can arbitrarily use their "personal ratings" criteria to manipulate who gets in and who does not. Students can score very high in academic achievement scores, but because they are in a certain ethnic group, they can be scored low on "personal ratings" - unless, of course, they are the children of a famous politician, actress, or movie producer, but that's another story. This subjective process is used to manipulate admissions in order for Harvard to accomplish its goal of diversity over equality – the Civil Rights Act and the Constitution be damned.

With their personal ratings formula, Harvard can eliminate an applicant because of their ethnicity, even though the student is a valedictorian with impeccable personal accomplishments. Where is the equality in that? Diversity for diversity's sake actually violates the basic rights of certain applicants who get excluded because of their ethnicity or gender. How is it not a violation of the Civil Rights Act?

In 2017, a group of Asian students filed suit against Harvard because their personal ratings had been used against them for no apparent reason other than to exclude Asian students. The quotas for Asian students were maxed out. Apparently, the admissions group at Harvard thought they have enough Asians, and they didn't need any more. That seems more like exclusion than inclusion – maybe even racist?

In court filings, the Asian group states, "Distinctions between citizens solely based in their ancestry are by their very nature odious to a free people whose institutions are founded upon the doctrine of equality. It demeans the dignity and worth of a person to be judged by ancestry instead of his or her own merit and essential qualities." Who could disagree with that?

Research performed by the plaintiffs found that Asian-American applicants had a 25% chance of admission to Harvard, 35% if they were white, 75% if they were Hispanic, and a 95% chance if they were African-American.

In another court case cited by the Asian students (Miller vs. Johnson), it states, "At the heart of the Constitution's guarantee of equal protection lies the simple command that the government must treat citizens as individuals, not as simply components of a racial, religious, sexual, or national class. Race-based assignments embody stereotypes that treat individuals as the product of their race, evaluating their thoughts and efforts – their very worth as citizens – according to a criterion barred by the government, by history, and the Constitution. Accordingly, any preference based on racial or ethnic criteria must necessarily receive examination." Now that makes pretty good sense to me.

Remember, Harvard has agreed specifically to uphold equality as a condition of receiving taxpayer funding. Therefore, the Asian students have every right to file a complaint against the university. Treating them as a group and then eliminating some of the group when the quota is reached should set off alarms that they were being targeted for discrimination. Again, shouldn't that be labeled racism?

This type of admission exclusion and manipulation occurs throughout the university community. A logical and reasonable conclusion is that this is wrong, unfair, exclusionary, and runs counter to what our Constitution and the Civil Rights Act stipulates. In order to achieve diversity, we cannot throw out the Constitution and we cannot ignore the Civil Rights Act no matter how guilty we feel about our past sins. Diversity must not be achieved at the expense or exclusion of anybody, no matter the good intentions or the misguided thinking that diversity trumps laws. It does not. And that is not to mention that diversity over everything else just lacks basic common sense and equal treatment.

If universities want to achieve diversity and assist students, they have every right to figure out ways to assist them. Where the rub comes with forced diversity is when that assistance or preference is at the **exclusion** or expense of someone else. That is discriminatory no matter how it is sliced and diced, and no matter how creatively the rationalization or justification is put together, it is still discrimination by definition.

The argument for diversity at the exclusion of others is that it's not discrimination; it's just showing preference for people who need some extra help. Opportunity plus extra preference at the exclusion of another equals discrimination in my book.

Most diversity initiatives are based on the thinking that we, as a society, must somehow make up for past sins committed against racial, ethnic, gender or social groups. In order to assuage our guilt, we are required to show preference to a certain group. In most realities, that type of policy leads to exclusion – not inclusion. What we are obligated to provide is fair and equal treatment and an opportunity for everyone to succeed. Again, inclusion through exclusion does not equal equality. Diversity forces people out so that others can be brought in.

The foundation of our society was built on the unassailable premise that all of us are created equal. If we start at that point and see other people through that lens, our society would be much better off. Yes, we have past sins and atrocities, but looking back should only be to see the error of our ways. We must learn from them, and then build a better future by treating EVERYONE as equals. This is only accomplished, in my view, by starting with the fundamental principle of equality – that is the only lens we should look through.

Yes, there will always be a segment of society that will carry prejudices, classify people, and try to engineer outcomes – today we call them neo-liberals. However, we cannot cop the attitude that equality is only applicable to certain groups; that is not conducive to unity and is antithetical to equal treatment for ALL.

We have come a long way as a country in terms of equality, and I do agree we must be ever vigilant in our pursuit of equality – it's an on-going process. What gets in the way is that we are only human from the outset. We are born imperfect. The great thing about our country is that we see our flaws and, as a whole, we try and eliminate our flaws.

I understand the feeling that we must do something to right the wrongs that have befallen certain groups of people - that's an honorable thing to try and do. However, in my estimation, the most critical point is that it cannot be at the expense of another group – that, to me, is counterproductive and exclusionary.

If we want to move forward and attain equality, we cannot start with the assumption that this group should have these rights and assistance, while that group does not. Trying to forcefully manipulate equality through exclusionary government programs and social intervention will never work as well as a purely organic inclusionary mindset where everyone can take advantage of freedom, equality, and opportunity offered to all citizens in our great country.

Multiculturalism is another central tenet of liberalism that is tied into diversity. It can be defined as "a social policy or educational theory that encourages the development of many cultures within a community or country." Like diversity, that's another nice idea, but it has its drawbacks as well. That is not to say that multiculturalism is catastrophic to a society, but too much focus on it can lead to separatism where certain communities of racial, religious or ethnic groups isolate themselves from the mainstream.

Our country has tolerated certain groups who chose to live in semi-isolation and not fully immerse into the community. As long as they do not cause a disruption and can coexist with the rest of the citizens around them, we do not force them to give up their culture or religious beliefs – as long as they follow our laws. The Amish and Quakers come to mind.

Most rational people are all for everyone maintaining their heritage and being proud of the culture in which they were raised. But when the culture runs counter to our laws and norms, as does Sharia law in Muslim communities, it creates a societal tension that can lead to serious issues and a clash with the community.

Groups can have cultural differences, but they cannot have their own set of laws. Would we tolerate fathers killing their daughters for having sex outside of marriage? Of course we wouldn't. It's against our laws, and frankly, it's barbaric. Yet that is what some cultures not only allow, but they require it.

We have existed as a country just fine with our Constitution, laws and moral norms. If individuals desire to live under a different set of standards, then they should simply find a country that supports those standards and move there.

Multiculturalism can be taken to extremes. When it is, it becomes detrimental to the well-being of a stable society. Multiculturalism cannot overtake or rise above our laws and moral norms. Everyone must live up to the same standards. It is acceptable if a culture or ethnic group wants to have their own traditions and customs, that is, as long as those customs and standards do not violate any of our laws.

What we need is the right to equal treatment despite differences, but the focus should be on the common threads that unite us. It is not the differences that define us or unite us; it is the common purpose of freedom of choice, law and order, plus equal justice that separates us from other countries.

Ironically, allowing too much multiculturalism can actually lead to racial tensions and disagreements in how the moral code is applied. One can see that a father may be deeply disappointed in his young unmarried daughter who had premarital sex, but murdering her is a violation of our moral code. The punishment does not fit the crime according to our laws and moral standards. Human life is far more sacred than the anger and vengeance a father may have.

In Canada and most of Europe, there have been problems with the focus on multiculturalism and allowing certain cultures to exist in their own communities. The mistake has been to allow cultures or ethnic groups to isolate themselves from the citizenry. This separatism is a choice that leads to alienation, fragmentation and societal tension.

Kenan Malik is a noted author, columnist for the *New York Times*, and lecturer known for his thoughts on diversity and multiculturalism. In an article on ForeignAffaris.com, Mr. Malik had some interesting thoughts on both.

"As a political tool, multiculturalism has functioned as not merely a response to diversity but also a means of constraining it. And that insight reveals a paradox. Multicultural policies accept as a given that societies are diverse, yet they implicitly assume that such diversity ends at the edges of minority communities. They seek to institutionalize diversity by putting people into ethnic and cultural boxes—into a singular, homogeneous Muslim community, for example—and defining their needs and rights accordingly. Such policies, in other words, have helped create the very divisions they were meant to manage."

The article continues: "A much-discussed 2013 poll conducted by the French research group Ipsos and the Centre de Recherches Politiques, or CEVIPOF, at the Institut d'Études Politiques de Paris (known as Sciences Po) found that 50 percent of the French population believed that the economic and cultural 'decline' of their country was 'inevitable' [due to the push for multi-culturalism] Fewer than one-third thought that French democracy worked well, and 62 percent considered 'most' politicians to be 'corrupt.' The pollsters' report described a fractured France, divided along tribal lines, alienated from mainstream politics, distrustful of national leaders, and resentful of Muslims. The main sentiment driving French society, the report concluded, was 'fear.'"

Interestingly, the French encouraged unfettered immigration and took a full assimilation tactic in trying to achieve multicultural balance. Immigrants were expected to learn and abide within the French culture, including the requirement to speak French. Things have not gone well. The "Orange Coats," made up of blue-collar workers protested the influx of cheap labor and the fact that wages were declining, along with taxes going up because of the rise in social program costs. The natives became restless.

The British, on the other hand, took a laissez-faire (to use a French term) tactic that essentially left immigrants alone, let them gather where that wanted, and the hope was that they would assimilate. It didn't work. Ethnic groups moved into certain areas and essentially took over, driving the natives away and isolating themselves.

Mr. Malik stated, "In the United Kingdom, multicultural policies were at once an acknowledgment of a more fractured society and the source of one. In France, assimilationist policies have, paradoxically, had the same result." That result is non-assimilation and self-imposed segregation.

The point is, as the French learned, the result of trying to force adaptation to a particular way of life is that the people within a culture or ethnic group don't want to choose to acclimate and assimilate. Humans don't like to be forced into accepting a way of life unless they consent to it – it must be their choice in order for it to work. They must have buy-in.

The opposite, as the British experienced, is to not stress that immigrants must have some semblance of acclimation and assimilation and to allow them to live in isolation. When that is permitted, humans will naturally segregate and sequester themselves. That accomplishes nothing in terms of having a common bond with the citizenry of the country in which they chose to immigrate. It does not contribute to unity – on the contrary, it promotes segregation.

Multiculturalism requires a balanced approach, but most important of all, it requires the desire of the immigrants to self-enjoin and become productive members of their new homeland – no matter their culture or background. Assimilating and respecting the societal norms are the keys to successful immigration.

Mr. Malik's article also stated, "Thirty years ago, many Europeans saw multiculturalism—the embrace of an inclusive, diverse society—as an answer to Europe's social problems. Today, a growing number consider it to be a cause of them. That perception has led some mainstream politicians, including former

British Prime Minister David Cameron and German Chancellor Angela Merkel, to publicly denounce multiculturalism and speak out against its dangers."

Mr. Malik continued, "How did this transformation come about? According to multiculturalism's critics, Europe has allowed excessive immigration without demanding enough **integration**—a mismatch that has eroded social cohesion, undermined national identities, and degraded public trust..."

Europe has taken on vast millions of immigrants and the results have been disastrous in the minds of many native citizens. In several European countries, immigration was encouraged due to declining birthrates and the need for cheap labor. It was an economic decision versus being a culturally beneficial decision.

There is no doubt that the divide in multiculturalism has caused a transformation that the natives have had to deal with. The cultural conversion has not gone as planned, and the strain has affected the natives while having little or no beneficial economic impact – in fact, it has been detrimental to the citizens. Well-meaning leaders in many European nations thought it was a great idea, only to discover that it was not. Societal manipulation through forced diversity and multiculturalism does not work and the evidence is obvious.

Mr. Malik had more to say: "Moving forward, Europe must rediscover a progressive sense of universal values, something that the continent's liberals have largely abandoned, albeit in different ways...To repair the damage that disengagement [brought on by multiculturalism] has done, and to revive a progressive universalism, Europe needs not so much new state policies as a renewal of a civil society."

Diversity and multiculturalism are a slippery slope, and where they can run off the rails is if immigrants and minorities do not feel the need to assimilate and adapt to the cultural norms that are pre-established. A country can have diversity without the need for multiculturalism – and diversity is not a requirement for the toleration of different cultures.

On the other hand, monocultural countries like China do not have the problem of assimilation. If people immigrate there, they either get along or they are thrown out, sent to a "re-education camp", or possibly executed. We don't see people lined up at the border to get into China do we? I wonder why...

The only way multicultural societies can be successful is for those groups that immigrate to assimilate seamlessly. The strength of our country and the ties that bind us are not found within ethnic groups of various cultures. Our strength lies in our ability to be tolerant, yet adamant about abiding by our laws, and insuring equal treatment of every citizen. Diversity and multiculturalism must take a backseat to commonalities and unity.

The USA has always been a multicultural country because of the vast numbers of people that migrated here. What was pervasive throughout the first 200 years of migration was the immigrants' love and respect for their new country. They came here for what America offered and stood for. Their intent was not to take over or transform the country - they just wanted to acclimate, assimilate, and enjoy the wonderful benefits of a free society that offered unlimited opportunity. Our ancestors focused on what they had in common. They were not obsessed with their differences, diversity or multiculturalism; they were driven by and united through their commonalities.

The reason people want to come here is for the freedoms we enjoy. The oneness we feel regarding freedom and equality is the glue that holds us together. It's that common thread that is woven into the fabric of our country and our culture.

Immigrants have always come here for these very reasons: We have the freedom to choose our own destiny. We have the freedom to be successful if we want to be. We have the freedom to live whatever lifestyle we want. We have freedom of speech. We have freedom of religion. We have fair and impartial laws. And everyone receives equal treatment. Yes, there are instances where we have come up short on equality, but we are far better than most other countries, which is why billions of people would love to live here.

We cannot let our country be divided into groups, categories and clans because, as we have seen play out in Europe, it just doesn't work. The failure of European immigration was because the focus was always on differences rather than commonalities and universal values.

This whole all-out push in the USA for diversity just so a company or governmental agency can say it adheres to diversity standards is unnecessary. We must let diversity happen organically and stop dividing people into groups or categories and force-feeding our country with multiculturalism. As said earlier, the end result of forced diversity and multiculturalism is exclusion, and it does not accomplish the intended goal – there are always unintended consequences and unintended victims.

Those of us who are not in a minority group are now considered outsiders by left-wing liberals. The neo-liberal attitude has devolved into if we are male, we are the wrong gender. If our skin color is white, we are the wrong color. If we are a Christian, we have the wrong religion. If we are successful, we shouldn't be. If we are happy, that's out of line. If we're not a victim of something, we need to be. Those are the messages "the majority" are subtly and constantly being told by neo-liberals and leftists.

I'm sorry, but I disagree with the Left's mindset and portrayal of who we are and what we represent. As a whole, we in the majority are a good and respectful people. All the people I know have no problem with any minority. The assumption is because of OUR skin color, we are automatically judged as insensitive, we are bigoted, we are racist, or just not very good people. To that way of thinking, we all should be calling BS! We are good people and to be accused otherwise is an insult to us all.

Leftists are always pushing for and insisting on more diversity and more multiculturalism, when in fact, the emphasis should be on quite the opposite – and that is UNITY and EQUALITY. When the focus is on the wrong thing, the end result is not going to be what they are seeking.

The bottom line is that forced diversity distances minorities from the mainstream while multiculturalism forces a separation from the mainstream. Neither one is beneficial to the cohesion of a society.

A lot of people who are classified as the majority are beginning to think that no matter what they do to be receptive to and supportive of minorities or immigrants, it will still never be good enough for some on the left. We should all hope that this judgmental and divisive attitude brought on by the obsession with diversity and multiculturalism will go away soon, because *"I Know We Are Better Than This."*

Chapter 16

Ethnic Tribalism and Identity Politics

Many neo-liberals are intent on putting all people into categories - they admit that. They play the game of identity politics. So, what is identity politics? It is defined as, "Political attitudes or positions that focus on the concerns of social groups identified mainly on the basis of gender, race, ethnicity, or sexual orientation."

This is how the website reference.com describes it: "Identity politics involves embracing these divisions as an essential part of identity, which means the identity of a single person is necessarily politicized by the social categories to which he belongs."

Mark Lilla, a liberal academic and Columbia humanities professor stated, "Identity politics on the left was at first about large classes of people ... seeking to redress major historical wrongs by mobilizing and then working through our political institutions to secure their rights. But by the 1980s, it had given way to a pseudo-politics of self-regard and increasingly narrow, and exclusionary self-definition that is now cultivated in our colleges and universities. The main result has been to turn people back onto themselves, rather than turning them outward towards the wider world they share with others. It has left them unprepared to think about the common good in non-identity terms and what must be done practically to secure it—especially the hard and unglamorous task of persuading people very different from themselves to join a common effort."

Identity politics, by its very nature, leads to exclusion and division. It sets into motion ethnic tribalism and separation. This eventually leads to groups competing against each other, hating each other because they are different, and the outcome inevitably leads to jealousy and hostilities against each other. It has happened repeatedly throughout history, from ancient tribes to modern-day liberals.

The neo-liberal community regularly practices bigotry with its brand of identity politics. Here are some examples. If we are a black conservative, we are identified as not black enough. If we are a gay conservative, we are not gay enough. If we are a conservative woman, we are not allowed to be a member of the feminist's club. If we are a conservative black gay woman, that is just so egregious that these types of people are completely shunned by neo-liberals and not recognized as actual human beings – they are the ultimate defectors in the cause of identity politics.

Neo-liberals can deny that this happens, but sadly, it does happen every day in the world of liberalism. That is the truth. Within neo-liberalism or the "woke" elitists, they are utilizing identity politics in an attempt to shut down free thought and free speech. This is the weaponization of identity politics. If we do not meet their standards and toe the liberal line, our label of black or gay or feminist is summarily removed and replaced by the label of traitor to the black, gay or feminist cause.

Identity politics has absolutely nothing to do with virtue, although that is what those that are fully immersed will claim. Categorizing people and then attacking those foolish souls that believe in conservatism, for example, is the polar opposite of being virtuous. It is political bigotry plain and simple.

Liberals have fired their identity politics bullets at Clarence Thomas, Ben Carson, Condoleezza Rice, and many other black political figures that have dared to hold conservative viewpoints and be a minority - it's just not acceptable to neo-liberals. Hollywood elites black-list conservative actors and actresses and prevent them from working. Conservatives in Hollywood are not judged by their talent, they are first judged by their political point of view. Does this type of behavior have even a modicum of virtuousness? Obviously not. Sadly, these sanctimonious Hollywood people are practicing political discrimination, but they are too busy virtue-signaling to even notice their own hypocritical sins. If any other group were treated like conservative Hollywood people, Lord knows the neo-liberals would be in a tweeting frenzy along with marching in the streets, carrying signs, and screaming about unfair discrimination.

What puzzles me is that liberal Hollywood elites cannot see the error of their ways, even when it's staring them right in the face. Hollywood discriminates against conservatives – it's the truth. The first step on the pathway to recovery and atonement begins with admitting there's a problem. Let the confessions commence in Hollywood. Yeah, right.

Identity politics in its very essence is divisive – that is its essential purpose – to categorize, classify, pit one group against another, while treating one group one way and another group another way.

The truth of the matter is that identity politics leads to disunity. Inciting people to battle against each other does not sound like a real good plan for building trust between ethnic groups. How can anyone claim that identity politics is conducive to having a peaceful coexistence? Women are pitted against men. Blacks against whites. Straights against gays. Atheists against religious people. Criminals against the cops. Conservatives against liberals. Democrats against Republicans. Rich against the poor. This list could go on and on ad infinitum – hopefully the point is obvious.

It takes far more hard work to live in the world of identity politics than to just accept everyone for who they are and what they believe. To me, it seems like an exhaustive endeavor to play the game of identity politics that ultimately leads to endless frustration and unhappiness. Has anyone ever seen a happy identity politics person? They are always on edge, in a bad mood, and complaining about something.

If history has undoubtedly shown identity politics to be divisive, then why on Earth do we think that identity politics is a productive activity for our country? To me, logic would dictate that identity politics is not conducive to unity, peace and harmony, which all progressive neo-liberals say is their ultimate goal for their ideology. There seems to be a stark irony in the reasoning and justification of identity politics.

Identity politics purports that our ethnicity defines us at the time of our birth, and our value to society is based on our ethnicity. It seems to me that a very famous person who is revered by Democrats once said, "I dream of the day when people are judged by the content of their character, rather than the color of their skin." Yes, that was Martin Luther King, Jr. in his iconic, "I Have a Dream" speech.

Ironically, civil rights activists and MLK were pushing for people to NOT be categorized – they wanted EQUAL treatment – not SPECIAL treatment – there's a big difference. They did NOT want to be known as a black person – they wanted to be known as simply a person who was equal to everyone else. They had already been isolated and categorized – they wanted freedom FROM their black ethnicity, not BECAUSE of their black ethnicity. Neo-liberalism wants to put black people back into a group and isolate them from other groups, which is the polar opposite of Dr. King's dream.

In identity politics, these groups are favored over those groups, and some groups are punished just for being a member of an ethnic group that is deemed evil or privileged. According to what neo-liberals believe, what matters most is our genetic makeup, not our personhood. They are encouraging the "weak" groups to attack the "strong" groups. The weak groups are the victims, and the strong groups are the oppressors. Minorities are the victim groups and the white majority is the group classified as the oppressors.

Neo-liberalism not only dictates that all groups are to be treated differently because of their ethnicity, it rewards some groups and punishes other groups – again, based on the color of their skin or their ethnic identity and not based on the "content of their character."

An interesting question is, exactly who gets to be the judge as to what group wins and what group loses? Is it going to be dictated by the "holier-than-thou" group because they know better? Perhaps a self-assured group of pompous politicians?

It seems to me that some people think white people (full disclosure, I am white) are to blame for all of society's problems from social justice to income inequality. To some on the left, white privilege is so pervasive that it is ruining our society by causing minorities to live in poverty, drop out of school, do illegal drugs, have babies out of wedlock, and commit murder or other criminal activities. The view of neo-liberals (made up ironically of mostly whites) is that all minorities, all women, all ethnic groups are victims - except for white people, and especially white males.

Since liberals want to categorize and classify those that are not white as victims, does that mean that ALL white people are oppressors just because we exist? The answer most progressives would give is "yes, except for me because I am 'woke'." That's strange, because I don't recall ever oppressing anyone, nor do I know anyone who has oppressed someone else. It seems to me there should be some hard evidence to prove white people are oppressing minorities by simply being white – which is exactly what leftists believe.

So, all white people fall in the "white oppressor" category, and the reason they are in that category is that they have "white privilege". It seems pretty obvious that this kind of thinking sounds a lot like racism. One ethnic group is being attacked by others just because of skin color. Is that not a prime example of racism? Where does the logic go wrong? And does it just apply to all white people? It seems as though the message from "woke" white people is, "It's OK to be racist against white people - it's justified because they are white – and I am not a racist, I just hate white privileged people even though I am one, so I hate myself because I am white."

One might ask if there is a special category for certain whites who are victims, such as those in poverty. When do white people get to have an acceptable identity? What does it take for white people to redeem themselves and renounce their white privilege? Who is the judge that will tell white people they are redeemed? Is there a sword white people must fall upon? Who gets to decide if I am a good white person or a bad white person? And how long will it take in a neo-liberal world for white people to eventually become the victims themselves rather than being classified as the oppressors? Would it take the destruction of a small grocery store owner's business by a vigilante group simply because he is white? Doesn't that make the store owner a victim of racism? Or is that merely justifiable behavior in the world of neo-liberalism? Who has the answers to those questions?

We are all different – we are individuals. When groups are labelled and put in a box, it is by its very nature a contentious act. We need to adopt the attitude that we are one nation, one people. When that happens, we are far better off. That sets a foundation from which we can work together. Mutual trust is a requirement for a peaceful society. Reaching out is more conducive to achieving compromise than using identity politics to build walls that divide people into groups.

The incessant attack on white Americans by neo-liberals only leads to more division, and white people will naturally react to these attacks with disdain at some point. Their only option is to defend themselves, and paradoxically, it creates an attitude that white people must stick together in order to survive, leading to more white resentment, which is what progressives are trying to eliminate.

Asad Haider, author of the book, *Mistaken Identity*, stated this in an interview on newhumanist.org/uk: "The problem with this identity politics is that it does not account for intra-group differences, it does not provide a basis for forming coalitions and solidarities across groups, and it reduces politics to gaining recognition rather than transforming the social structure."

He continued, "I have always been dismayed when call-outs begin at a political meeting, because it means that the actual project of working for change will be obstructed by a potentially endless process of exposing everyone's privilege. We are all privileged and corrupted in various ways, and these public performances of trashing and shaming do not address the problem which comes with every coalition, which is that everyone is vulnerable and taking a risk. As the civil rights activist and black feminist Bernice Johnson Reagon said in her speech 'Coalition Politics: Turning the Century,' coalition work is 'dangerous.' There are no 'safe spaces,' and there's nowhere you can go where you will just find people who are like you." It is evident that identity politics leads to segregation, not integration. Paradoxically, this is another unintended consequence of identity politics."

If there is a method to the identity politics madness, a lot of us regular, peace-loving people would like to know exactly what all this is going to accomplish. Maybe I've missed it, but to my knowledge, no one has clearly articulated how identity politics is going to be a great thing for our country. I truly am having trouble understanding how classifying, categorizing, separating, victimizing, grouping, galvanizing, and attacking ethnic groups are at all beneficial. Maybe some people like me are not "woke" enough to understand this, but it certainly looks to me like there is nothing positive in identity politics for our society.

Neo-liberalism embraces a divide and conquer strategy. As mentioned, they need to put everybody in a group, divide and separate them, pit these groups against those groups in a battle of victims versus oppressors. They will say anything that is necessary to incite certain groups. They will put a full-frontal assault on the oppressors, and whatever incidental damage the oppressors suffer is inconsequential as long as the chosen "victim" group conquers the "oppressor group".

There are so many dangers hiding within identity politics. The same scene has been acted out time and again throughout history, and the results have been catastrophic for those countries that chose to go down this road.

Here's a statement that sums it all up: "There's not a black America and white America and Latino America and Asian America; there's the United States of America." That statement came from then Senator Barack Obama in his keynote address at the Democrat Party's National Convention when John Kerry was nominated for president. A lot of people would never have thought that he was against identity politics. Evidently, he is (sarcasm intended).

Brett Easton Ellis, famed novelist and author of *American Psycho* and social provocateur had some harsh words regarding identity politics: "This is an age that judges everybody so harshly through the lens of identity politics that if you resist the threatening groupthink of 'progressive ideology,' which proposes universal inclusivity except for those who dare to ask any questions, you're somehow [screwed]." Ellis says, "Everyone has to be the same, and have the same reactions to any given work of art, or movement, or idea, and if you refuse to join the chorus of approval you will be tagged a racist or a misogynist."

Somehow, I just can't wrap my arms around this concept of ethnic tribes. It seems counter-intuitive to what neo-liberals are ultimately seeking. Is there a beneficial end to the means of ethnic tribalism and identity politics? Is it simply a way to sow public discord between groups of people for political gain or to obtain power over a group of people?

One aspect of identity politics is that it entails people voting for a candidate based on one particular issue. In practice, that means that a feminist would only vote for a candidate that supports the feminist ideology. Black voters only vote for Democrats. Gays only vote for a gay rights advocate. Those votes are cast based solely on one issue, not the sum of a candidate's positions, and politicians try to play the identity card as often as they can because it guarantees votes from an ill-informed, single-issue electorate. As Charles Barkley told Alabama Senator Doug Jones, "We need to start holding you Democrats accountable, because they've been taking black people's votes—and they only talk to black people every four years. All of these politicians only talk to black people every four years because they want their vote." Barkley accused Democratic lawmakers of abandoning black communities once the race is won. "When they get elected, they do nothing in the four years in between," he stated.

Heather MacDonald, author of *The Diversity Delusion*, in an interview with Tucker Carlson stated, "I think what we are witnessing is the most dangerous import from 'the academy' into the real world [is] students [in college] are taught from the moment they arrive on campus two things, and two things only…which is that the most important thing about themselves is their group identity, defined redactively by melanin, and that racism, sexism based on those characteristics are the defining features of American society. [They are] taught to believe that when they face any kind of disagreement, they reflexively accuse their ideological opponent of bigotry and hate. And that works wonderfully on a college campus – you accuse a [university] president of racism and he immediately crumbles and orders another million dollars of diversity bureaucracy. You accuse a corporation of racism and it folds as we saw with Nike and a preposterous claim that the Betsy Ross flag is racist. It works with politicians with Biden repudiating his justified support of the federal crime bill that saved thousands of minority lives.

"The question is, will this work on the rest of us. If it does, civil society is over, because this is a totalitarian power play. It is an attempt to shut down any kind of dialectic search for truth and to occupy a sole ideological ground. And that's a recipe for a society to halt dead in its tracks and go in reverse."

"You know, there's been political disagreements long before identity politics [which] is an act of narcissism to think that everything is about yourself to immediately say 'it must be because of my gender and race that I am being disagreed with, and you must be a bigot to disagree with me.' No, that is not the case. These are issues that deserve to be thrust out into the public forum. And again, if they are not, we are approaching a totalitarian state very quickly.

Wrapping up her comments, Ms. MacDonald stated, "Racism is no longer the predominant characteristic of America, if it ever was … It was never THE defining feature – it is not. It [America] still remains the land of opportunity. The alternative explanation is there are profound behavioral differences and choices that individuals make that determine social outcomes. We have to fight back against this [identity politics] narrative…because if they win, we lose our civilization, we lose meritocracy, and we lose freedom."

The foot-soldiers of the neo-liberals that practice identity politics march in the streets and are told by the politicians and activists to revolt. Divide. Disrupt. Tear down. Riot. All the while the politicians are gazing out their window and watching from their ivory towers as property gets destroyed and people get hurt because of identity politics. No worries, it's just the collateral damage of identity politics at work. Is this really what we want to sign up for? *"I Know We Are Better Than This."*

Chapter 17

The Myth of Socialism

Socialism is rearing its ugly head here in the USA. The push for socialism comes from the leftists who think that collectivism and government control are the panaceas that bring nirvana to a society. Anyone that buys into the idea that socialism is the end-all, cure-all, best way to be governed is grossly ill-informed and/or sadly mistaken. Unfortunately, the ideals of socialism are best left for a discussion in the classrooms of universities versus being adopted and practiced in the real world.

Socialism doesn't work because its basic premises of collectivism and government control of everything is diametrically opposed to a basic human instinct, and may I say a basic human right, and that is FREEDOM. Who in his or her right mind would want to choose the enslavement of socialism over freedom?

Collectivism is idealistic and does not take into account reality and reason – it resides somewhere up in the clouds of idealism or somewhere in the dreams of those who believe in the fairy tale of a socialistic Camelot. The ideal of collectivism crashes to earth when people wake up from the hypnotic slumber. Reality and common sense eventually set in for those that have given away their freedom when they get fed up with the constraint and control inflicted upon them.

Mark Levin on his radio show had an interesting take on how socialism creeps into people's lives when he stated, "The diabolical genius [of socialism] is that it provides the emotional and intellectual roadmap for autocrats to persuade millions of people to support their own enslavement to [a socialist] government…But they are persuading millions, not only in this country, [but also] tens of millions, hundreds of millions overseas." And I might add, hundreds of millions of people were convinced socialism or communism was great, but they highly regretted it after the fact. Perhaps it's a little bit of "be careful what you ask for."

Let's break it down to the basic tenets of socialism. Here is my top 10 list of what we can expect in a socialist state:

1. The government is in control of everything in commerce because it is for the good of the collective
2. There is no private property ownership - the government owns everything because it is good for the collective

3. The government does not allow any dissent or freedom of expression because it is not good for the collective
4. What people think and do is dictated by the government because it is good for the collective.
5. Religion is not allowed for the good of the collective.
6. Creativity and art are not allowed unless approved by the collective.
7. Moral authority and justice are dictated by the government for the good of the collective
8. Food is controlled and distributed by the collective.
9. What is taught in schools is controlled by the collective
10. All weapons, including for self-defense, are confiscated for the good of the collective.

I could go on, but the point is obvious.

Sadly, far too many people in our world are enticed by the golden glow of socialism, only to discover that they have bought into fool's gold that was sold to them by the charlatan purveyors of the big lie that is socialism.

Now let's look at the chain of events that occurs when socialism is adopted.

1. A leader rants about bringing revolution and socialism, promising free stuff, equality, and social justice and then gets elected. The people buy into the notion that giving up freedoms, which is essential for the implementation of socialism, is a good idea.
2. The leader and all his cronies take control of the government and establish themselves as the ruling class that they say will lead to peace and social order.
3. The leader removes any type of weapon or means of self-defense and establishes a police state – the people are disarmed.
4. The government seizes property and businesses because the state must control all commerce while the ruling class begins to accumulate wealth.
5. Once complete control is achieved, the leader declares supreme leadership and exercises martial law, and a full authoritarian state is then established.
6. The working-class people who elected the leaders begin to suffer from oppression, poverty, and begin protesting their deteriorating conditions. The protests are summarily beaten down.
7. The leaders further assert power over the working class by exterminating those that disagree with them, using lethal force when necessary. Public executions are a good way to keep the populace in fear and in line.

8. The working class suffers even more while the ruling class continues to further enrich themselves – the rich get richer while the poor get poorer.

9. A revolution FROM the revolution begins to break out and internal class warfare begins. As we have witnessed in numerous examples, things can get pretty bloody and lots of casualties will be the result.

10. The Socialists are thrown out of power after the populace realizes they made a big mistake, and the leaders are either hung in effigy or, if they are lucky, exiled to another country. What's left is economic ruin, pervasive poverty, and utter chaos. People do prefer freedom and democracy over socialism. The most disturbing thing is that the populace had to learn the value of freedom and democracy the hard way – by giving it up.

The most recent example of this chain of events occurred in Venezuela. Nicholas Maduro, the Venezuelan socialist dictator, was elected to office and immediately disarmed the country – he took all civilian weapons away. Maduro created "disarmament centers" where Venezuelans could relinquish their arms without any punishment. Everyone was commanded to hand over their weapons. Here's what he said, "Let us chase after the dream, after the utopia, the utopia of a Venezuela in peace." He characterized the disarmament to be part of "the movement of peace and life. Disarmament must come from the conscience of the youth."

Now one might ask, why would a dictator like Maduro do that? Could it possibly be to have complete control of the citizens of Venezuela? After all, a revolution armed with rocks and voices is not going to make any headway against the government that has all the weapons.

It's a perfect example of how an armed electorate was convinced to give up their ability to defend themselves, ultimately resulting in a "democratic" socialist government that has deteriorated to such a point that it is literally a crime against humanity. Authoritarianism took over and the results were abysmal for the Venezuelan people. They were once a prosperous nation that has deteriorated into total disarray at the hands of socialism. The same pattern occurred in other countries like the Soviet Union, North Korea, China, Viet Nam, and many others.

As we have seen throughout history, once the Collective has conquered the individual, then it's time for getting down to business and having the ruling class (the state) run the show. Everyone is equal in this collective paradise (and equally poor). Everyone makes the same salary (except, of course, the ruling class). Individuals must perform the job that the state dictates (except, of course, the ruling class). Individuals must think whatever the state tells them to think (except, of course, the ruling class). All people must speak whatever the state tells them to speak (except, of course, the ruling class). All citizens must give all their money to the state (except, of course, the ruling class).

Hmmm… this is sounding a lot like a socialist dictatorship, where the ruling elite get to set all the rules, and the rest of the population must live by those rules whether they like it or not. Socialism sounds rather oppressive to me.

Let's face the facts about socialism – **it just doesn't work**. Again, it's a nice idea to be discussed and debated in classrooms, but it is wrought with enormous flaws, and the road of history is littered with failed attempts to make socialism work.

All the communist/socialist countries are a prime example that if we give up control of our freedoms, we lose control of our destiny. Our future is dictated by the ruling class, and if we're not one of the chosen few, we are screwed and destined to live an unhappy, unfulfilling life that is a constant struggle. Just ask the Venezuelan people, the North Koreans, the former Soviets, et al.

There are six countries remaining that are communist/socialist: China, Cuba, Venezuela, North Korea, Laos, and Viet Nam. Does anyone have a warm fuzzy feeling about those countries in terms of freedom and democracy? The people in those countries prior to communist takeover were told that life would be hunky-dory – the Communists said to just put them in power and they would make life so much better for everyone.

They promised equal jobs, equal pay, affordable food, great healthcare, and all government services that will be the best ever. That sounds like the Democrat party doesn't it? The people bought into it and look what they ended up with – a totalitarian ruling class that lives high on the hog while untold millions of people starve and suffer. It's the usual modus operandi. It starts out as socialism and ends up in totalitarianism, and it happens EVERY time.

Some people say communism is not the same as socialism, and some say socialism is not the same as communism. To those who say communism is not socialism or vice versa, let's have a neutral party tell us what they mean. Merriam-Webster's dictionary says communism is "political and economic ideologies that find their origin in Karl Marx's theory of revolutionary socialism, which advocates a proletariat overthrow of capitalist structures within a society, societal and communal ownership and governance of the means of production, and the eventual establishment of a classless society."

Here's Webster's definition of socialism: "Any of various economic and political theories advocating collective or governmental ownership and administration of the means of production and distribution of goods; a system of society or group living in which there is no private property."

These two ideological terms are indelibly interlinked with each other and there is no denying it.

I have seen the result of communism with my own eyes while visiting China. I have seen the looks on the faces of many Chinese people up close and personal. What I saw was despair, anxiety, and anguish. Imagine how the North Koreans feel. Needless to say, it's not a happy sight. I also spoke to several Millennial-aged young people who warily but carefully shared their views on the Chinese government. I could tell they were afraid to speak openly. They are completely controlled by a dictatorial regime that has no sympathy for their plight. The government tracks them and monitors their phone and email. There is no freedom of the press. There is no freedom of expression. Everything is controlled by the state. Does that sound like what we want?

Sadly, government has failed the working-class people miserably in every communist country. There is no freedom or democracy in those countries. Their elections are a joke. Prosperity is closely confined to the ruling class, and the rest of the populace can just fend for themselves.

Recall that Robin Hood robbed from the rich and gave to the poor. Quite the opposite is true for socialist and communist regimes. I would classify them as undertaking "reverse Robin Hoodism" by robbing from the poor and giving to the rich.

Do we think North Koreans would choose their current plight versus having freedom? What about all the Cubans that have escaped to the US? What about all those that died trying to cross the Berlin Wall? Why did they risk their lives? They did it to escape oppression and gain their freedom. If socialism or communism is so great, the walls they built would have been to keep people out, not to keep them in.

Ayn Rand said it this way: "When one observes the nightmare of the desperate efforts made by hundreds of thousands of people struggling to escape from the socialized countries of Europe, to escape over barbed-wire fences, under machine-gun fire—one can no longer believe that socialism, in any of its forms, is motivated by benevolence and by the desire to achieve men's welfare."

To further prove the point of how socialism and communism have failed miserably is evidenced by the countries that have tried them and said thanks, but no thanks. Thus far, there are 43 – here's the list if for those that care to read it:

This list is from the website infoplease.com:

- *Formerly part of the Soviet Union:* Armenia, Azerbaijan, Belarus, Estonia, Georgia, Kazakhstan, Kyrgyzstan, Latvia, Lithuania, Moldova, Russia, Tajikistan, Turkmenistan, Ukraine, and Uzbekistan.
- *Other Asian countries:* Cambodia, Mongolia, and Yemen.
- *Soviet-controlled Eastern bloc countries:* Bulgaria, Czech Republic, Germany (East), Hungary, Poland, Romania, Slovakia.
- *The Balkans:* Albania, Bosnia and Herzegovina, Croatia, Rep. of Macedonia, Montenegro, Serbia, and Slovenia.
- *Africa:* Angola, Benin, Dem. Rep. of Congo, Ethiopia, Somalia, Eritrea, and Mozambique.
- *Belarus, Afghanistan* (yes, it's true)

Let's count them up. That's 43 failures and 6 dysfunctional existing communist or socialist countries – that's not a very good track record. Zero for 43 – that's a really bad batting average. Is there any more compelling evidence that socialism and communism don't work?

Ronald Reagan characterized communism in this way: "How do you tell [someone is] a Communist? Well, it's someone who <u>reads</u> Marx and Lenin. And how do you tell an anti-Communist? It's someone who <u>understands</u> Marx and Lenin."

There are some countries that call themselves "socialist," but most, if not all are not truly and completely socialist. Proponents of socialism point to Denmark, Sweden and Norway of examples where socialism has worked. Their economy is based on capitalism – not socialism. Not to mention the total population of these countries combined is less than half the population of California and 3% of the total US population.

Those countries have social medicine where the government controls healthcare or they might enjoy "free" college tuition. That's really nice. However, with all those purportedly great perks offered by the government come high tax rates. Somebody must pay for all that free stuff. Would we be willing to perpetually give up 50 to 60% of our income to have "free" healthcare and "free" college?

Let me get this straight. People only go to college once and that has a finite cost, but they still pay for everybody else's education for the rest of their lives. Does that sound enticing? What happens if individuals don't want to go to college? Do they still have to pay? Of course they do. It's all for the good of the Collective. Somehow, that just doesn't make good sense to me.

The idea of simply taxing the rich to pay for everything does not hold water either. If we confiscated the entire wealth of Jeff Bezos, Bill Gates, Warren Buffet and the top 10 richest people, it would probably pay for everyone's health care and college tuition for a year – maybe two. Then what? Take the wealth of the next 100 people? And then the next thousand after that?

Far too many billionaires and celebrities tout socialism as the answer to mankind's problems. One day, perhaps they will realize they should be careful with what they ask for. What are they going to do when they get a 90% tax on their wealth? Does anyone think that is going to go over well? Then why are so many of them intent on promoting socialism and neo-liberalism when all it's going to do is cost them a LOT of money? That just strikes me as strange and ironic – maybe a bit moronic. They support candidates who want to hammer them with higher taxes. It just seems to be a bit weird – maybe even masochistic. The logic doesn't add up. Perhaps they know they will be part of the ruling class that takes over.

If billionaires and celebrities want everyone to have free health care and free college, why don't they volunteer to give up their extravagant lifestyle for the good of the Collective? It seems to me that's a valid question. They call capitalism evil while extravagantly enjoying its benefits. We can hear their lame excuses: "Yes, I make way too much money, but hey, it's not my fault the laws say I can keep most of the money I make. If they want me to pay more taxes, change the laws." Are they ignorant of what they are asking for by supporting neo-liberals and socialists that want to severely raise their taxes? It makes a person utterly wonder about their sanity.

Rebecca Walser, a noted tax attorney stated in a Fox Business Channel article, "…in the US, a single person earning $60,000 a year using the standard deduction would only be in the 12 percent marginal tax bracket and would pay an effective tax of around 10.75 percent. But in Denmark, where health care and education are 'free', earning the US equivalent of $60,000 puts that person's tax rate right around 60 percent. Does this 60 percent tax on a person making $60,000 sound like taxing the rich?"

Ms. Walser concluded, "This tax-the-rich line of thought is a façade, obscuring the fact that by rich they really mean even those making $60,000 per year. Because massively taxing the super-rich, or even the top 1% would not begin to provide the funding required for the government programs of a socialist system."

Margaret Thatcher famously spoke about socialism when it rose to popularity in the UK: "I think they [socialists] have made the biggest financial mess that any government's ever made in this country for a very long time, and socialist governments traditionally do make a financial mess. They always run out of other people's money…They're progressively reducing the choice available to ordinary people."

Also, knowing that governments can be inefficient and ineffective in administering government-controlled services, does it really seem like a good idea to turn over our health care to a bunch of bumbling bureaucrats who don't really care personally about us and our family's health?

Also if we cede total control of our education system to be funded and administered by the government, it opens the door to not only poor education (which we are currently experiencing in far too many school districts), it exposes students to being educationally manipulated – in other words, brainwashed. Is that really what we want? Local control is far better for true education than centralized governmental control.

Somehow, I just can't get my arms around and embrace those two "free" things and feel good about socialism. Whenever the government tells us we're getting something "free," does anyone really believe that? Free isn't really free because somebody somewhere has paid the price. I guess the attitude is, "If I didn't have to pay for it, it was free." Little do they realize they pay for it dearly in taxes and in freedom to choose.

People in the USA who sing its praises and want socialism are seeking an ideal that is unattainable because to achieve collectivism, sacrifice must be made by everyone – some more than others. No problem; make the rich people pay for it. Well, as stated earlier, that's just great until we run out of rich people. Then what? Everybody at the bottom of the money chain must pay more. Ultimately, the middle class and the poor people end up getting the short end of the stick because taxes must be raised higher and higher in order to support the Ponzi scheme perpetrated on the populace by those in charge.

As we have seen, what usually follows in socialist countries is dissention and discontent amongst the people as a result of the repression and over-taxation. The populace eventually gets their belly full, and the revolution commences. If the people are strong enough and capable of overthrowing the government, they can rid themselves of the tyrants and end up (hopefully) free to choose a new form of government that allows the people to have control through democracy. This scenario of control leading to misery and then leading to revolution has been played out repeatedly as witnessed by the list of failed governments mentioned before.

We are spoiled by freedom. In Cuba, Venezuela and other socialist countries, food is rationed. Imagine what would happen if we went to the grocery store and could only buy one chicken, two pounds of rice, two pounds of vegetables, one quart of milk and that's it for our family's meals for the week. That is exactly what is happening in Venezuela and Cuba. Just think how we would react to that. And oh, by the way, using electrical power is rationed. How do we think Millennials would react to being able to use their phones for 30 minutes per day? We all know their heads would explode and they would not be able to cope with such a tragedy. And then there's the medical side which would also have to be rationed. However, all this rationing is OK because it is for the good of the Collective. Socialism means pervasive sacrifice, and I doubt ANY free American citizen would tolerate what socialism requires. Truly, it's a waste of time to even be talking about socialism.

I heard a young lady in a TV interview say socialism would work just fine in our country because we are smarter than the Russians, the Cubans, the Venezuelans, the Chinese, and all the other citizens that thought socialism was a great idea. Obviously, she is misguided and has not looked at the history of socialism, or she is bigoted against all those people. It is pure folly to think that giving up freedom and ceding control to the collective is a good idea. As mentioned previously, socialism still has a batting average of .000. The naiveté displayed by her and all the other socialism activists is not only shocking, it's also a sign that they are trying to live in an alternate reality that cannot and does not exist.

Helen Raleigh is a senior contributor to The Federalist. An immigrant from China, she is the owner of Red Meadow Advisors, LLC, a Colorado Registered Investment Advisory Firm, and an immigration policy fellow at the Centennial Institute in Colorado. Ms. Raleigh has first-hand experience with communism, having grown up in China under the Communist regime. She characterizes communism and socialism as a "bait and switch scheme." In an editorial, she described how families eked by on very limited resources and lived in one-room bungalows with no kitchen. Her family cooked in a communal kitchen, and what food they were able to get was strictly controlled by the government handing out food stamps, which was the only way food could be acquired.

Ms. Raleigh described how electrical power was cut to their community one day a week – and sometimes more. She is worried that too many people in the USA are embracing socialism and stated, "Immigrants like me came to the U.S. to escape socialism, not to encounter another round of a so-called socialist experiment. We know all too well where it will lead us. Socialism has been tried too many times in different places, by different people of different cultures and languages – Russia, China, Cuba and Venezuela just to name a few. No matter where it is implemented, the result will be the same – individual freedom will be destroyed and ultimately there will be death, starvation and misery."

Another thought … if socialism is so great, why has it not taken over every country on the planet? It has certainly been around long enough to have established a reputation and achieved validation. Results matter, and the results of socialism are disastrous. Something then must be fundamentally wrong with socialism. That something is that it runs counter to human nature. Humanity yearns to be free – not to be controlled. We are born free and we should always stay that way.

When one recalls the nightmare of the desperate efforts made by hundreds of thousands, even millions of people struggling to escape from the socialized countries of Eastern Europe, South America, Asia, and the Soviet Union, it is a stark reminder of what communism and socialism did to its people. They tried to escape through digging tunnels, climbing over barbed-wire fences, and dodging machine-gun fire. The price of freedom was costly, but those who tried to escape felt like the reward was worth the risk. Some made it, while most did not. One can no longer believe that socialism, in any of its forms, is motivated by benevolence, nor by the desire to improve the welfare of the people. In socialism, misery loves company.

Consider Mao and all other communist dictators who sought power by putting people in groups much like what neo-liberals or progressives do by adopting identity politics.

This tactic used by Soviet Communists put a wedge between various factions. Divisiveness becomes an asset of the government that is deployed whenever there is a hint of disagreement among ethnic, religious or political groups. Public discourse becomes more heated and polarizing, and it paves the way for the government to step in and take control of the population, giving a whole new meaning to the phrase "divide and conquer."

Communist leaders know that by putting people in various groups, it makes it easier to manipulate them or attack them. There is no need to understand them or listen to them; it is far easier to group them all together in order to use them against other groups. That is the Communist ploy to brainwash one group to be in opposition to another; they want to sow radicalization and social tension.

In twentieth-century Communism, it was the working class schlubs against those evil oppressors in power who were replaced by, you guessed it, more evil oppressors. When they gave up their freedoms, they gave permission for the government to enslave them.

Such radicalism seeps into groups because members want to make sure their voices are heard above the crowd; they scream louder and/or execute protests that can result in property destruction and violence against other groups in order to get maximum attention.

Today's radical leftists pleading for socialism exert pressure by categorizing people and pitting them against each other in much the same fashion as has been practiced by communism since the turn of the twentieth century. It becomes blacks against whites, cops against criminals, liberals against conservatives, religions against atheism, men against women, straights against gays – it goes on and on. By creating political discord and wreaking societal havoc, it allows the government to become the arbitrator and pick the winning side. It's all about division and then control.

Leftist liberalism holds the view that everything is always wrong, which coincidentally is one of the other tactics used by many Communist dictators. Change is necessary because everything is wrong. President Obama forwarded the position that we must "fundamentally change America". I ask this poignant question, "In a country as successful as America has been in the last 250 years, is it necessary to throw out the baby with the bathwater?" Far too many people have the view that "fundamental change" is necessary because we are so screwed up that we need to trash the Constitution, re-write our history in accordance to the neo-liberal stance, put everybody in groups, and have everyone adopt the same groupthink viewpoint. For neo-liberals, that is Nirvana.

Neo-liberals think that life would be perfect here in the good ol' USA if we all only believed in neo-liberalism, which is essentially equal to socialism. We would all think alike, dress alike, make the same amount of money, and all hold true to the belief that we are all the same, and agree that differences only lead to disagreements and strife. Everyone should think and feel the same. Competition is cruel and winning should not be tolerated.

However, communism and socialism are diametrically opposed to how we humans like to think and act as we please. Total control of the populace is the position that communism must have for the ideal to be accomplished. Neo-liberals want to manage and control us just as communist regimes have done.

Neo-liberals will argue that they don't really want full government control – they only want enough control that they can regulate thought. What they aren't saying is that the more government control we surrender, the more freedoms we give up – they are inversely related.

How many neo-liberals really and truly want the government to control everything? It sounds nice, looks nice, but under the sheep's clothing is a wolf that is ready, willing, and able to devour its prey. Power corrupts absolutely, and absolute power corrupts absolutely. Haven't we learned that yet? Are we really that ignorant to buy into the belief that communism or socialism is really the be-all, end-all, highest form of government? If so, I have a bridge I'd like to sell the neo-liberals...

Even a casual look at history would lead most people to think that a socialistic society runs counter to the human need to be free. In my opinion, if we really want to experience total government control, I suggest we move to China in order to live under an oppressive, controlling form of government. Or perhaps a long trip to Venezuela will be enlightening. How about North Korea? I don't see people lining up for that.

When a leader has complete control over a populace, bad things always happen. Groups of people are extinguished at the whim of the government. Cultures and ethnic groups are snuffed out because they differ from what the government wants as is evidenced in Hitler's, Stalin's, and Mao's tactics.

What is most worrisome is that currently our youth often are taught by dishonest professors who magnify the glories of socialism while touting the promise of a fairytale social philosophy. If I were a betting man, I'd bet a lot of money that none of these socialist professors tell their students that communism and socialism are responsible for the slaughter of more than 100 million "non-combatant civilians." And I doubt they mention that Venezuela used to be a thriving country until socialism took over and now it's in shambles. I'm pretty sure they would not teach about the starvation and the abysmal health conditions that socialism brings.

Communist and socialist governments must coerce their citizens into behaving as the leaders want. They must use force in order to silence any opposition and get rid of the non-cooperative citizens or the ethnic groups they don't like. Extermination is required, and they justify it because it's "good for the collective."

Here are a few statistics that should be the final nails in the coffin for those that defend socialism and/or communism. While Hitler led the National **Socialist** German Workers' Party (commonly known as Nazi's), he killed 11 million citizens. While Stalin led the Union of Soviet **Socialist** Republic, he was responsible for killing 30 million people, including 2 million Germans alone. Mao Tse Tung ruled over the People's (**Socialist**) Republic of China and was guilty of killing 45 million people. Those three leaders alone presided over the killing of 86 million people, and that is not counting Cambodia (1.8 million), Viet Nam (1.3 million), and many other murderous communist/socialist regimes – including Cuba and several African nations. Along with these numbers attributed to communist and socialist democide, genocide and politicide, add another 38 million who are estimated to have died from starvation that was intentionally carried out by these regimes. All those people slaughtered or starved were mere collateral damage on behalf of the Collective.

After reading those numbers, anyone who thinks socialism and communism is how we should be governed is not only grossly misguided and ignorant of the facts, I would go so far to say they are psychotic.

A good example of the use of force to control the population is what happened at Tiananmen Square during May and June in 1989. A groundswell of support for freedom and democracy swept into most parts of China, including Beijing, Shenzhen, Guangzhou, and other major cities. The focus was on Tiananmen Square, and we know a lot more details of the protests that broke out because there was a historic meeting of Soviet Union's Mikael Gorbachev and Communist China's leaders there during that time. Tiananmen Square was the usual place for such pomp and circumstance of a state visit to Beijing, but the choreographed reception for Gorbachev and his entourage had to be moved to the airport because the Square was occupied by thousands of protestors.

Many of the press contingencies from around the world became more interested in what was happening in the Square than what was going on at the airport. Protests of hundreds of thousands of people and even millions across the country were unheard of in China. Dissent, of course, was not allowed, and the punishment would result in a ticket to one of two destinations – either the gulag or an appointment to meet our maker in front of a firing squad.

A small Statue of Liberty made of Styrofoam was erected by some of the protestors in the Square. Along with democracy, the millions of protestors were demanding something that the Communist regime had never given their people – respect.

The Chinese government was hesitant to quash the protests because world attention was focused on them, so they let the protesters do their thing until the summit was over and the press traveled back to their own countries.

On the evening of June 3rd, after three weeks of protests, the Communist government's patience had run out, and they began to forcibly disperse the crowd and silence the protesters. Tanks and armored personnel carriers moved in along with several thousand troops. Bullets started flying indiscriminately into the crowd, and the death toll was never reliably reported, but estimates ranged from 300 people massacred to several thousand. That's not to mention the full number of people that were injured. It has been estimated that more than 10,000 were arrested, but it could easily have been far more, and no one will ever know the true numbers. We will never know because the Communist government tightly controls what the press is allowed to say – and that includes foreign journalists.

This is what happens when an all-too-powerful government has absolutely no regard for the lives of their citizens and how they want to be governed. How the Chinese Communists treat their people can only be characterized as immoral and inhumane. I'm sure this book would not be well-received by the Chinese government, nor will it be available at any bookstores in China or for sale on Alibaba. Thank God I live in a country that allows me free speech and the ability to write and publish a book.

Does anyone really think that, outside of those in power, anyone in China would choose a brutal Communist regime over freedom and democracy? Of course not. People want respect from their government, not mistreatment and massacre. There are two things to remember: totalitarian governments are a direct result of socialism or communism as is evidenced in China, and dictators have no respect for their people; they don't value human life – the Collective is more important than the individual, and the despots make up the rules and strictly enforce them.

It appears we are not only forgetting about but also not being taught about the devastation brought on by communism and socialism. I'm pretty sure that if one of those radical professors that tout the beauty of communism or socialism bothered to ask someone who has lived under a repressive regime if he or she would prefer freedom over socialism or communism, the answer would undoubtedly be freedom – I'd bet my house on that. I can envision those professors brushing that choice aside and then start making excuses for the failures of socialism. I would do the same if I were trying to defend a baseball player that had a .000 batting average – he'll get a hit next time up even though he's 0 for 43.

Some people may say, "Oh, we would never allow a dictator to take over the country; there are too many protections in place." When those protections are gradually eliminated one by one, the populace doesn't even notice until it's too late. Socialism initiates a slow death spiral that has always led to totalitarianism. That's the way it has worked in EVERY country where it has been tried. Socialist professors and activists would never admit it, and anyone that negates history is utterly and irrevocably in denial.

We need to correct our path away from socialism and head more toward individual freedom. Our democratic, capitalistic, freedom-loving country has done pretty well since 1776. The good that we have done is unsurpassed in history. Why on earth would we want to change that? Yes, we can use some trimming around the edges, but the tree is strong and sturdy with deep roots. Let's not cut it down or poison it with an ideal that has never worked. All a communist or socialist government wants to do is to enslave the populace. Who in their right minds would think that's a good idea? It baffles me.

I believe freedom is a gift from God. I believe it's embedded in our DNA to want to live free. Those who have freedom are dearly fortunate. Those who don't have it dearly crave it. We cannot let the notion that socialism is the panacea that cures all our cultural problems further creep into our lives and slowly take away our freedoms. Surely, we are smarter than that. Once again, *"I Know We Are Better Than This."*

Section 4
The Trouble With Academia

Chapter 18

Liberal Academia and its Influence

The main purpose of higher education is to launch students into the workforce where they can build a career, raise a family if they want, and live comfortably. That's not to mention the satisfaction and pride that comes with graduation – it's a personal accomplishment. Education is about learning how to apply one's skills while being able to reason and express personal opinions. However, things are changing in the world of education.

Academia in the US is playing an enormous and influential role in a manipulating generational change among our youth. This has been happening for more than 60 years, and it seems to be accelerating at a rapid pace. There is no doubting this trend, and the statistics that follow are revealing, enlightening, and shocking – except to the die-hard liberal. However, even the most adamant liberal may be surprised to learn what's going on in our entire education system, affecting students from kindergarteners to doctoral students. Many public school teachers, professors, and administrators are using indoctrination.

A research paper written by Mitchell Langbert, Anthony J. Quain, and Daniel B. Klein entitled, "Faculty Voter Registration in Economics, History, Journalism, Law, and Psychology," showed some startling statistics. This is from the Abstract: "[In our paper] we investigate the voter registration of faculty at 40 leading U.S. universities in the fields of Economics, History, Journalism/Communications, Law, and Psychology. We looked up 7,243 professors and found 3,623 to be registered Democratic and 314 Republican, for an overall Democrat-to-Republican ratio of 11.5 to 1. The Democrat to Republican ratios for the five fields were: Economics 4.5 to 1, History 33.5 to 1, Journalism and Communications 20.0 to 1, Law 8.6 to 1, and Psychology 17.4 to 1.

"The results indicate that Democrat-to-Republican ratios have increased since 2004, and the age profile suggests that in the future they will be even higher. The data supports the established finding that Democrat-to-Republican ratios are highest at the apex of disciplinary pyramids, that is, at the most prestigious departments. We also examine how Democrat-to-Republican ratios vary by gender and by region. People interested in ideological diversity or concerned about the errors of leftist outlooks—including students, parents, donors, and taxpayers—might find our results deeply troubling."

Also from this study, some of the more prominent universities and the ratios of registered Democrats vs. Republicans are: Columbia, 30 to 1; Brown, 60 to 1; Boston University, 40 to 1; USC, 26 to 1; UC-Davis, 26 to 1; University of North Carolina, 23 to 1; Penn State, 6 to 1; Harvard, 10 to 1. The universities from the 40 institutions they studied that were the most balanced were Ohio State at 3.2 to 1 and Pepperdine, 1.2 to 1. The study was a good cross-section of different parts of the country, and with a sample size of 7,243, the data is reliable.

The National Association of Scholars performed a study in 2018 and discovered that 39% of elite liberal arts schools didn't even have one registered Republican on staff. Huh? How can that be true? But it is.

More from the NAS study: "For 2004 such a ratio was estimated at 8 to 1 (Klein and Stern 2005, p. 264), but now we are comfortable with moving the estimate up to 10 to 1. The reality is that in most humanities/social-science fields, a Republican is a rare bird. In fact, registrants either to the Green Party or Working Families Party equaled or exceeded Republican registrants in 72 of the 170 departments (that includes Economics). That is, in 42 percent of the departments, Republican registrants were as scarce as or scarcer than left *minor-party* registrants."

"Once the apex of the disciplinary pyramid becomes predominately left-leaning, it will sweep left-leaners into positions throughout the pyramid (or, at least, it will exclude vibrant dissenters)."

The paper outlined how left-leaning professors and administrators heavily favor the hiring of staff that agree with their political and social viewpoints. They concluded, "In our view, today the groupthink mechanisms continue to heighten the one-party nature of academia."

To further the point, a study by Spaulding and Turner in 1968, showed academic historians had a Democrat-to-Republican ratio of about 2.7 to 1. The noteworthy rise in the ratio to 33.5 to 1 in the 2016 study shows a stark movement to the left.

Another interesting trend is that right-leaning conservatives and even moderate professorship applicants don't have much of a chance at being hired. They are frozen out of academia because of their political beliefs. This is a good way to maintain control of the party line – don't hire anyone unless they embrace neo-liberal ideology.

To put the problem into further perspective on how skewed the system is, in a study in 2014 from the general US populace, conservatives outnumbered liberals 34% to 24%, with the balance of 32% claiming they are moderates. This is obviously far from being representative of the political make-up of college campuses. One would assume that academia would be representative, or at least close to reflecting the general populace. As the statistics obviously show, that is not the case. It's completely upside-down.

According to the Higher Education Research Institute, the ratio of liberals vs. conservatives in the student population as they entered a college or university is far less than what it is among academia. However, as students progressed through their college years, more of them that claimed to be moderates leaned to the left as a result of liberalism being embedded in higher education.

Another study showed that after a lot of liberal students graduate, they hit the real world and begin to see things differently. Many of them move from liberalism to conservatism. There are car payments, a mortgage, groceries, a spouse, and kids. Life situations can alter one's ideals. Also, many students raised in a conservative environment return from college with a more liberal, if not fully liberal mindset. However, studies have shown that as they advance in age, conservative views are regained. The real world outside of academia is where real-life learning takes place. Life and circumstances tend to change one's perception of reality. What they are taught at the university may not jive with who they become and what viewpoints they adopt later in life. Some remain propagandized, but many ultimately reject liberal ideology.

Unfortunately, higher education has become an incestuous quagmire of liberalism where administrators carefully select professors that will preach the gospel of liberalism at the expense of providing a full spectrum of thoughts and ideas.

By adopting these hiring practices, the goal of liberal university staff is not to educate – it is to indoctrinate. This intentional tactic erodes the lofty goal of exposing students to ALL viewpoints and ideals in order for the students to come to their own conclusion as to what they believe and what type of citizen they become.

The studies mentioned earlier show two major takeaways that are pretty clear - academia is not just leaning left; they have taken a hard left turn. There is also blatant prejudice in academia in hiring and the singularity of ideology– all we can call it is prejudice and political discrimination. If applicants are not a member of the liberal groupthink bandwagon, they can forget about being hired.

This is from a *Washington Times* article by Bradford Richardson and Jennifer Harper citing an academic study: "When asked to assess which factors are responsible for the negative view of higher education, 86 percent of college and university presidents cited the perception of liberal bias on campus. Seventy-seven percent said they are worried about the way conservatives view higher education, and 65 percent said the perception that colleges and universities are intolerant of conservative ideas is having a major impact on higher education."

That is a surprising and revealing indictment on the system itself – admitted to by the academics themselves. I don't think there's a stronger case to prove that liberal bias is rampant in academia – they even recognize it.

The following graph from the HERI Faculty Survey, Higher Education Research Institute at UCLA shows the striking trend that is occurring:

Professors are getting more liberal

Ideology among college and university professors, 1990 – 2014

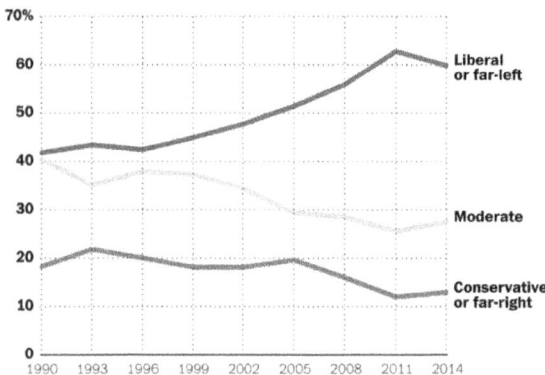

Those liberal professors and administrators that preach so loudly against prejudice and exclusion are guilty of the very things they say they despise. One would think these "well-educated" members of academia would be honest enough with themselves to realize the incestuous nature of what's going on. It is incestuous – evidence proves it. This is not healthy for our colleges and universities, let alone our country. The last thing we need is an educational system that promotes and practices indoctrination.

A group of academic faculty members that call themselves the Heterodox Academy did a study, and they argue that homogeneity in higher education is becoming a bigger problem in areas outside of education. The study concludes: "With relatively few right-leaning voices in the professoriate, particularly in the humanities and the social sciences where ideas matter most, many college students receive less than the intellectually rigorous education that they deserve."

The study also states: "American politics seems to work best when the two main factions are animated by rigorous thinking and serious ideas. And if there's no home for conservative ideas at today's colleges, it stands to reason that our political discourse will be poorer for it."

Robert Lichter, a professor at George Mason University said, "What's most striking is how few conservatives there are in any field [of academia]. There was no field we studied in which there were more conservatives than liberals or more Republicans than Democrats. It's a very homogenous environment, not just in the places you'd expect to be dominated by liberals." "In general," says Lichter, who also leads the nonprofit Center for Media and Public Affairs, "even broad-minded people gravitate toward other people like themselves. That's why you need diversity, not just of race and gender but also, maybe especially, of ideas and perspective."

It's pretty obvious to see how things are recognizably skewed towards liberalism in our educational system. These studies paint a stark and undeniable problem. It does not take a rocket scientist or a master statistician to see there is a major disparity. With all the influence throughout our entire education system, this movement can be interpreted as – let's call it what it is - social engineering, which eventually leads to the suppression of speech and free thought. Our youth are being socially engineered to believe neo-liberalism is the only ideology worth considering and adopting.

Kim R. Holmes, the author of *The Closing of the Liberal Mind* and a distinguished fellow at The Heritage Foundation said, "If the culture at large neither cares about morality anymore and, on top of that, the education is being cheapened, it's no longer about trying to teach people to think critically but about trying to indoctrinate them to a certain point of view. The American public over time is going to decline in the ability to be self-governing, and, ultimately, that's a threat to democracy."

The exchange of ideas and open thought that teaches critical thinking is essential for a society. However, with the overwhelming level of liberalism in education, that skill is getting lost; it is a troubling trend. Anyone who cannot see the significance of this is probably a neo-liberal that thinks this is the way it should be.

Upon closer scrutiny, we discover that the pervasive influence of educators is far more akin to social manipulation than it is to free thought. The studies shown here prove that the problem of liberal dominance within higher education is getting worse, not better. When liberal ideology monopolizes campuses, the lengths to which they will go to defend their turf has played out across the country.

During the past few years, American colleges and universities have been marred by the banning of conservative speakers. All of this leads to "institutional bias," and it will continue unchecked unless colleges and universities are exposed under a hot white light.

Educational institutions ideally would be (and must be) free of any political bias. If educators choose to have an ideological bent, they should leave their bias at the door and keep it out of the classroom and curriculum. Examining differing sides of thought is at the very core of education.

Imagine a science teacher with a bias against seeking new theories and questioning current scientific orthodoxy. What if a professor had told a young Einstein that he should not be looking for how to disprove the then current scientific dogma, he should just accept it? Any type of bias or shutting down the exchange of ideas has absolutely no place in the educational community. Education is about expanding the mind not limiting thought.

What right does a teacher or professor have to stand in front of students and say, "The way I think and what I believe is superior to any other viewpoint, and it is unnecessary for you to question other thoughts and positions – just blindly and unquestioningly believe as I do." In most universes, I would think that an attitude like that would be a fast track out the door. Not so. That type of thinking is on the welcome mat of virtually every college and university.

Educators are not doing a good enough job teaching students to be free to draw their own conclusions. Not enough professors are challenging students to be innovators and free thinkers. There is a great benefit to society in having a strong educational system with open idea-sharing. Ultimately, it culminates in a population full of strong contributors.

As previously discussed, far too many students and young people lack the ability to exercise critical thinking. Along with study skills and organizational skills, the ability to use critical thinking should be taught throughout a student's education. By doing so, students would be better equipped to think for themselves as college students and adults.

Emotional attachments and ideological bigotry have replaced rationality and reason. When looking at the decrease in critical thinking from a cause and effect standpoint, we must look at the root cause in order to find out why we are where we are. There is obviously strong evidence that one can easily conclude, and the cause emanates directly from our educational system – and it only gets worse the farther we climb up the educational ladder. The effect, then, is a whole generation of indoctrinated students who are unable to use critical thinking.

Ultimately, the cause for less critical thinking can be laid directly at the feet of our colleges and universities – for not teaching it and for not using it.

The effect of this decline can be easily linked to the slowly evaporating right to free thought and free speech on campuses. It is certainly not a leap to say that this pathway of limiting speech and controlling thought leads straight into groupthink and social engineering.

As statistics cited in this chapter have shown, colleges and universities tilt so far left that students are not allowed to think for themselves. I repeat: the professor knows everything and there is only one way to think. Obviously, this violates the whole premise of education. Of course, there are good teachers, but there are enough of the fully indoctrinated ones to see a trend that started some sixty years ago, and the problem is getting worse. If educators are not challenging students to open their minds and think for themselves, they are doing a major disservice to students, and these professors should pack up their briefcases, take their ideological bigotry with them, and go find another profession.

As stated earlier, what if Einstein didn't have the freedom to challenge his professors and their theories? Imagine being a fly on the wall when those late-night discussions occurred between Einstein and his professors and colleagues. They probed. They questioned each other. I'm sure there was a lot of hearty debate, perhaps even heated. They challenged each other, and the result was historical.

Our students are also losing the art of being intellectually discerning. They are losing the will to probe, plus they are being taught a dogmatic and close-minded version of the truth by professors with an agenda. Challenge and debate are being shut down. We cannot condone or accept this. We cannot allow ourselves and our children to become mind-numbed robots whose only alternative is to accept the academic dogma that is stuffed down the throats of our students and ourselves.

Purportedly, academia is made up of the smartest and most open-minded people we have in our society. They are the sculptors of the minds of our youth. They are supposed to be a cross-section of the populace that seeks knowledge and truth. Unfortunately, what we often get is a clannish bunch of ideologues that are intent on sticking closely together in order to manipulate students away from free thinking and toward academic groupthink. Is that what we really want from our educational institutions? Is that what's best for students and our society? I think not.

Unsurprisingly, there are many liberal professors that are also teaching students that we are a bad nation with a bunch of bad people. They say there are problems all over our country and that there are no civil rights, racism abounds, and inequality is everywhere. There's no social justice, there's white privilege, there's income equality, there's this that's wrong, there's that that's wrong. We are just a bunch of horrible people – except for those that are intellectually superior neo-liberals. They are "woke" and we are not. This gets pounded into students' brains on a daily basis in far too many classrooms. Who in their right mind thinks that teaching students to hate their country and the people in it is a good idea? These professors have the right to think what they want, but they are just plain wrong in sowing hatred toward our country in my humble opinion.

Jason D. Hill is a distinguished professor of philosophy at DePaul University. He stated, "We are witnessing a generation that will not tolerate other perspectives, students who will not hear opposing ideologies…The gravest internal threat … is leftist professors who are waging a war against America and teaching our young people to hate this country."

By denigrating our country and conservative political philosophy (as so many liberal professors unashamedly do) it is 180 degrees out of phase with conventional wisdom and educational norms. If students stand up and defend our country, they are summarily attacked and ostracized. They are not free to say what they want to say.

An open mind that seeks learning is totally betrayed by these liberal professors that quash free speech, quash freedom of thought, and disparage our country. On one hand, they will flaunt their freedom of speech and thought, and then shut down anyone who chooses to voice an alternative viewpoint. Radicalism amongst the "professorhood" has no place in an educational institution. Despite this, it takes place every day somewhere in the university universe.

How can professors espouse freedom of thought while limiting the scope of ideas? It is simple to see that this type of educational philosophy is restrictive and counterproductive. How is this justified in the minds of university staff? The only conclusion one can draw is that they have chosen indoctrination as being more important to society than education. They are making that value judgment. I repeat - the abandonment of freedom to draw one's own conclusions and beliefs is an egregious assault on students and on our society as a whole.

So many of the liberal professors will march in the streets wanting an end to "fascist thinking," while at the same time espousing a fascist position by limiting freedom of speech in their classrooms. Forgive my incomprehension, but I truly don't understand how that works. Does anyone besides me see any irony in this way of thinking? It is anti-fascist people using fascist tactics. Regretfully, administrators allow this to occur on their campus way too often.

A definition of fascism is: "forcible suppression of opposition and strong regimentation of society." Part of the Italian root word of "fascio' has to do with "bundling." Fascism is also used in a governing context which has to do with the government being all-knowing and all powerful with a supreme leader that dictates thoughts and ideas that must be embraced. Remember Hitler? Freedom of speech is not tolerated in fascism. The people are looked at as a bundle — one body that must be controlled by the government using absolute force.

As we look at our educational institutions, the idea of fascism starts to creep into our thoughts of what political views are predominately adopted by administrators and professors. Again, while advocating freedom of expression, they are putting boundaries on what students can think and say. That is educational fascism, and sadly, that is where we are today in far too many of our institutions of higher learning – and even in our public schools.

The idea is that if we all think like educators want us to, we would have a perfect society – we would be totally peaceful with no disagreements, no strife, no one going rogue in debating or questioning anything. Do we really want to live in a country like that? I think not.

This whole groupthink mentality runs counter to our human spirit. We are all individuals. We all have our own brain and we should be free to think as we want and come to our own conclusions about anything and everything. We do not want to be manipulated and coerced into how we should think – at least most people don't. Taking away our freedom of thought and expression strips us of our human dignity. We would become slaves to those in power if we allowed that to happen, yet we have essentially turned a blind eye to that which is happening in our educational system.

The liberal takeover of education has been a very slow process over many years, but it is happening, and we need to realize what's going on, and be vigilant about stopping it. My hope is that we come to our senses and right the ship. If we are unable as a society to tolerate and support freedom of expression without retribution, we are headed for a day of reckoning that will not end well.

Back in 1722, a 17-year old youngster sent some of his own opinions to a newspaper editor. He submitted these opinions anonymously, using the name of Mr. Silence Dogood. One of the statements poignantly said, "Without freedom of thought, there can be no such thing as wisdom." That young writer was later identified as none other than Benjamin Franklin. Perhaps it would be appropriate for all left-wing educators to go the chalkboard and write that statement a thousand times – maybe it would eventually sink in and make some sense to them. It might even lead them to an enlightenment.

Learning is a wonderful thing. Freedom is a beautiful thing. A society that encourages learning and the expansion of thoughts will be a successful society because that is how we as humans advance ourselves – I believe it is in our DNA. As discussed before, we have seen governmental entities (or I should say regimes) throughout history that indoctrinated through education and manipulated their constituents. Fortunately, most of them did not last too long because the people got fed up with the suppression and control.

China is the longest-running society that rules with an iron fist and tells their citizens what to think and what to learn. At some point, their citizens will revolt, but the power of the Chinese government is preventing that from happening. When the revolution does come as they always do, it will be a bloody battle between a dictatorial government and the spirit of freedom. We have already seen what the Chinese government is capable of in terms of 45 million citizens that were slaughtered, and more recently, what happens to dissent as was witnessed in the Tiananmen Square massacre. And that's not to mention the horrific concentration camps (or as they call them, re-education camps) where millions of people are brutally held captive and tortured.

I do hope liberals will at some point realize that the effect of government-controlled, mind-numbed robots immersed in groupthink is really not as attractive as it seems. Anyone who wants to live that way without freedom of thought and expression can board an airplane and get to China in about 12 hours. I suggest they try living under the oppression of an all-powerful government and see if it might change their perspective in a pretty short time. America looks mighty good to those Chinese people that yearn for freedom.

Academicians should know better than to force their liberal ideology on students, but unfortunately, they just can't seem to help themselves. By abandoning freedom of choice, freedom of speech, and discouraging critical thinking in education, administrators and professors commit sacrilege against the very ideals of education. It's a crying shame that it is being tolerated, and in some cases, encouraged by educators and administrators. Far too many people are not even aware of how our educational system is practicing liberal indoctrination. What I have laid out is not a conspiracy theory – it is facts and data that are irrefutable.

We need to hold educators and administrators accountable. Large donors need to step in. The Feds should intervene. Parents and their students that finance this charade should demand a change. Educators and administrators need to be unmasked for who they are and what they are doing.

We are letting it happen by turning a blind eye to the problem. If we continue to ignore the problem, things will only get worse. What's behind the mask is the evil of indoctrination that is highly detrimental to our freedoms and our country. *"I Know We Are Better Than This."*

Chapter 19

When Will the Bubble Burst?

The total of outstanding student loans has increased to $1.5 trillion and growing. In 2006, the average student loan was $20,000. In 2019, the average has risen to $31,000. That is a 50% increase in 13 years, and it far outpaces income growth during that time period.

Let's look at a few more statistics from 1987 through 2017. According to the US Census Bureau, household income rose 135%. According to the Case-Schiller National Home Price Index, housing rose 188% over the same period. According to Medicare and Medicaid, health care costs increased 276%. Wow, you might think – that is a LOT – and we feel it in our wallets. But wait - college tuition at state universities rose 549% according to The College Board. Amazingly, that is DOUBLE the increase in health care costs. No one seems to notice, and no one seems to care – we just let it happen and saddle students and parents with increasing debt.

Just like the home loan bubble, the student loan business is heading for a meltdown. We can see the same pattern playing out. Our government loan guarantees in the real estate market meant that people who normally could not afford to buy a house were given access to loans they couldn't afford to repay. We brought that catastrophe upon ourselves. All the geniuses in Washington DC thought it was a good idea that all people should be able to have their own home, and then the bubble burst because of a high rate of loan defaults.

It is not a far stretch to see what's coming in student loans. We have made it so easy and have encouraged kids to go to college. Then we charged them an enormous amount of money, burdening them with a huge debt. One-third of them don't even graduate – mostly because they can't afford to take on more debt, or college just wasn't really their thing. The 6-year graduation rate was 59 percent at public institutions, 66 percent at private nonprofit institutions, and 26 percent at private for-profit institutions. The end result is tens of millions of young adults strapped with high debt and no degree to show for it.

More than 2 million graduates owe more than $100,000. Doctors that make it through medical school and residency end up owing $200,000. Fortunately for them, they can afford to pay off their loan, but those that don't make it through will be broke for a long, long time. And what about those students that end up working at a fast food restaurant because their degree is in a discipline with no jobs? They're most likely not going to able to pay the bills with a degree in French literature or art history. Is it any wonder that so many graduates unable to live on their own? Imagine trying to finance $50,000 or $100,000 in debt on a slightly above minimum wage. The system is doing a great disservice to our youth.

Then there are many Democrats that want to rescind all student loans and provide financial amnesty. So, who is going to pay for that $1.5 trillion? Perhaps those that propose this think it's just like writing off a bad debt. I'm sorry to inform them, but of course Mr. and Mrs. Taxpayer will pay for it either in the form of higher taxes or an increase in our national deficit (which is out of control to start with), and perhaps even both.

What about those who recently paid off the student loan debts? Do they get shafted? Or perhaps the Democrats will give them reparations. But hold on a minute – if they get their money back, what about me? My college was paid for long ago, so why can't I have reparations, too? Where does it end? Who wins and who loses? And who is to decide?

This whole notion is fraught with problems, but scarily, it's only a Congressional vote away. If it does happen, I want my college funds to be refunded along with every other person who has ever graduated and those that didn't graduate. Why not? It's only fair, and Democrats are always all about fairness. Oh, I forgot, there must be some that suffer so others can be advantaged.

The primary culprit that is culpable in this scam of high-priced education is in our colleges and universities. After all, they control the cost of a degree. Parents and our entire culture put pressure on everyone to go to college. Isn't it ironic that they are required to go to college and are sacked with huge debt, while colleges and universities are enjoying the benefits of the scam? A lot of professors are enjoying a hefty salary that is put on the backs of students and their parents. A very large number of professors are making six figure incomes (some even seven figures) while teaching four or five classes a week – some may even teach less than that! From 1987 to 2012, the number of administrators increased two-fold. Add to that the fact that the cost for textbooks has tripled in the last 20 years, and it becomes obviously apparent exactly what's going on – there are lots of administrators and educators that are enriching themselves and expecting students and parents to pay for it.

It seems to me that this is purely and simply an exploitation of our youth. It's not right, and eventually, we taxpayers are going to be stuck with the bill. Can we really afford another trillion-dollar boondoggle? It seems to be inevitable, but I could be wrong. However, if I were a betting man, I know what I'd put my money on.

How is it that university systems such as Harvard, Yale and so many other major universities have billions upon billions of endowments sitting in the bank or in investments, while charging students an inordinate amount of money for the privilege of attending the university? Is it really necessary for them to have all this money while so many of their students struggle to survive while in school and then graduate with $100,000 and more in debt?

Think about it. You have exceedingly wealthy institutions with more money in the bank than most corporations. I thought higher education was a non-profit enterprise. With all this untold wealth, why is the cost of higher education so high? It seems to me that universities would gladly be noble institutions eager to help students get a good education, but evidently, it's more important to build a large bank account and endowment. Instead of using their billions of dollars of assets to assist more students in obtaining a college degree, they sit on all this money like a bunch of fat cats whose only interest is in building a bigger endowment - all the while charging students enormous sums of money that strangle them for many years to come. Is there any sanity in that?

Here are some statistics sourced from bestschools.com:

Harvard:
Endowment: $36,021,516,000
Average annual tuition per undergraduate student: $48,949
Average salary of full professor: $221,382

Yale:
Endowment: $27,176,100,000
Average annual tuition per undergraduate student: $51,400
Average salary of full professor: $216,189

University of Texas:
Endowment: $26,535,095,000
Annual cost of tuition per undergraduate student: $36,744
Average salary of full professor: $116,119

Stanford:
Endowment: $24,784,943,000
Annual cost of tuition per undergraduate student: $49,617
Average salary of full professor: $234,549

Princeton:
Endowment: $23,812,241,000
Annual cost of tuition per undergraduate student: $47,140
Average salary of full professor: $206,496

According to the national Center for Education Statistics, the grand total of college and university endowments in 2015 totaled $547 billion. That's more than half-a-trillion dollars – and it continues to grow!

So, if contributors to these endowments gave their money to further the cause of education, why is it that this money is not used to further the cause of helping students get a college degree? Yes, there are scholarships, but the average Joe or Joline can get very limited financial assistance outside of loan guarantees. They must pay for their education and incur a huge debt so that professors and administrators can live well, the board of regents can brag about their endowments, and large donors can get great PR with large donations.

The neo-liberals that want free college for everyone may be looking in the wrong direction for funding their idea. As discussed previously, many professors make $200,000 per year – some even more than $1 million. Does a single professor have enough knowledge and wisdom to impart on students that's really worth that much money? Of course, the universities use these high-dollar professors to attract students so the universities can charge an enormous amount for tuition. Where else can they get the money for these professors besides from students and their parents? Why are administrators willing to fork over that much money for professors and finance it on the backs of poor college students? And why are there so many high-salaried administrators that bring very little value to actually educating students? It makes absolutely no sense whatsoever in my rational estimation.

It seems like a scam. Isn't the goal of administrators to educate as many worthy students as possible? That would be a good way to spend half a trillion dollars – not to mention the millions of dollars donors provide to build beautiful buildings so they can get their name on it.

We know that an educated society is stronger at its core than an uneducated society. I would hope we can all agree that our country's constituents are better off if money is used to advance the society rather than build an inordinately gaudy endowment fund.

In one of his articles, Kurt Schlicter, author, stand-up comic and contributor to thehill.com summed up the current state of our colleges and universities this way: "It [academia] exists to mass produce ignorant future elitists and to provide jobs for liberal indoctrinators fueled by our tax money. The state and private schools both take our dough directly as well as through guaranteed student loans. Student loans are a giant scam, of course. Students get grifted into chaining an anchor around their necks in exchange for credentials most don't even need. Colleges can raise tuition as high as they like because the government will just back the loans these suckers take out. It's a great system, if you're an academic. Not so much if you are a student or a taxpayer." I would also add parents.

Here's how it all looks to me. There are loan repayment problems with students being burdened with large debts; there are ideological issues with educators; fat-cat professors and administrators are living quite nicely off the backs of taxpayers, parents, and students; and there are restrictions of free speech and free thought on campuses. Does anyone not see what a mess colleges and universities are in? And we let it happen. Given all that is wrong in our educational system, I just have to think there's a better way. *"I Know We Are Better Than This."*

Section 6
The Media Mess

Chapter 20

The State of the Media Today

Historically, the media has been a part of the truly amazing checks and balances part of our Constitution – freedom of the press. For more than 200 years, newspapers reported the news. Newspapers were a part of the people's voice. They sought "truth, justice and the American way."

George Dealy, long-time publisher and owner of the *Dallas Morning News* was an icon in the newspaper business for many decades. He wrote this foundational statement which was inscribed in granite on a three-story tall façade outside of their original headquarters. "Build the news upon the rock of truth and righteousness. Conduct it always on the lines of fairness and integrity. Acknowledge the right of the people to get from every newspaper both sides of every important question."

In days gone by, journalists used to be journalists. Reporters reported the news. Editors kept reporters in line and challenged any story that didn't meet the appropriate standards for validity and truth. Editors were tough guys that pushed reporters to be accurate and fair, often throwing reporters out of their office for not having multiple sources and impeccable factual background for their stories. All journalists were expected to be transparent, unbiased, and neutral. There were high standards and expectations from the media and they proudly held themselves to these high standards. Things have changed in the past three decades.

Unfortunately, our college and university journalism schools have spit out an entire generation of political hacks that disguise themselves as journalists - which is why they have garnered such a dismal reputation and rank slightly higher than Charles Manson in most popularity polls. Why is this? What has transpired over the past thirty years or so that has brought about this horrible reputation? It started, in my opinion, when journalists started wearing their opinions on their sleeves and began inserting their opinions in order to fortify a political stance.

At first, journalists tried to oh-so-subtly slant the news. Iconic news anchors such as Walter Cronkite, Edward R. Murrow and others were left-leaning, but they generally kept their personal opinions to themselves – they reported the news and there was no exaggeration, partisanship, or pontification. It was the news. Reporters were the same; they reported the news. They all attempted to stay within the boundaries of journalism's duty to simply report the news, not embellish or slant it.

Now, far too many mainstream media "journalists" (I use quotes because I use the term loosely to describe this class) have deteriorated into a bunch of partisan hacks that have an agenda, and they "report" the news through the filter of their own beliefs and interpretations of the "news" (I use quotes again because actual news reporting is becoming a lost art).

A truthful story in what used to be the golden age of journalism is now reported with bias, too often filled with subtle opinion or even outright prejudice. Many times the utter blather and hyperbolic talking points are fed to them by politicians or political parties, and they gladly spew out the party line at the expense of real news reporting. No longer are news stories "slanted". All too often, they are fully tilted in the direction of which political side the "journalist" supports.

This whole journalism issue with a total lack of journalistic integrity is not only bothersome to most people (look at the polls) – it is antithetical to the "free press" ideal laid out in the constitution. Journalists are free to say what they want – we do have the first amendment - but when it purports to be unbiased "news" that is fully slanted in one political position or another, integrity is lost, and their believability becomes highly suspect, which leads to abysmal press' approval ratings that are below Congress.

The audience that remains listening is more than likely only listening because they, too, espouse the beliefs or political positions advocated by the talking heads. Do not mistake these statements as being anti-free speech – quite the contrary. Free speech for a journalist should entail factual-based, unbiased reporting of what we should and need to know. And we don't have to know EVERYTHING – just the important stuff will suffice, thank you very much.

If a judicial system was one-sided, it would reasonably lead us into thinking that there would be a total lack of fairness and equality - fairness and equality being the operative words - let us remember that thought. Without fairness and equality, there would be no justice. Justice should always be on the side of truth. In our courts, we are judged by our peers, and justice is to be administered on a fair and impartial basis – without prejudice! Fundamentally, there is no fairness and equality within prejudice. Prejudice intentionally excludes fairness and equality.

I'm speaking to the media now: "Must you continue to dumb us all down? Must you completely insult our intelligence? Must you take a side of the story and beat us all into submission? Surely, there are other things to talk about from a newsworthy perspective besides what politician is running around having affairs, embezzling money, etc., etc. ".

CNN, MSNBC, and other network news outlets turned into anti-Trump TV 24/7/365. No need for any other news items, they just go over and over and over the same thing, with virtually every newsperson and "expert commentator" regurgitating the same talking points. What would they have done if Trump was not elected? I suspect many of them would be unemployed. These channels are guilty of making outrageous claims in order to attract an audience that they pander to and then continuously club their audience over the head with the same mantra.

The Media Research Center periodically studies media bias and has found that generally from 90 to 94% of all coverage on TV was bias-slanted against President Trump. Every liberal thinks Fox news in in the tank for President Trump, yet the Media Research Center found that Fox News was far more balanced at 52% negative, 48% positive. Which news organization was more "Fair and Balanced?"

CNN, MSNBC, and the mainstream media are unabashedly, unashamedly biased when it comes to anything remotely related to conservatism. Negative stories about conservatives are the mainstay of the mainstream media. The sad thing is that they just can't help themselves. It's an obsession that is insatiable. It's a derangement. As a viewer, people may have a problem if they are totally immersed in the circus and their life is consumed by watching the political performers act out the drama center stage on cable news.

On top of that, what is becoming more clear is that Google, Facebook, and Twitter are not only left-leaning (they have openly admitted that), they are left-tilted. More stories will be appearing about how these three companies are attempting to influence elections, showing a preference for liberal ideology and controlling speech. All three have crossed the line.

It's funny how Democrats complain that corporations should not have any influence in the election process, yet they admittedly support the "Social Three" and their right as corporations to promote whatever ideology they choose to support – as long as it fits the leftist agenda. Hmmmm… smells like collusion to me. I'm sure if the shoe were on the other foot, the Dems would view things a lot differently. It's strange how we can be overly tolerant of misdeeds and miscreants if they benefit our side. It's almost as if we say, "Yes, I know that it's not right, but we are willing to accept it because it benefits our agenda."

There are many media outlets that echo the views of various politicians, and of course, the politicians use these media outlets as a tool to their advantage. As previously mentioned, many of the cable news channels and mainstream media companies are unequivocally slanted in support of the Democrat party. Consider what the Democrats would think if the media were tilted 90% negative against them. One can safely assume that they would certainly decry corporations or the media as untruthful and biased – maybe even call them "fake news". They would be screaming to the high heavens how it was all unfair and not truthful. The point is, their viewpoints would change if the shoe were on the other foot.

A wise person who really wants to understand what's going on always looks at these scenarios from the perspective of "What if that were me being attacked incessantly? How would I feel? What would I think? How would I react?" If the media had attacked President Obama on a daily basis like they have done to President Trump, the Democrats would have screamed bloody murder and would have thrown out racism and every other card they could throw. Negative coverage is constantly hurled at conservatives and right-leaning media folks at every chance the liberal media has. Everyone knows that. I know that. It is plainly and painfully obvious.

When it's our side that benefits, there is a willingness to smile and say, "I knew it." Unfortunately, many people are willing to look the other way without questioning the validity and veracity of media reporting because it reinforces what they believe. A wise person always questions – that's how wisdom is acquired – we examine the facts, question and test them, make an evaluation, and then come to a judgment or conclusion.

Instead, the mainstream media practice what I would classify as "opportunistic journalism." A shining example of this is the mainstream media's coverage of the Jussie Smollett story. They were quick to incite and call this whole incident a reflection of the systemic racism that exists in our country. Politicians and pundits were complicit in jumping on the hate crime and racism bandwagon. All the leftists responded to the incident at warp speed. They called it a deplorable racist attack perpetrated by President Trump's "Make America Great Again" gang running amuck in downtown Chicago on a frigid night with a chill factor in the minus 50-degree range.

The initial story was never questioned as true "investigative" journalists would do. Strangely, the local Chicago media were skeptical and got it right, but the national mainstream media didn't take the time to stop and consider the holes in Mr. Smollett's story. There were simple questions to ask about the two purported male assailants: Who in his right mind would be walking the streets of Chicago (a heavily left-tilting city) with MAGA hats in -50 degrees chill factor weather, carrying bleach (which freezes around -19 degrees) and a noose (they just happened to have with them), looking for a gay black man to beat him up at 2:00 AM in the morning? Did that sound truly plausible from the outset? And then why would the victim of this hate crime want police to turn off their body cameras during questioning?

Of course, none in the mainstream media stopped to question the veracity of the accusations because it was a perfect scenario for them to launch into an all-out assault that fully supported their anti-Trump agenda – it was hate-crime nirvana for them - a gay black man beaten up by two white men wearing MAGA hats splashing bleach and carrying a noose. It was a perfect storm, so they ran with it with 24-hour coverage, interviewing every left-wing politician, every Hollywood star, every race-baiter they could find, and every leftist talking head they could dig up and put on the air or quote on their website or in their newspaper.

There was no need to stop and consider the facts and look at the incident with a modicum of common sense because the fact that it supported their agenda was far more important than the real truth. We have seen this play out on a number of occasions - the gullibility of left-wing media is unsurpassed when it comes to anything supporting their agenda. They are off to the races at warp speed to use a story to their advantage. It truly is appalling, and the funny part of it is that they actually think that everyone believes them. It's purely and simply delusionary and narcissistic, but that's how they roll with reckless abandon. They seem to be puzzled why their credibility is so far under water that they can't even see the surface.

When the dust settled and the truth came out, how many left-wing media talking heads, Hollywood stars, and politicians came out and said they were wrong for jumping to conclusions? The answer is zero, because they would then have to admit they were wrong and gullible. They merely made excuses for Mr. Smollett and tried to position him as a victim. Sorry, but common sense says that an accuser can't be a victim of a crime if he fabricates it and it's completely false – as I am sure we will find out.

This was also an opportunity for politicians to make political points, get their base riled up, increase their audience reach, pad their fund-raising coffers, and increase their website clicks or increase their TV profile. To them, all is fair in the war of political discourse – truth and intrepid reporting is unimportant. Pushing an agenda is far more critical.

This incident reeked of journalistic opportunism. Instead of waiting to hear all the facts, the media turned out-and-out lies into facts without any proof or evidence – it's really pretty plain to see if we look at this with open eyes. It was shameful for Mr. Smollett to perpetrate this charade, and it was shameful for the media and politicians to seize the moment for their own benefit. What makes it even worse, in my mind, is that Smollett KNEW this would set the media into overdrive and instigate a full-frontal attack on President Trump and his supporters – it was intentional, and it was calculated, although very poorly executed.

When the media is in constant negative mode against any party or politician because they disagree with them ideologically, their bias becomes very obvious. Their prejudicial tendencies begin to surface through the bigotry they display. The primary reason for this tactic is to forward their cause, no matter the cost. It shouldn't be that way, but it is in today's media climate. It's sad but true.

However, those that agree with the media constantly berating politicians with whom they disagree accept it because it supports their beliefs. The position adopted by these people is, "It's alright, I accept it and tolerate it because I support their way of thinking – and it doesn't matter if they are right or wrong." It should not be accepted and tolerated. It's just plain wrong for the media to be biased and the audience that buys into the propaganda is complicit in supporting this nonsense.

Here's a prime, unmistakable example of liberal bias in the media and how they go to great lengths to protect one of their own. Angela Alioto is a prominent Democrat and civil rights attorney in San Francisco. At a Democratic County Central Committee meeting with African American union members, she used the "n" word not once, not twice, not three times, but SIX times. Full disclosure – Ms. Alioto is a white liberal. She was trying to make a point, but the audience was aghast and asked her to stop using that term. After three local newspapers and a few local TV stations covered the story, Ms. Alioto issued an apology stating, "I went too far, and I profusely apologize that I offended anyone. She also stated, "My clients say that word. The 'n' word doesn't mean anything [to them]. You do not sugarcoat or whitewash that word when you're in litigation mode."

Her remarks where offensive in the first place, but then she further stepped in the pile of dog poo with her strange apology. To make a point, if a conservative or Republican had said that word six times in a public meeting, that person would have been shamed to high Heaven for being insensitive and racist. It would have been front page news in the *New York Times* and *Washington Post*. It would have been the top story on CNN, MSNBC and all the national network news programs. The View would have talked about it for days on end. On Politico, Huffington Post, Yahoo and other liberal websites, there would be story after story raging about endemic conservative racism. Every journalist or commentator would have ranted and raved.

I wondered how all these outlets covered this story, so I did a Google search. I found nothing in the *New York Times* or *Washington Post*. There was no mention on CNN or MSNBC or any other the national network news stations. The View did not discuss it. There were no references on Politico, Huffington Post, Yahoo and any other liberal websites. Does that not strike us as a bit strange? Not one mention? Of course, understanding the bias of the mainstream media, we would know exactly what went on – they were protecting one of their own – it's way too obvious.

If that is not a shining and revealing example of media bias, then I don't know what is. It is blatant, it is undeniable, and the depths of hypocrisy are indicative of exactly what kind of journalists work at these media outlets. Perhaps more importantly, it's an open exhibit displaying what kind of people they really are. The message is loud, clear, and totally indisputable. Excuse me, journalists and media outlets – your bias is showing.

True journalists cannot properly do their job if they are not honest and forthright. In the media business, just like any other business, integrity does matter. However, when their bias is on display, it's insincere to claim they are honest journalists. The media should serve as a watchdog on our government rather than a lapdog to those they fawn over or protect.

Absolutely slobbering, the media fawned over candidate and president Obama. One cable news host stated, "I got a tingle up my leg when he (Obama) spoke." He was their superhero flying in to fundamentally change the world. He was touted as the greatest president ever, even though evidence and performance prove to the contrary. None of that even mattered to the media because he was one of them – a left-leaning champion riding in on a white horse to save the planet.

Facts don't matter to the left-wing media because emotion and ideology trumps truth and reality. Instead of reporting the news, the media has become "interpreters" of the news, folding in their ideological positions and providing their slant on what they want us to believe. Yes, there are opinion shows as well as news shows, but mainstream media has somehow devolved into using these interpretative tactics, mostly because they believe we are not smart enough to understand the news as WE see it. We must be TOLD by them how to interpret the news. It has sadly become pervasive and customary on nightly newscasts, newspapers and websites.

If the media disagrees with or has it in for a public figure, all too often it turns from disagreeing on a particular point of view and then goes directly to personal attacks. The underlying message is that, "You should not believe this person," or "You should not agree with this terrible person who doesn't know anything and doesn't believe as we think he or she should believe." We are instructed not to believe this individual who is supposedly a racist, a misogynist, a liar," or whatever useful label can be applied based on the situation. Unfortunately, politicians are just as guilty as the media in this matter.

An undeniably shining example of media bias is the continuing saga of personal attacks on Justice Brett Kavanaugh. On September 14, 2019, an opinion piece was published in the *New York Times* (a now unmistakably left-tilting newspaper) that featured an accusation that was made by someone who "heard" that Bret Kavanaugh had exposed himself to a female at a drunken frat party some 30+ years ago. Note that there was no factual or evidential basis for the accusation; it was a second-hand account of what someone "heard" from another person.

The female "victim" stated to several friends that she did not recall the incident, and she declined to be interviewed by the reporters, who just happened to be writing a book soon to be released intending to smear Mr. Kavanaugh. Take a wild guess as to who was the publisher of the book. Yes, it was the *New York Times Publishing*. In the "editorial" that they published, the accusation was purported to be true, but the editorial staff conveniently left out important information.

In commenting on how journalists and editors can frame and manipulate a story, Cal Thomas, a renowned long-time columnist for the Chicago Tribune stated, "As with much of the media, bias is not only expressed in how and what is covered, but even more in what is omitted."

Sadly, the *New York Times* is now more akin to a tabloid than a revered newspaper. They intentionally omitted the fact that there was no corroborating evidence, no witnesses, and the "victim" never recalled the incident. They ran the story anyway with the undeniable intent to hype the two reporters' upcoming release of their book and to damage Mr. Kavanaugh's reputation. Embarrassingly, the next day the *New York Times* admitted they left out those facts that there was no corroborating evidence, no witnesses, and the "victim" never recalled the incident. The *New York Times* editorial board did issue an apology and included the missing sentence, but it was too late because the damage was done. My conclusion (along with many others) is that it was a pre-ordained, calculated move with clear intent to smear Mr. Kavanaugh and to sell more books – it's as obvious as it is deplorable.

The authors of the book stated that the *New York Times* board of editors made the decision to remove the sentence that described this accusation. The statement from one of the authors, Kate Kelley, said, "During the editing process there was an oversight and this key detail, about the fact that the woman herself has told friends she doesn't remember it, and has not wanted to talk about it, got cut." Kelly said as she smirked, "It was an oversight and the *Times* adjusted it and we're very sorry that it happened." Robin Pogrebin, the other author of the book stated, "We thought we had [read the final version]." Sadly, the only conclusion to logically draw is that the editorial board from the *New York Times* maliciously made the call to remove the clarifying sentence.

Since 1896, the newspaper's slogan has been "All the News That's Fit to Print." It seems to me they violated that premise when they calculatedly published this accusatory editorial that was not worth the ink and the paper that is was printed on. Perhaps a better slogan for the *New York Times* is, "All the news that's fit to print based on our biased political agenda." Seems as though that is more appropriate.

In my opinion, this was a glaring example of the weaponization of a media platform whose sole intent was to inflict harm. It was an attack by *New York Times* editorial board whose singular purpose was to execute a political assassination on someone they disagreed with – again, it was all too obvious. Their attack was not only shameful, it was patently dishonest and utterly diabolical. With the damage done and their goal accomplished, all they had to do was issue a little apology and they got away with it.

The *New York Times* and the mainstream media are continuing to perfect the art of self-inflicted degradation. Again, this is reflected in the fact that most people have lost all confidence and respect for these biased malcontents who purport to be "journalists" and the corporations that pay them.

One of the reasons this is happening in the media is that many of them have become indoctrinated by college and university journalism professors who have taken it upon themselves to train their students to only believe one political viewpoint. Too many of these professors preach that it is the job of a reporter to report the news in a fashion that moves the cause of neo-liberalism forward. All too often, students are not taught to seek the truth and question; they are taught to adopt the neo-liberal stance and protect it at all costs. All too frequently, they are subtly taught how to slant reporting by not interjecting pertinent facts that may take away from the neo-liberal views. The Smollett story and the *New York Times* story are glaring examples of media bias. A whole book could be written about the sins of the news media.

Let us hark back to an earlier point that fairness and equality are necessary for justice. Prejudice must be totally absent in order for fairness and equality to rule the day. It is blatantly obvious that the media are totally and unapologetically biased. People who deny that are either uninformed or totally biased themselves. It is impossible to call it fair and equal news reporting when there's 90+% negative coverage for Republicans and conservatives. That's undeniably obvious.

To further examine the bias, let us look at political donations made by journalists. The Center for Responsive Politics describes itself as a "nonpartisan, independent and nonprofit...research group tracking money in U.S. politics and its effect on elections and public policy." The data tracked election donors working for ABC, CBS, NBC, The New York Times, or The Washington Post between 2008 and 2016. A whopping 94% made contributions to Democrats. MSNBC analyzed the partisan divide in donations from newsroom anchors, reporters, and editors who were identified in FEC documents between January 2004 and the first quarter of 2007. Of the 143 journalists in the donor pool, 87 percent (125) donated to Democrats and liberal causes.

Another study from The Center for Public Integrity identified about 430 individuals working in journalism who contributed to either candidate between January 2015 and August 2016. The study showed 96 percent of the donations went to Clinton, and 4 percent went to Trump. There's a distinct pattern here that is not only hard to deny, it is troubling.

Back when Ronald Regan was president, the press was certainly unfriendly towards him, and there were news people whose primary mission in life was to bash one of our greatest presidents - they literally had it in for the man. However, there still was some modicum of media dignity and decorum back then. Unlike today, it wasn't completely blatant; it was subtle. Now we see CNN reporter James Acosta verbally assaulting a president simply because the reporter's hatred for the man is uncontrollable. There is no restraint, and the left-wing ideologues think it's acceptable and justifiable behavior. In reality, it is shameful behavior. Acosta's bias is so deliberately obvious it's laughable.

When George Bush came into office, any type of propriety was thrown out the window by the left-slanting press, and it only worsened when President Trump took office. During President Bush's tenure in office, the media incessantly hurled personal attacks that he was dumb, uneducated and illiterate. That was the narrative that echoed through the mainstream media. However, that conclusion was drawn by the media without proper vetting.

Their false caricature of Bush was of a good ol' country boy dolt, when in fact he was a more avid reader and deeper thinker than he got credit for. In 2006 he read 91 books. In 2007 he read 51 books, and in 2008 he read 40 books. These were not Dr. Seuss books, either. How many of us are that hungry for knowledge? He was an avid fan of history and read a lot of biographies. He and his chief of staff, Carl Rove, had an on-going contest to see who could read the most books in a year. Rove always won, but Bush had the goal of reading a book a week. Now, I ask, how many of our vaunted journalists would have been able to keep up with Mr. Rove and Mr. Bush? It's a pretty good bet that 99% of all journalists would have trouble keeping up. But then again, reading and learning are far less important than pushing an agenda.

The point is, the media spread the false narrative that Bush was not very bright, when in fact he was a very learned man. But when the narrative is pounded over and over again, the unwashed masses accept the narrative. Opinions on President Bush were unapologetically manipulated. It certainly appears that the "truth" was never the goal of the media when it came to characterizing President Bush. The goal was to paint him as an unlearned hick from Texas because that matched the media's goal of denigrating him to the point where anyone thinking Mr. Bush was a bright man was an idiot who didn't get the memo that Mr. Bush was an ignoramus. The media had every right to disagree with Mr. Bush's policies but attacking someone's intelligence is less than sophomorically petty – it's deceitful and disgraceful.

If the media were truly trying to convey the "truth," they would not have reported something that is contrary to reality. It was a baseless personal attack that had no merit, but it was executed to support their agenda. Anyone saying otherwise is not informed on the subject. It is fair to disagree with someone's viewpoint, but there is no justification for out-and-out misrepresentation – there really is no excuse for it.

Most of the media have devolved into a bunch of political hacks disguising themselves as journalists. Isn't it ironic that they denigrated President Bush, yet a true journalist would have reported the truth about the man? Anyone could certainly disagree with his viewpoints and decisions, and most of the media did, but it takes a poor excuse for a reporter (and a person) to use personal attacks in order to advance a false narrative. In most circles, we call that lies and deceit, but in journalism these days, they dishonestly call it "reporting." And it's a far too common practice.

The media manipulate us unwashed masses by an unwavering narrative and agenda. They try and influence opinion intentionally, and to make matters worse, they do it with malice. They have an agenda and they are intent on pushing that agenda until everyone believes them. How sad is that? Agree or disagree with Mr. Bush and his policies, it's not hard to zero in on and see what the media was trying to accomplish – and they did it with no shame whatsoever! In fact, many were proud of their successful mischaracterization – it was funny and entertaining to them, and they felt they were justified in doing it because it furthered their neo-liberal ideology. Sadly, it made them feel self-important.

The media wield so much power to manipulate that if unchecked, they can be dangerous to a democracy.

Here is a shining example of how the liberal media outlets are lockstep in trying to influence what people think about President Trump. According to Grabien Media, an online media production and news prep service, during the week of July 14 through July 21 in 2019, MSNBC and CNN (both radical left-wing outlets) repeated the word "racist" 4,100 times when referring to President Trump. Let that soak in. That's nearly 600 times per day. Does that strike anyone as strange? Can anyone figure out what their intent was? It's a very obvious case of opinion manipulation through continuous repetition which is more closely characterized as propaganda. That is what we are getting out of far too many media outlets. Again, if you repeat something incessantly, people will start to believe it, even though it may not be true.

Spreading a false narrative can have enormous effect on either events or people. It can change the course of history! With this much power at the hands of the media, who is it that provides the checks and balances? Is it the role of the government to regulate the media in our country? No, it is ours. As consumers of the news and readers or viewers, we need to hold the media accountable for their misdeeds and misinformation. We should expect better behavior and expose their bias.

The general public is not as stupid as the media think. We recognize manipulation, but some readers or viewers consume media only to validate what they believe. These people only seek out the media that they agree with. But the general public can discern BS from truth and reality. They know when they are fed a line of BS. If they get tired of it, they tune out, which is why the mainstream media are suffering in terms of people seeking out different places to find the news – not to mention their abysmal approval rating which has been in decline for many years, hitting all-time lows in 2018. The trend line continues a downward slant. Is it any wonder why that has happened?

My take on it is that the media has come out of the closet as left-tilting neo-liberals. No longer is news reported without a slant. It creeps into not only WHAT is reported, but HOW it is reported. Headlines can tell how an article is positioned politically using a few simple words – and the slant often starts in the headlines. This is a technique to get us to read the article if we agree or disagree with the headline. Again, it is subtle manipulation based on an agenda. It's wrong, but unfortunately, we tolerate it far too much. We should reject it.

What's also intriguing to me is how one event that happens can be talked about for days – even weeks at a time. News people say the same thing repeatedly as if to think that we didn't listen or didn't understand the first twelve times they said it. Is that really necessary? Should every talking head from "journalist", to athlete, to political spokesperson, to activist, to psychologist, et al. be voicing their biased opinions? Do we really need all that? Does it make us any smarter or any wiser? I suppose the press think that we really like it because they continue to vomit this stuff up, and too many people sit back and happily consume it.

It's pretty clear that reporting the news fairly and objectively has been overtaken by bias. It seems as though editors and reporters must take every opportunity to make us think a certain way and to make us believe what they believe. That is NOT news reporting; it is propagandizing, and it has no place in our society. They must put their big boy pants on, rise above partisanship, and simply report the news – that's what they are supposed to be doing. Opinion shows or editorials are one thing, but when one purports to be a journalist or news person and can't help but weave an opinion into a story, that changes things.

Propaganda is very dangerous to a democracy. Something repeated over and over again, despite it not being true, can make it seem to be true, and the masses will eventually accept it as fact. Repetitive speech in its intent is to assist the listener in recalling what the speaker said. Orators repeat things for one reason – to reinforce their message. It's like hearing a song repeatedly. We learn the song and we sing along with it. It becomes an embedded part of our memory that elicits emotion. It pops into our head when we're not expecting it. It just keeps playing. The same is true for propaganda.

The attempt is to alter reality and truth which leads to manipulated thinking on a mass scale. The goal is to get the listener to set aside logic and reason and not question whether a statement is fact or not. When we lay down our skepticism and fully embrace what may not be factual, we have given in and we have been manipulated.

In that vein, some people also tend to easily believe propaganda if they fully trust the source, and what is said fits with what they want to believe. If they want it to be true, they can be easily programmed to believe propaganda. By doing that, they are laying down their skepticism simply because it makes them feel more comfortable, and it's what they want to believe. Critical thinking is abandoned and is replaced by gullibility.

The other aspect that neo-liberalism is tapping into is the use of Hollywood stars and extremely famous people in other areas of the world of entertainment. Why would this group be such a target – to get famous people touting the leftist viewpoints and ideologies? And why are they such an important voice in public discourse? It's because schlubs that do not pay attention to politics and what's going on in the country will be easily manipulated and will swallow the propaganda hook, line and sinker. The only reason is because they are fans of the famous person. The people who don't pay attention are an easy target that can be quickly and easily picked off by an often-ill-informed celebrity that has bought into propagating the propaganda and uses fame as a tool.

186

ESPN learned a hard lesson when it began allowing its on-air people to put forth a political viewpoint. Rather than nipping it in the bud and telling its sportscasters to stick to sports and leave the politics outside the studio, the network allowed left-wing viewpoints to be aired. Within a few months of Tweets and on-air political rants, ratings began to plummet. Its audience tuned out because ESPN was gradually turning into a left-wing propaganda machine.

ESPN's president Jimmy Pitaro finally put a stop to it and said he wants "fair and balanced news, not politics." It was interesting that he used the phrase "fair and balanced" since that is a Fox News term. Pitaro said in a *Los Angeles Times* article, "Without question our data tells us our fans do not want us to cover politics." Duh? Some of their audience will never be recovered, and their ratings declined all for the sake of neo-liberal politics.

There are times when left-wing media people just can't help themselves. Sometimes they become completely unhinged. They totally forget about reason, honesty and decency. I recall the White House Correspondents' dinner in 2016 when a full-frontal personal attack was launched against the White House Press Secretary Sarah Sanders who was sitting at the head table. It was disgusting as much as it was disturbing that a comedian would stoop so low and lose all decorum, let alone humanity. Her "performance" does not even merit mentioning her name. She wasn't funny – it was an out-and-out brutal verbal assault on Mrs. Sanders that went way overboard.

In front of the audience in attendance, and then on national television, Mrs. Sanders was ridiculed, disrespected, and every woman's organization should have flocked to her defense and should have spoken out against such rudeness and vitriol. Perhaps I am mistaken, but aren't women's organizations supposed to have the backs of ALL women? Aren't they all supposed to stick together? We must conclude that they only are organized to support liberal Democrat women, which sends a loud message that their support is bigoted. How else can one characterize it? It's the only conclusion one can reasonably come to. Since Mrs. Sanders worked for President Trump, she was no longer worthy of protection from women's rights organizations – she was not a member of the approved ideological clan.

If the NAACP only supported and segregated a certain group of black people, they would be castigated. Yet it's acceptable for women's organizations to segregate conservative women and treat them differently than liberal women. ALL women should show respect for ALL women; otherwise, the bigotry negates any good that women's organizations bring to the betterment of women. But I digress.

The comedian, who shall remain nameless, should have been ashamed of herself, but, of course, she had no shame, no couth, and a total lack of respect for another human being. The whole routine spewed hatred. I suppose she couldn't help herself due to her Trump Derangement Syndrome – it's a psychosis that leads to insanity, and the main symptom is despicable public behavior.

Our news used to be fed to us in the morning and in the evening in small doses. Now we have the news blaring at us all day, every day 24/7. To spend our days enthralled by the day's events and all the craziness that we subject ourselves to is a form of masochism. There is constant negativity being shoved down our throats, whether we like it or not.

The vast majority, even maybe 90% of the news we hear is bad news. We are told about all the murders, the robberies, the divorces, and the car wrecks. We watch the news and see the muck and mire we are up to our neck in. Are we tending towards being masochists? The definition of masochism is, "a person that enjoys feeling pain." If the shoe fits…

It has become a cultural addiction. Do we somehow get satisfaction from subjecting ourselves to the incessant ranting and raving of biased reporting and commentary? Is it not puzzling why we find it fascinating to witness horrible behaviors of some members of our society, and we must see it or hear it again and again ad nauseum?

All this negativity fools us into thinking that the world is a miserable place and we are all totally worthless. No wonder we are a confused, sometimes neurotic group of humans. No wonder we view things so pessimistically. No wonder we don't like each other. If I were an alien from another planet and was looking around, I wouldn't like us either.

Another disturbing aspect is that the media today has an enormous effect on our society. Hark back to 100 years ago. The media was nowhere near as influential, and they were at least somewhat beneficial to society and had a positive image. Now, forget about it. As all the polling has told us, the media as a whole is highly disliked, not trusted, and considered detrimental to the well-being of our society. I wonder why?

Think about it if we reversed what's going on. What if we were constantly bombarded by positive news? Think about how much better off we'd be. Instead, we are watching ourselves self-destruct in front of our own eyes as we watch it play out on a video screen. Anyone that thinks this is a healthy thing for our society is horribly mistaken. It's not.

That all may sound too far out there and an exaggeration for some, but looking at it from a macro perspective, one cannot deny that we are witnessing ourselves in a bad car wreck and watching it in super slow-mo. For some twisted reason, we have allowed this to happen to us. It shouldn't be this way, and we do have control of it if we choose to exercise that control.

Ted Koppel is a professed liberal and widely respected mainstream media newsman with 25 Emmys. He was the top news anchor for ABC and hosted Nightline for 25 years. Mr. Koppel made some comments that raised not only the eyebrows of those in liberal media news, it raised their ire. In a speaking engagement for the Carnegie Endowment, Mr. Koppel stated, with all sincerity, "I'm terribly concerned that when you talk about the *New York Times* these days, when you're talking about the *Washington Post* these days, we're not talking about the *New York Times* of 50 years ago. We are not talking about the *Washington Post* of 50 years ago. We're talking about organizations that say Donald J. Trump is bad for the United States." He continued, "We have things appearing on the front page of the New York Times that never would have appeared 50 years ago." Mr. Koppel was specifically referencing the fact that opinion and biased reporting now appear on the front pages of these once-respected newspapers. Opinion used to be confined to the editorial pages, but not anymore.

Referring to President Trump's denigration of the media because of the negative coverage he receives, Mr. Koppel added, "But the notion that most of us [reporters and news people] look upon Donald Trump as being an absolute fiasco, he's not mistaken in that perception and he's not mistaken when so many of the liberal media, for example, describe themselves as belonging to the 'Resistance'. What does that mean?" His point was that journalism isn't about "resistance," it's about reporting the news minus any personal opinions.

What it also means is that the vast majority of the mainstream media have a political agenda and slant the stories they produce or write as their contribution to resisting anything and everything that President Trump does. It's a nonstop, full-on assault on the presidency, and it is an insult to real journalism and an insult to the American ideal as I perceive it.

Jill Abramson, the former managing editor and executive editor of the *New York Times*, released a book called *Merchants of Truth*" that labels The *New York Times* as "unmistakably anti-Trump."

Speaking of the *New York Times* she stated, "Given its mostly liberal audience, there was an implicit financial reward for the Times in running lots of Trump stories, almost all of them negative." She also said, "Some headlines contained raw opinion, as did some of the stories that were labeled as news analysis…The more anti-Trump the Times was perceived to be, the more it was mistrusted for being biased." Sadly, things won't change even though the truth is plainly obvious that the *New York Times* is clearly predisposed to forwarding the neo-liberal or progressive agenda.

Lara Logan, former CBS and 60 minutes reporter has plowed new ground for women in media. She was the chief foreign correspondent for 5 years inside Afghanistan, and while in the middle of the Egyptian uprising she was captured by militants and gang-raped and beaten because she was a female news person. Ms. Logan had some strong words to say about the journalistic integrity of her cohorts in the media. On Mark Levin's *Life, Liberty and Levin* television show, Ms. Logan stated, "I know I'm not the only journalist who's watching in horror as opinion and pejorative language is passed off as fact, where anonymous sources are given complete cover to do political assassinations without any regard for the consequences of what they are doing."

She stated, "Journalists are walking hand-in-hand with propaganda groups and pushing forward narratives that are not based in fact, that are not based in honest journalism, that are nothing more than political targeting, thinly disguised as journalism today."

Ms. Logan has been attacked by liberal journalists for her stance on the state of the media. She was emphatic in saying, "I want to make it clear here, I'm an independent thinker, OK? Nobody owns me – I'm not owned by the left and I'm not owned by the right."

She continued, "What bothers me is that one political ideology dominates almost all of your academic institutions, and that same political ideology dominates all of your newsrooms. When they're all singing from the same hymn sheet, all their butts are covered, aren't they? Nobody's challenging them; nobody's holding them to account for what they're reporting…so when you stay inside the bubble and inside the narrative that dominates the media industry, it's a safe place to be because nobody's coming after you.

"What's changed today is that you now have a press corps that's working hand-in-hand with propaganda organizations [like Media Matters] with a political agenda…too many journalists today are political operatives now. They have forgotten how to be journalists – they have forgotten what we are supposed to be as journalists, and they have become political operatives. They have a pre-determined outcome for all of their reporting."

Ms. Logan continued, "I'm very 'concerned,' using Ted Koppel's word, by the number of journalists who have taken a political position and still expect and demand the legitimacy of being 'objective and independent' and being open and balanced and fair. These are not people that are open-minded." She later stated, "They don't want alternative points of view, they most especially don't want conservative points of view."

Michael Tracey, an independent journalist stated, "[the] Trump-Russia [thing] has come more to resemble an article of religious faith, than a set of journalistic, political, or legal claims. And a religious faith, by definition, is just not falsifiable; meaning countervailing evidence can never undermine the court premise upon which believers rest their faith."

Regarding journalists who hate President Trump and were obsessed with the Russia collusion investigation, Mr. Tracey continued, "It's almost like they are in a church and, you know, chanting these excerpts from a holy text."

It did seem as though they were all reading from the same script. They brought up the same points on every show and each guest seemed to nod in agreement and echo the same thoughts. I can certainly see Mr. Tracey's point, and it is perfectly clear that most, if not all, of the mainstream media were participating in the church ceremonies, regurgitating the same talking points incessantly and all singing from the same songbook. It is profoundly obvious what went on, and anyone that claims it did not happen is in denial.

The left-wing talking heads all over the cable news channels and even the prime-time national news people were saying the same exact things repeatedly as if it were a mantra chant. This kind of journalism is either religious zealotry, a psychosis, or an unabashed attempt to brainwash viewers. Perhaps it's all three.

Rather than rooting for judicial prudence, they were rooting for a guilty verdict. The mob was in attack mode and they threw every stone and pursued every avenue to discredit the President and claim he colluded with the Russians. It was shameless and relentless. It was also an assault on true journalism and another insult to the intelligence of the American people.

Yes, we have freedom of the press, but we do have the remote control as a defense mechanism, and we can certainly occupy our time in a more productive endeavor than watching and listening to political pabulum and fake news. Social manipulation and brainwashing intentionally perpetrated on the public should not be tolerated.

The strategy neo-liberals are using is to get the mainstream news media on their side, which they already have done. Then they get the educational system nodding robotically in agreement with the propaganda. Next, they get the entertainment industry behind them echoing the talking points. Lastly, they exert control over who can use social media. Pretty soon, they have changed an entire generation's thinking. It's a slow and subtle process of brainwashing through the use of propaganda. However, there's hope. As affective as the propaganda from the left has been, there are still enough people who are more cynical and don't buy into neo-liberal ideology as it is touted today.

Again, I reiterate, these knuckleheaded talking heads and left-wing writers have every right to spew their nonsense, but the general public should turn off the mainstream media. The only way to counter the out-of-control media is to stop watching. A lot of people have already stopped watching CNN as is evidenced by their ratings which are abysmal. And the only people who don't know the whole channel is biased are the liberals that watch it. When it comes to the current state of journalism, it's a mess, but most importantly, it is also a threat to our democracy.

Welcome to the new world of reportage where honesty and integrity have been replaced by religious fervor and political bias. It's a sad state of affairs, but it's indicative of a trend towards more distinct and divisive polarization within our country. And the media is feeding the fire.

We cannot sit idly by and allow the media to turn into a pack of political hacks. If we do so, we are supporting their addiction to bias and bigotry, while the truth is being sacrificed for a higher cause – political propaganda. Like a rabid dog, they have turned on the American people and are more interested in political ideology and zealotry than they are good and honest journalism. *"I Know We Are Better Than This."*

Chapter 21

Domination by Device

The most important tool a dictator or demagogue must use is control of the masses. Power must be gained by force and then maintained by whatever means is necessary in a totalitarian state. Power equals control, and control equals power.

In today's world, control of HOW things are communicated (the physical mediums such as cell phones, tablets, computers, and televisions) is critical for anyone wanting to seize control either quickly or very gradually to intentionally manipulate the masses.

Controlling WHAT is being communicated (the message) is also vital in taking over a populace and then maintaining power. To be a dictator in today's world, unless one cannot authoritatively exert control over those two things, the medium and the message, they will probably not be able to stay in power and enjoy the comforts of the castle very long. That is why dictators throughout history have seized the media – it is essential to maintaining power. Hitler did it. Mussolini did it. The Soviet Union did it. China did it (and still does). Every totalitarian government has done it. It is crucial for maintaining control. China is a shining example of a modern-day government exercising both means of control – the medium and the message.

The Chinese people are under strict control when it comes to what they say and what they view on their computers, cell phones, and tablets. They use a point system, and if citizens speak against the government, they will have privileges taken away like invalidating their passport if their "social score" drops below the acceptable level. They also reduce the time citizens are allowed to use their phone or tablet as punishment if they rack up too many negative points. The Chinese government monitors and controls the populace by device.

Since we have adopted the cell phone and other electronic media and made it such an integral part of our lives, it actually sets us up to be manipulated and controlled if we are not careful. China has realized that technology is a perfect way to "manage" the populace – it's an unprecedented tool, and they are all in with its use. That is domination by device.

Imagine our government having full access to our phones, tablets, laptops and PC's and being able to intrude into our lives. Imagine if an Alexa-type device was required inside every home and residents were not allowed to turn it off. Perhaps China is not too far away from doing exactly that.

I read an interesting interview printed in the *Moscow Times* featuring Patriarch Kirill, head of the Russian Orthodox Church. In it, he put forth the idea that a dictator and even the Anti-Christ could conceivably come into power by controlling us through our own electronic devices. It's an interesting thought that deserves some careful consideration.

Patriarch Kirill stated that he was not entirely against gadgets – his fear was centered around "falling into slavery" to cellphones and other electronic devices. He pointed out that the collection of all user data, including "location, interests and fears," could theoretically be manipulated to the point of control. "Control from a single point is a harbinger of the coming of the Anti-Christ," Kirill stated. "The Anti-Christ is a personality that will be at the head of the World Wide Web, controlling the entire human race." He concluded, "If we don't want to bring the apocalypse closer, there should be no single center [of information flow]."

Before anybody scoffs at the Anti-Christ comment, we should truly stop and think about what is possible these days. Even if we remove the Anti-Christ portion, the idea that we could be controlled through our own devices should give us all pause. His point is well-taken and we must always stop and ponder the possibility that he may indeed be right – even if he is wrong about the Anti-Christ.

Here in the good ol' USA, similar but less obtrusive control is happening right under our noses, and sadly, most people do not see or even realize or care what's going on. We have long been manipulated through advertising. Politicians are attempting to brainwash us by saying something over and over again and having the media incessantly repeat it until we accept it as "truth."

We are undoubtedly already being manipulated by mainstream television news organizations and their websites along with social media. Neo-liberal slants and even political rants have become more frequent and acceptable at the major news outlets.

As discussed previously, far too many television companies, large circulation newspapers, and social media companies slant so far left that it has become blatantly obvious. However, they are unabashedly, unashamedly, and dishonorably practicing manipulative bias. They would never admit they are biased because they can't be biased if they are always correct in their viewpoints. They are correct and anyone who thinks differently is just plain wrong and should be ashamed. As a result of this bias, we are required to view things through the neo-liberal left lens. I wonder how that would go over if all news had to be presented from a conservative bias. I doubt that any liberals would find that acceptable – but I could be wrong.

As stated earlier, the control of and access to information wields great power. When combining the control of the medium and the message, things can get pretty serious. Looking at today's mainstream media, it's not a leap to say that we are approaching a monopolistic mainstream left-leaning media. Neo-liberals have taken over except for talk radio which conservatives dominate with Rush Limbaugh, Sean Hannity, Mark Levin, Dennis Prager, and others.

Fox News is the only major outlet where conservative views are heard, and the left-wing folks are in a constant attack to try and shut down the only major alternative news viewpoint. This battle headed up by Media Matters and other websites is as ugly and bigoted as it gets. Isn't that nice of them to want to shut down anyone that disagrees with them? That sounds so fair-minded and rational doesn't it? It's really not an obsession; it's a justifiable crusade in their minds.

Without those limited outlets, the conservative perspective would never be heard. Anyone who doubts that liberals don't control the message is sadly mistaken. It's a fact – liberal media people know it except they would never admit it because it would further deteriorate what the American people think about them. Poll after poll shows that the masses have a very poor trust factor with the media already, and it is trending further down because liberal media people wear their guilt on their sleeves – they are very easy to spot for most rational people.

As cited earlier, Media Research Center's on-going tracking of President Trump's coverage shows that consistently more than 90% of his media coverage is negative. According to another study, liberals outnumber conservatives in the media 5 to 1.

Despite the amount of negativity thrown at candidate Trump during the election cycle of 2016, he amazingly won. They aimed their entire arsenal of media weapons at President Trump during the campaign – and they are still firing off as many rounds as they can muster on a daily basis. On many occasions, they have literally embarrassed themselves with bogus stories and outlandish rhetoric aimed at doing one thing – get President Trump at all costs. They are obsessed. It really is pathetic when we think about it. No one, let alone a president, should be treated that way.

Even Politico, a left-slanted website, concurs regarding media bias. They wrote an article on the concentration of media that emanates from the left-leaning two coasts that stated, "The national media really does work in a bubble. Not only is the bubble real, but it's more extreme than you might realize."

The point of the Politico article is that mainstream media is controlled by large east and west coast organizations which have a very large concentration of liberals working there – liberalism is pervasive across all levels of the mainstream media companies from top to bottom.

One of the portions of the media market where this has also played out is the demise of small-town local newspapers in flyover country between the two coasts. The control and influence have shifted to the large newspaper corporations, as small to medium-sized markets have lost their local newspapers. This leads them to rely on the national media for their news.

The danger that comes into play through media bias is that the general public is only hearing news from one viewpoint and from one angle – and it is a slanted perspective. Most news consumers are lazy. The vast majority do not seek out the other side of the story or alternative opinions. This leads to the populace being exposed to manipulation. It happens and that's the spooky part ... and we subject ourselves to this because?

Most revolutions happen from the bottom up. The masses that have been abused and the peasants eventually get their bellies full of the elites and they revolt. What seems to be happening is that the elites from Washington DC, Hollywood, mainstream media, and Silicon Valley are trying to wield their power to track us, spy on us, tell us what to do, influence elections – all of which is a fast track to ultimately controlling us. This is opposite of revolutions that emanate from the bottom up; it's happening from the top down.

Thousands, even millions can be riled up and ready to riot in less than an hour through social media. A new term was recently minted – flash-mob. Does anyone really not believe the masses in our country can be manipulated simply through their cell phones and social media?

To further reinforce the top down effect going on is that the Big Tech companies are influencing our politics, telling us what to buy and where to buy it without even asking our permission. In addition, they are dictating what we should be thinking. The revolution is being pushed UPON us, and we don't even see what's coming. In fact, way too many citizens are getting in line and obediently following their every command. The most effective form of manipulation is to do it and not have the people even aware of what's going on.

There's another aspect that is reaching farther and farther into our lives. When we stop and truly think about how much control that Google, Facebook, Twitter, and Amazon have, it should set off some alarms. I don't really think this is merely conspiratorial talk; after all, there are millions of homes that have invited a new resident into their homes with Alexa, Google Home, etc. These devices are an open invitation for those companies to join the family. Numerous reports have shown that these companies or their contractors are listening to what is being said in user's homes. Did these users sign up for that? I suppose if we are comfortable with that, so be it, but there should be some caution because it makes us vulnerable.

Another major problem with social media companies is that the only accountability they have is with their shareholders. They are not accountable to us citizens, and most importantly, they are not accountable to the government. That gives them a license to use us, manipulate us, and enjoy the benefits of a huge revenue stream from OUR private information. Oh, let me restate that – it's our not-so-private information after we sign up with one of them. I think everyone would agree that we should be able to, at the very least, opt out of various products and services that they provide to their customers; it's our data they are using to make billions of dollars, and we ought to have control of it. However, by clicking on the "agree" button, we consent to this abuse, and I would say 99% of all users never read exactly what they are agreeing to because the "agreement" is a long and tedious document written in lawyer-speak that few people can fully understand. When we start to read the document, our eyes cross and our brain tells us that this is not fun, so we just click "agree". The sad thing is that is exactly the outcome these companies are intending – make it so complicated that users just get frustrated and say yes.

So, it boils down to us having no control over our data, and our government has no control over these social media companies. That pretty much means they are immune to privacy laws and they have free reign to do as they wish. These social media companies need to come clean about what they are doing, and if they won't do that, then the government needs to step in and protect its citizens.

Yes, we are culpable because we blindly sign up for social media sites and aps while not fully knowing what we are getting ourselves into and the privacy we are giving up. But the fact is, we are not slaves to social media and the aps we use, and we should not be treated as such.

I would suggest that everyone stop and consider the amount of data that is accumulated on us – and we voluntarily participate and make their task of manipulation far too easy. In giving up our privacy, we are ceding more than a modicum of control over our lives and opening the door to being "managed" by Silicon Valley elites. If that's what one wants to do, that's fine, but as for me, I am choosing not to participate.

It also becomes dangerous when these big companies can have the power to limit free speech by what news they want us to hear and whose opinions we should believe. Google controls the world of finding information, and if they choose to manipulate search results (which has been proven that they do), they control what we see. If we are profiled as an avowed conservative and they want to convert us, they can simply control the news they want us to view or hear. They possess a very extensive profile on us – they know what sites we visit. They know what we search for. They know just about everything about us.

Facebook is an admitted manipulator and plays the role of censor whenever it's convenient for them and their ideology. They know who our friends are, and they know what we like. Twitter is the same. Let's examine that a bit further.

Here's more on Google that needs to be recognized. Google technologies have infiltrated virtually every school in the country.

Google, as part of their strategic plan, has captured a virtual monopoly to hook into every aspect of a student's life – and they start young, as in pre-school. Many educational institutions require a student to have a Gmail account. Students use Google Cloud, Google Drive, Google Docs, Google Vault, Google Sheets, Google Slides, Google Hangouts, and all of this is running on a Google Chromebook. It's been estimated that Google has 80 million students and teachers using Google services, and there are 30 million Chromebooks used by students – many of which were given to the students for free.

An on-line tool called Canvas is a learning management system that stores test scores, quiz results, homework assignments and grades, plus a lot of other personal information. And then there's Class Dojo that collects and stores a student's psychological profile, family information, personal messages, and behavioral data. The question every parent who has a student should be: Do I want a single company, unregulated by the government, to have that much information at its disposal? All that data is out there begging for a company to manipulate students or a hacker to break in and steal away every bit of private data on both students and parents. We must stop and think – is this really a smart thing to do?

As we discussed earlier, the Big Tech companies are easily able to manipulate content that students see. They can ban people, words, ideas, opinions, and manipulate search results. They can easily be the self-proclaimed referees of speech and thought. All they must do is execute that power – and they do.

Of course, they promise they don't sell our private info (ooops, they all are guilty of that). They say our data is safe (ooops, hackers have already breached private data many times). They can basically take over and run our lives (ooops, they already do for many people who are fully entrenched and live in the world of Google Home). It just seems logical to me that they wield far too much power and we should not let it be happening, no matter how much convenience Google offers.

The other major aspect is the encouragement of our young students to be engaged with a Chromebook or other tablet device all day every day. Whatever happened to direct interaction with the teacher and the other students in the classroom? Kids already spend far too much time on their phone or tablet. All we are doing is increasing screen time when we should be decreasing it. I cover this topic more extensively in another chapter called "Unsocial Media." It is shocking to discover how screen time has been highly detrimental to not only our youth, but to adults as well.

Currently, the Big Tech companies are monopolies in their business segments. There is no doubt that no competitor of Google is even in the same hemisphere. There is no more influential platform for sharing information than Facebook. Amazon and Walmart on-line are taking over retail. Twitter has little competition for conversations.

Please recall that the Bell telephone companies and Standard Oil were broken up out of fear that they could wield too much power and influence. It's time we did the same with Big Tech.

This monopolistic advantage of the Big Tech companies should be at the top of the list for those in Congress. It's a problem that our government must deal with – they cannot just ignore what these corporations are doing. Aside from the fact that they are all left-tilted entities that think they have the right to control what is said on their websites and search engines, other reasons should be worrisome. They can subtly (or maybe not so subtly) tell us what we can read and what we cannot. They are the judge, jury and executioner of what is acceptable speech and what is not.

These corporate giants get away with it due to a special "carve-out" on how they are classified by the Federal government. The "Communications and Decency Act" classifies these companies (along with countless others) as "non-publishers," meaning they are not responsible for content – they are just a provider of a "platform" – just like a full-regulated utility – except they are not regulated.

Where the rub comes is that they DO control what is being "published" on their "platform." They serve as a censor. They are making editorial decisions which negate their classification of being a non-publisher. Consequently, they fall under First Amendment protections and are not allowed to limit speech. If they want to act like a utility, then they should be held accountable as a utility. Conversely, if they want to act like a publisher, then they should be treated as a publisher.

Without any protections against censorship, there is no legal recourse against them if they choose to limit free speech. If they want to terminate the right of people to provide their opinions under the First Amendment, they cannot be sued for censorship because they are a non-publisher – meaning, we are all at the mercy of the Google, Facebook , and Twitter's editorial boards – which, by the way, makes them a publisher. They are no longer an impartial, disinterested, open "platform". From a legal perspective, that's an important distinction because it's an artificial protection that is not granted under our Constitution.

Electrical utilities can't cut power to someone who doesn't agree with their political views. The major telecom companies are not allowed to monitor conversations and censor what we say over the phone. They are non-publishers – they are true platforms and they have no right to censorship as a utility. In my opinion, the same is true for Google, Facebook, and Twitter – they need to be treated as a utility if they want to maintain their non-publisher status. That means they should be out of the business of limiting speech and shutting down those that don't toe the neo-liberal line.

Providing these companies with the ability to sway elections and control what we see or read goes way too far. Media outlets become the arbiters of information and can ultimately control how we think and what we think. It is strikingly ironic that the media exists because of our free speech protections, yet social media outlets participate in limiting free speech. That just doesn't seem right.

Another point to consider is that because of their carve-out exemption, they have literally become more powerful than our government when it comes to controlling speech. As a whole, the social media sector has taken over control of censorship, while replacing, subverting, and superseding the government and the First Amendment. They dictate what they determine is acceptable speech, and they are accountable to no one. That seems to be too much power in the hands of a few tech companies, does it not? That's not only true in the USA, but GLOBALLY, although Europe seems to be a lot tougher on Big Tech companies than our lame and timid Congress. The only conclusion I can draw is that these big tech companies spend a lot of money lobbying and contributing to political candidates – the vast majority of which goes to Democrats. By dangling enormous amounts of money in election contributions in front of politicians, the Big Tech companies buy their loyalty and manipulate these politicians like puppets on a string, insulating themselves from oversight and regulation.

Perhaps someday, the general public and our political leaders will realize the dangers presented by these companies and other media outlets that practice censorship and control.

We have never been to this place before in our country's history – this is totally new territory. But this is the 21st century, and this is where we are.

Google is the search engine; Facebook is the sharing medium; Twitter is where conversations take place. What if Google decides one day that Democrats and liberals are going to be eliminated from search results? What happens when one day Facebook decides that postings related to global warming are automatically deleted? What if Twitter suddenly decides to control all conversations by banning words like progressivism or liberalism? All Hell would break loose.

Selective limitation of speech is no freedom of speech at all. We must safeguard our right to freedom of expression – we cannot let a bunch of tech titans tell us how we are all to think and speak. We cannot sit idly by and let this happen.

If individuals don't believe the conspiracy, then they should at least be aware of what is possible with today's technology. We carry around cell phones with us all day, every day, or keep them in our homes. We are setting ourselves up for being vulnerable to manipulation. All the Big Tech companies are perfectly capable of exercising control – it's pretty obvious they are doing it already with targeted ads, suggestions for what to eat and what to do, all the while knowing where we are and what we are doing.

The top-down control exerted by a group of elitists is the first step in executing a strategy for controlling the masses. We know it is possible. There is evidence that it is already happening and that it will likely continue to happen. We need to get a grip and realize what's going on with the media and big tech companies. It's only going to get worse if we allow it to happen.

As Patriarch Kirill suggested, the dissemination of information from a single source (Big Tech and Big Media) and through a single medium (cell phones, tablets) is enabling vulnerability to manipulation. In my opinion, far too many people are happily (or perhaps not knowingly) letting it happen. We have let the genie out of the bottle, and we need to take back our privacy and freedom of speech as quickly as possible before the genie ends up taking over complete control and dominating us through our devices. Why would we choose to remain vulnerable and continue to let this happen? *"I Know We Are Better Than This."*

Chapter 22

Unsocial Media

Social media came upon us with a rush and abandon that we had not ever seen from a technology. The craze became so pervasive that the lives of people were altered – and not in a positive way. Far too many people took things to an extreme and were putting in four to five hours on social media each day. Some people use social media to subtly brag about their lives with an underlying message to their "friends" that "my life is great and yours is not." To some, it became a social hammer that was continuously beating down people and taking over their lives. It became self-deprecation. Friends became enemies because of social media. Marital relationships have been fractured. Lives have even been lost because of the effects social media has on people. What positive good social media has brought us has been far outweighed by the negatives. It was a nice concept that turned into a nightmare.

A study by Millennium Cohort Society of 11,000 girls aged 14 has shown a distinct trend that the more these young ladies used social media, the more depressed they became. UK Professor Yvonne Kelly who drove the research said, "The link between social media use and depressive symptoms was stronger for girls compared to boys." She continued, "For girls, greater daily hours of social media use corresponded to a stepwise increase in depressive symptoms."

Social media has been a driving force in lowering self-esteem. The constant semi-conscious comparison of one's life with everybody else's is a set-up for making one feel inferior. The University of Copenhagen conducted a study of 1,039 adults and concluded that social media reinforces insecurities and contributes to what they called "Facebook envy". Social media has taken "keeping up with the Jones's" to a whole new level.

Social media has had a negative effect on human interaction, as has text messaging. We humans need personal contact. We need to look in each other's eyes and communicate. If the primary means of human interaction is through a cell phone, we become more isolated from each other. Isn't it a strange dichotomy that a technology whose purpose is to extend our communication capabilities actually makes us become lonelier and further withdrawn?

Selfies posted on social media have become all the rage. So many people are more interested in getting a perfect selfie in front of a famous landmark than merely enjoying the experience of the marvel. Selfie sickness robs us of the happiness usually derived when visiting a beautiful natural wonder. Our amazement and awe are replaced by a selfish obsession to document the visit and post it on social media so our friends can be jealous rather than simply enjoy the moment.

Another aspect of social media doing harm is cyber-bullying. In the good ol' days, bullies were usually confined to a classroom, a school, or a local neighborhood. Now, social media bullying has a much broader impact which can even reach to thousands of people. There is very little that can be done to defend ourselves if we have been cyber-bullied on the internet or social media. It used to be that bullies were taken care of on the school yard or the front yard through some sort of confrontation, sometimes ending in some level of violence. Things were usually quickly settled.

Bullies now have a much broader audience to receive their attacks, and the result can be catastrophic when teens, and even adults, take their own lives because of bullying. Bullies are often empowered, because they can remain anonymous and say virtually anything, including threats of violence, without any consequences. Sadly, one study showed that only 10% of parents who have had a son or daughter that were bullied even know about it. Many of them only learn about it after it is too late.

Bullying can be manifested in other ways within social media. In an article on Quillete.com, Barrett Wilson used a pseudonym, because he was afraid of the backlash he might suffer from calling out those that participate in mob bullying. He was fired from a company that he described as being in the "social justice industry", because he began to question the motives and tactics of that company. He is now a food delivery driver to try and feed his family, because he was ostracized and unable to get employment in his profession. It's a pretty good guess that he was a writer on a liberal elitist website.

In the article, he stated, "I was publicly shamed, mobbed, and reduced to a symbol of male privilege. I was cast out of my career and my professional community. Writing anything under my own byline now would invite a renewal of this mobbing—which is why, with my editor's permission, I am writing this under a pseudonym. In my previous life, I was a self-righteous social justice crusader. I would use my mid-sized Twitter and Facebook platforms to signal my wokeness on topics such as LGBT rights, rape culture, and racial injustice. Many of the opinions I held then are still opinions that I hold today. But I now realize that my social-media hyperactivity was, in reality, doing more harm than good."

He continued, "The only causes I was actually contributing to were the causes of mobbing and public shaming. Real change does not stem from these tactics. They only cause division, alienation, and bitterness. How did I become that person? It happened because it was exhilarating. Every time I would call someone racist or sexist, I would get a rush. That rush would then be reaffirmed and sustained by the stars, hearts, and thumbs-up that constitute the nickels and dimes of social media validation. The people giving me these stars, hearts, and thumbs-up were engaging in their own cynical game: A fear of being targeted by the mob induces us to signal publicly that we are part of it.

"There's no such thing as due process in this [media] world. And once judgment has been rendered against you, the mob starts combing through your past, looking for similar transgressions that might have been missed at the time. …Social justice is a surveillance culture, a snitch culture. The constant vigilance on the part of my colleagues and friends did me in. That's why I'm delivering sushi and pizza."

Mr. Wilson stated he had a dream that while he was delivering food and following the app he was using, his car became a tool of destruction. When he awoke, he said he was "thrust back into the reality of the living world—where I could understand the suffering, carnage and death I would have caused by my in-app actions. There were bodies strewn along the streets, screaming bystanders, destroyed lives, chaos. My car, by contrast, was indestructible while I was living in the app."

The article concluded, "The social justice vigilantism I was living on Twitter and Facebook was like the app in my dream. Aggressive online virtue signaling is a fundamentally two-dimensional act. It has no human depth. It's only when we snap out of it, see the world as it really is, and people as they really are, that we appreciate the destruction and human suffering we caused when we were trapped inside."

As we all have witnessed, hate-speech used in cyber bullying toward someone's appearance, sexual orientation, religion, gender, race or disability is on the rise, and females lead the way. A full 60% of all social media hate-speech is perpetrated by females, while 40% is done by males. Females are also more apt to use social media than males in their bullying. High school-aged girls are also twice as likely to commit cyber bullying than boys. Shockingly, 75% of 17-year-old girls and 85% of boys have experienced some sort of cyber bullying or trolling. All these statistics show a disturbing trend. Is this how we want our teens to behave?

Social media can even affect our health by robbing us of our sleep. When we are trying to go to sleep, it makes it more difficult when we are fraught with anxiety about what all our friends are saying and doing, and it keeps our brains on high alert. Some social media users even wake up in the middle of the night just to check their phones. Sleep deprivation is not healthy and can lead to depression and an increase in anxiety disorders.

Origin, which is the research arm of the Hill Holiday marketing company, found that 41% of young adults aged 18 to 24 feel depressed, anxious or sad whenever they visit social media platforms such as Facebook, Twitter, Instagram and Snapchat.

A recent study of 1,500 Facebook and Twitter users by the UK disability charity, Scope, showed that 62% of those surveyed reported feeling inadequate. A feeling of jealousy was experienced by 60% from comparing themselves to their friends or acquaintances. To many social media users, it has become an addiction, resulting in self-inflicted torture.

Depression is increasing in our teen-agers here in the USA. Estimates say there are 3 million teens that are clinically depressed. In 2018, it is estimated that 13% of 12 to 17-year-olds suffered from depression. One in ten college students is affected by depression. Suicide is the second leading cause of death for those aged 10 through 17. The suicide rate for teen-aged girls climbed to 5 in 100,000, doubling the rate from 2007. For boys, the rates increased by 30% to 14 per 100,000. It's certainly not a leap to say that social media and screen time has had a major impact on those rates.

Jean Twenge, a renowned professor at San Diego State University has done extensive research into behaviors and patterns among Millennials and iGen (her term for the generation that has never experienced life without the internet and smart phones).

In an article in *The Atlantic*, Dr. Twenge spoke about the iGens versus the Millennials, "Psychologically, however, they [the iGens] are more vulnerable than Millennials were: Rates of teen depression and suicide have skyrocketed since 2011. It's not an exaggeration to describe iGens as being on the brink of the worst mental-health crisis in decades. Much of this deterioration can be traced to their phones."

She continued, "But the twin rise of the smartphone and social media has caused an earthquake of a magnitude we've not seen in a very long time, if ever. There is compelling evidence that the devices we've placed in young people's hands are having profound effects on their lives—and making them seriously unhappy."

Her advice to iGens: "If you were going to give advice for a happy adolescence…it would be straightforward: Put down the phone, turn off the laptop, and do something—anything—that does not involve a screen. Once again, the effect of screen activities is unmistakable: The more time teens spend looking at screens, the more likely they are to report symptoms of depression. Eighth-graders who are heavy users of social media increase their risk of depression by 27 percent, while those who play sports, go to religious services, or even do homework more than the average teen cut their risk significantly."

Our thinking patterns are affected by the Tweets we read, the Facebook posts we read, and the people we follow and the blogs we read. Our minds are poisoned by videos on Snapchat and YouTube. Our self-worth is dictated by Facebook and Instagram. Jac Vanek, noted millennial podcaster even observed, "You are the books you read, the films you watch, the music you listen to, the people you meet, the dreams you have, and the conversations you engage in."

Thankfully, social media usage has seen a declining trend, but it is still far too pervasive. The decline is mostly because many people are getting tired of punishing themselves. Interestingly, those that are putting in too much screen time use a similar excuse as those that suffer from various addictions: "I know I shouldn't be doing it so much, but I just can't help it."

Our world has become addicted to an electronic drug. Addiction is defined as "the persistent and compulsive use of a substance (or device) known by the user to be harmful." As hard as it may be to admit it, we are a flawed and vulnerable group of people that has formed a new addiction. We can do better, and if we don't want to recognize our faults and shortcomings, we will cease to advance, and the trajectory of our upward evolution will take a downturn. This will lead to an era where we are not so kind to ourselves. But first, we must confess our addiction and make a concerted effort to change our behaviors. We need to use technology responsibly, not carelessly. If not, an unfortunate outcome is as predictable as it is likely.

All statistical markers among Millennials, iGen, Gen X, and even older adults point to less social interaction, more loneliness, more depression, less happiness, and higher suicide rates. Parents need to get a grip on managing screen time, and both young people and adults need to understand the damaging effects they are bringing upon themselves. Recognizing and responding to the negative effects of social media and screen time is an absolute societal necessity. We need to adjust before too much damage is done. *"I Know We Are Better Than This."*

Section 6
The Climate and the Earth

Chapter 23

Global Warming and Mother Nature

Before I get into the subject of climate change, let me first explain that I think the "save the planet" movement has raised our awareness that Man creates a lot of waste and we could be a lot smarter about what we do with our garbage and how we treat our environment. When I say "we", I mean the entire world – not just the USA.

It is a noble endeavor to be environmentally conscious and to be a good steward of our resources – it's the right thing to do. We should give a big thanks to the environmentalist community for changing our perception of how we should treat our planet.

When I visit one of our beautiful state or federal parks and see that people discarded trash carelessly, it makes me angry. We all should take more pride in what we do with our garbage and leaving it for someone else to pick up or leaving Mother Nature to absorb and cleanse itself of our trash. It is abominable. Yes, we need to take care of our environment and anyone that disagrees is misguided.

There is no doubt that Mankind's mistreatment of our valuable resources needs to be addressed, and we are doing that. But some of the claims of how much effect we are having are debatable.

First things first. We cannot make an informed decision without honest examination with emotion removed. Let's start with that premise. Is climate change real? Is there unassailable evidence? Is everyone over-reacting? Are we under-reacting? Those are good questions to ponder.

I have tried to examine the subject from five different angles in five different chapters – the science behind climate change, the CO_2 issue, the religion of climate change, the pollution problem, and the renewable energy push.

Those reading this that believe in man-made climate change will hopefully read this chapter and not bail out – there's more info out there from numerous scientists that has not been widely disseminated. I tried to lay out a pragmatic view of what the "other side" (who are not-so-lovingly referred to as "deniers") thinks about climate change. If some are unable to open their minds and look at all possibilities, then I can't help that. People will believe what they will believe. If individuals want to be close-minded, then they have my permission to move on to the next chapter. If people continue reading, they might learn something that they would never hear from the mainstream media, global warming activists, or politicians.

On one side are the believers, and on the other side are non-believers. To some, climate change has become a religion. They have placed their complete faith in it – it consumes many people. It's a strange form of worship of a phenomenon they firmly believe is fact, or as they say, it is "settled science". However, more on that in another chapter.

I, too, was a global warming advocate early in the movement. I wrote a song about the rainforests being burned down. I watched the PBS programming. I watched "The Blue Planet" and the "Nature" series on Discovery channel and believed the message that we were destroying our planet at a shockingly fast pace – all of this due to carbon dioxide emissions from cars, planes, factories, coal plants, etc. I thought the Sierra Club was committed to reducing global warming, although I stopped short of sending them any money. I thought Al Gore was going to be a folk hero.

Then over the years, I started looking into the actual "settled science" because it seemed as though the folks touting global warming were on a warpath for those that showed any skepticism whatsoever in order to protect their theories (and their jobs). It made me stop to think that perhaps there was something else going on. Maybe there was an agenda. Maybe the science wasn't settled. Maybe too many people were emotionally attached to this THEORY. So, I began to question it and started looking at things through a different lens.

I also came to look at things from a larger time perspective. We all know for a fact that our Blue Planet goes through warming and cooling cycles. It just makes logical sense that we cannot come to any certain conclusions with such a small data set as 50, 100, or even 200 years. Yet that's what we are supposed to believe according to global warming scientists. Mankind's entire existence on this planet is but a blink of an eye when considering the life of our Earth, and our impact seemed to have been over-exaggerated.

Scientists who want to prove their projections about global warming attempt to do something that is at best pure speculation. That *something* is trying to predict and extrapolate what Mother Nature and our planet are going to do.

Since the time that the first bunch of rocks in our early solar system collided to form the Earth, our planet has changed every second of every epoch. The earth is in constant change. Things may seem to be stable, except for those times when Mother Nature rears the ugly side of her head, but our planet evolves at its own pace, and it does it ever so slowly. If we can't control it, how can we accurately predict it? I think that is a pretty reasonable question to bring up.

There was a feeding frenzy that ensued and still exists today regarding the subject of global warming. When a scientist tries to prove a theory, the lazy thing to do is to take initial evidence that confirms a theory and role with it as fact, and then take the firm position that it is "settled science".

True scientists will spend a great deal of time trying to disprove their own theory and get other scientists to assist in either confirming or disproving the hypothesis. That's what scientists do. They must ask themselves is the data flawed in any way? Where might my hypothesis have gone wrong? Scientists need to be doubters, not activists. We all know that statisticians can take data and twist it around to prove just about anything they want. The same is true for global warming scientists.

The scientific community has been trying to disprove Albert Einstein's theory of relativity for 100+ years, and physicists will continue to try and poke holes in his theory. It's not a personal vendetta against Mr. Einstein; it's just science. Some scientists have claimed to have proven Einstein wrong, but so far, the theory has stood the test of time, and an inordinate number of brilliant scientists will continue to test the theory. Is $E = mc^2$ called "settled science"? Many astrophysicists don't think so. If it were, no scientist would have to work on disproving the theory. Gravity is "settled science". The speed of light is "settled science". The Earth is round is "settled science". Even Einstein's equation is a THEORY of relativity – it's not "settled science". As Yogi Berra said, "It ain't over 'till it's over."

Someday someone may prove Einstein was incorrect, but as it stands right now, it's a pretty solid theory whose beauty, simplicity, and complexity are stated very succinctly and elegantly. It's hard to believe that the entire existence of the Universe is based on such an unpretentious equation. The amount of brain cells that have been used to try and disprove it is enormous. However, the theory has stood the test of time, and we will see if someone someday disproves it. Conversely, many climate scientists have determined that climate change is not worthy of any more questioning. The verdict is in. If Einstein's theory of relativity is not considered "settled science," why is it that so many people say global warming is "settled science"?

Another big problem is that global warming carries an enormous amount of emotional capital that has been spent on and attached to the subject. To the general public, the sight of a polar bear dying because of global warming elicits an emotional reaction. Those pictures have been used to try and move science from skepticism to emotionalism.

Alarmists back in the 60's and 70's predicted catastrophic damage was coming soon to "a theater near you". Please read on, because I want to make an important point in the discussion of climate change.

In 1970, Ecology professor Kenneth E.F. Watt at the University of California, one of the early prognosticators of global cooling boasted, "If present trends continue, the world will be about four degrees colder for the global mean temperature in 1990, but 11 degrees colder by the year 2000. This is about twice what it would take to put us in an ice age." This well-meaning professor touting gloom and doom certainly missed that one by a mile.

In 1988, James Hansen who headed up NASA's Goddard Institute for thirty years and is one of the best-known global warming scientists was interviewed by author and journalist Rob Reiss. Mr. Reiss asked Hansen to put into an everyday perspective how the "greenhouse effect" would affect his neighborhood. Hansen, who lived in New York City confidently stated, "The West Side Highway [which runs along the Hudson River] will be under water, and there will be tape across the windows across the street because of high winds. And the same birds won't be there. The trees in the median strip will change...There will be more police cars … [since] you know what happens to crime when the heat goes up."

Hansen also testified before Congress and stated that the Earth would be three degrees centigrade warmer within 20 years. Many climate change advocates claim that Hansen got it right, but other skeptics disagree with his statistical premises. Perhaps those temperature predictions are irrelevant since the effects of his predictions did not take place. Unless I am mistaken, the Hudson River has not flooded the West Side Highway. None of the changes he predicted came true.

Stanford University professor Paul Ehrlich, another global cooling doomsayer stated, "By the year 2000 the United Kingdom will be simply a small group of impoverished islands, inhabited by some 70 million hungry people. If I were a gambler, I would take even money that England will not exist in the year 2000 and give ten to one that the life of the average Briton would be of distinctly lower quality than it is today."

Frankly, I wish I could have taken him up on his bet. Ehrlich eventually threw in the towel regarding global cooling and changed his tune, later predicting that the Earth was headed for a catastrophic phase of global warming.

Michael Oppenheimer, Princeton University professor and lead author for the United Nations Intergovernmental Panel on Climate Change, made some dramatic predictions in 1990 while working as "chief scientist" for the

Environmental Defense Fund. He stated that the "greenhouse effect" would be "desolating the heartlands of North America and Eurasia with horrific drought, causing crop failures and food riots." He doubled down in 1996, adding that the Platte River of Nebraska "would be dry, while a continent-wide black blizzard of prairie topsoil will stop traffic on interstates, strip paint from houses and shut down computers." He also predicted that this climate problem would lead to this: "Mexican police will round up illegal American migrants surging into Mexico seeking work as field hands." Somehow, I think he might have missed those predictions by more than a mile.

Let us fast forward to claims by the UN Environmental Program in 2005 which issued some dire predictions that many coastal areas will be under water by 2010. They published a map showing the cities that would be inundated. They predicted that 50 million coastal residents would become "climate refugees." After realizing they made a giant leap to these conclusions based on highly flawed "data," the UN tried to cover up these outlandish predictions by removing the map from its website and removing all traces of their study because they "didn't want to cause any more confusion." Of course, they suffered embarrassment because we all know that anything posted on the internet lives forever – much to the chagrin of a lot of famous people and organizations.

Do all these predictions not seem like scaremongering to anybody?

Other dire predictions from the UN included a 2007 report that was originally heralded as preeminent proof by many global warming activists, calling it undeniable that global warming was "settled science." In the report, it forecasted that all Himalayan glaciers would be melted by 2035. The UN has since retracted their claims.

In 2000, the Climatic Research Unit (CRU) at the University of East Anglia predicted that snow would disappear in the UK. Strangely, over the past decade, the UK has seen a stark increase in snowfall.

University of East Anglia was in the eye of the hurricane (pun intended) of what came to be known as "Climategate" back in 2009. A small group of professors from this university were famous for their data that showed a "hockey stick" rise in global temperatures. Their "study" was the basis for much of the global warming hysteria that Al Gore and every other activist used to prove the planet was doomed, and it was all mankind's fault. An email server was hacked and some of the small group's emails contained some eyebrow-raising statements about altering data, deleting emails that alluded to hiding data from public release, along with other admissions that they used unusual statistical techniques to come to their conclusions. Of course, they denied everything and stuck by their predictions, but there's no hockey stick increase going on.

Global warming advocates exonerated these scientists, stating that the emails were taken out of context, while the climate skeptics jumped on this incident as proof of evidence tampering. No matter which side was right, the broader lesson is that climate change science is not beyond reproach, and we should always question and challenge scientists who have an agenda. Climate scientists must conduct themselves as scientists – they are NOT politicians, although many of them in the scientific community have become more like politicians than scientists.

Under President Obama, White House Science "Czar" John Holdren stated, "A growing body of evidence suggests that the kind of extreme cold being experienced by much of the United States as we speak is a pattern we can expect to see with increasing frequency, as global warming continues." Isn't it fascinating that global warming climatologists and activists can predict that the world will suffer a lack of snowfall because of global warming and then turn around and claim that an increase in snowfall is because of global warming? Huh? How does that work exactly?

It appears a pattern is occurring. All those individuals are "experts" whose dire predictions of global cooling that were touted didn't come true. Then the focus became global warming, and it now appears that we are in a slight cooling cycle. It seems as though whatever the alarmists try to predict, the opposite happens. Maybe that's why people fall off the climate change bandwagon.

And then there's Mr. Climate Change himself, Al Gore (formally known as Mr. Global Warming). Mr. Gore won a Nobel Prize and an Oscar for his movie, *Inconvenient Truth*, while flying around the world in his fuel-guzzling private jet leading the crusade against global warming – ooops – climate change, while collecting $175,000 per speech. He made tens of millions of dollars in green energy investments while selling a flawed and bogus narrative. He has bilked rich and not-so-rich people who bought into his storyline by investing their money in green ventures that never really produced anything useful, let alone a profit.

Gore's doomsday predictions in the movie have fallen woefully short. Multiple articles have been written describing the fact that his batting average for predictions is .000. One of his predictions stated that the North Pole would be free of all ice during summer-times by around 2013 because of alleged "man-made global warming." Obviously, the penguins and polar bears still have ice to play on during their summer vacations.

Do these missed predictions not bother climate change activists? Evidently not. Does it cause people to pause and honestly question the veracity of the climate change mantra? Obviously not. Isn't there a point where people come to their senses and just stop listening to these predictions? So far it appears that the climate change zealots are not ready to give up their religion despite all appearances that they just might be being duped.

Climate change predictions are based on gathering data and then creating predictive models. As shown above, predictive models can be dubious at best, and pure conjecture at the least. Because weather is random, the models and the data are forever changing. Mother Nature and Planet Earth know nothing about "models," nor do they pay attention to what global warming scientists say or predict.

Climate change has become a global road show where the protagonists in this Kabuki act must increase the level of fear in order to raise money to finance their income and their zealotry. Some, like Al Gore and numerous other actors, have gotten rich by conning people into believing the story line. Remember, they always emphasize that it is "settled science", and if we show the least bit of skepticism, we are labeled a heretical "climate change denier" that cares nothing about saving our one and only planet. Fearmongering among the climate change community is out of control, and when any argument that is contrary to their belief is put forth, they either attack or close their ears, but mostly they attack. At that point, it truly is zealotry, and may I say scientific bigotry, in action.

As stated earlier, it is a religion with fanatical radicals waging war on the non-believers. Rather than seeking the truth in a calm and rational adoption of the scientific method, data needs to be altered and suppositions must be extrapolated without any unassailable data just to prove that they are right. Needless to say, their batting average on their predictions would never get them to the major leagues.

Show me a weather forecaster who gets it right all the time. They are pretty accurate in predicting weather from day to day, but they still don't get it right all the time. Local weathermen are working on data that is generated to make short-term predictions. Trying to accurately predict weather a week in advance gets to be pretty spotty, let alone a year or decade from now.

Because Mother Nature and the weather are so random, logic would dictate that it is very difficult to accurately predict future outcomes. How can randomness be factored into warming predictions? If randomness is factored into climate change models, the result would be an infinite number of potentialities. Therefore, predicting climate change becomes an infinitely difficult task with an infinite number of possible outcomes.

From the *National Review* article by Ian Tuttle: "A 2008 survey by two German scientists, Dennis Bray and Hans von Storch, found that a significant number of scientists were skeptical of the ability of existing global climate models to accurately predict global temperatures, precipitation, sea-level changes, or extreme weather events even over a decade; they were far more skeptical as the time horizon increased."

Before a Senate subcommittee, Sierra Club president Aaron Mair, stated the famous "Ninety-seven percent of scientists concur and agree that there is global warming and anthropogenic (man-made) impact."

President Obama tweeted the same number, and John Kerry used it in an international speech. It has been repeated by politicians trying to drum up fear, with their only intent to garner votes.

Did anybody take the time to research where the statistic came from? How about a fact check? Or was it merely a useful tool to forward the global warming cause? Like any other statement, whether fact or not, if we repeat it over and over again, people will just accept it as the truth. They want the "truth" to be what they say it is; therefore, what they say and believe is the "truth."

So where exactly did that statistic come from? John Cook, who runs a website called skepticalscience.com is one of the culprits for spreading this false premise. It was first stated in his summary of a paper entitled, *"Consensus on consensus: a synthesis of consensus estimates on human-caused global warming."* Sadly, I am not smart enough to fully grasp exactly what they mean, but I digress.

Read what they said carefully. Cook et al. (2013) found that "over 97 percent [of scientists they surveyed] endorsed the view that the Earth is warming up and human emissions of greenhouse gases are the main cause." Note it was also purportedly validated by the authors of the paper through their own study of many of the scientists who participated in their survey.

Got it? They claim that 97% of the scientists' papers that were REVIEWED and those that responded to the survey agreed with the premise. Does that mean they (et al) reviewed every paper ever written on global warming? Or was it 97% of the papers they CHOSE to review and those that responded to their survey agreed with the theory?

Here's another way to look at how the 97% number was extrapolated - let's do the math. Cook and a graduate student sent a 2-minute on-line survey to 10,257 "earth scientists." Are there really that many "earth scientists"?

The first question in the survey was: "When compared to pre-1800 levels do you think [note the word "think" – no scientific proof was necessary] that mean global temperatures have generally [another opinion word] risen, fallen or remained relatively constant?" Ninety percent of the responses they "selected" answered "risen."

Question 2 was: "Do you think [there's that word again] human activity is a significant [how does one define "significant"?] factor in changing mean global temperatures?" The surveyors said 82% of those they "selected" to use answered "yes". This is important: they only used the responses from the 5% who claimed to be climate scientists. So out of 10,257 surveys sent and 3,146 responses, the total they used was 79 people – and they used only those surveys that were favorable to the conclusion they were seeking to find. So, it might be considered a stretch to say 97% of all scientists agree that there is man-made global warming, let alone 97% of all climate scientists.

The whole "97% of climate scientists" talking point has been bastardized and spread around the world but that statement is just not true – plain and simple. Further proof is below.

From a Forbes Magazine article by Alex Epstein that also analyzed the Cook paper: "…when the study was publicly challenged by economist David Friedman, one observer calculated that only 1.6 percent explicitly stated that man-made greenhouse gases caused at least 50 percent of global warming. [The study by] Cook is only able to demonstrate that a relative handful endorses the view that the Earth is warming up and human emissions of greenhouse gases are the main cause. Cook calls this 'explicit endorsement with quantification' (quantification meaning 50 percent or more)."

Epstein continued, "He [Cook] had also created a category called "implicit endorsement" for papers they analyzed that may roughly imply (but don't say) that there is some man-made global warming and don't quantify it. In other words, he created two categories that he labeled as endorsing a view that they most certainly didn't."

Some scientists whose papers were used by Cook (et al) to "prove" CO_2 and its effect on global warming were wrongly classified. Here's what some of these experts said regarding Cook's 97% conclusion and how their papers were misused in the study:

Dr. Richard Tol, Professor of the Economics of Climate Change, Vrije Universiteit, Amsterdam said, "…[the] Cook survey included ten of my 122 eligible papers. Five of ten were rated incorrectly. Four of five were rated as 'endorse' rather than 'neutral'… I think your data are a load of crap… I think your sampling strategy is a load of nonsense."

Dr. Craig Idso, Chairman, Center for the Study of Carbon Dioxide and Global Change said, "That is not an accurate representation of my paper … It would be incorrect to claim that our paper was an endorsement of CO_2-induced global warming."

When asked if the paper was a true representation, Dr. Nir Shaviv, Ph.D. Astrophysics, Associate Professor, Racah Institute of Physics, The Hebrew University of Jerusalem responded, "Nope... it is not an accurate representation... Science is not a democracy, even if the majority of scientists think one thing (and it translates to more papers saying so), they aren't necessarily correct... the analysis itself is faulty, namely, it doesn't even quantify correctly the number of scientists or the number of papers which endorse or diminish the importance of AGW." (Anthropogenic Global Warming – in other words, man-caused)

Dr. Nicola Scafetta, a research scientist at the University of Napoli Federico said: "Cook et al (2013) is based on a straw-man argument..."

Willie Soon, Ph.D., Astrophysicist and Geoscientist, Harvard-Smithsonian Center for Astrophysics said, "No extra comment on Cook et al. (2013) is necessary as it is not a paper aiming to help anyone understand the [global warming] science."

Nils-Axel Morner, Professor Emeritus of Paleogeophysics and Geodynamics, Stockholm University characterized the study as, "Certainly not correct and certainly misleading."

Alan Carlin, Ph.D. Economics, MIT Senior Operations Research Analyst, U.S. Environmental Protection Agency (retired) stated: "If Cook et al's paper is so far off in its classification of my paper, the next question is whether their treatment of my paper is an outlier in the quality of their analysis or is representative."

One can easily see that the Cook (et al) study is obviously plagued with erroneously classified papers and is fraught with false assumptions. Its conclusions are baseless and its promotion by those in the media, politicians, and global warming advocates is disingenuous and purposely used to mislead the public. It has been a convenient yet faulty tool that has been used to promote a misleading and false message labeled as an "inconvenient truth." They purported that it was "settled science". It seems like the above scientists had a different version of an "inconvenient truth".

"The climate model's understanding of the atmosphere is incompatible with the data ... the data is being suppressed ... this is not about science and truth, it's about power and politics," stated David Evans who used to work for the Australian Greenhouse Office (the main modeler of carbon in Australia's biosphere) from 1999 to 2005. He has 6 degrees, including a PhD from Stanford.

Famed journalist HL Mencken stated, "The whole aim of practical politics is to keep the populace alarmed — and hence clamorous to be led to safety — by menacing it with an endless series of hobgoblins, all of them imaginary. The urge to save humanity is almost always only a false face for the urge to rule it." Others have said climate change is not about climate, it's about control of the populace.

I'm beginning to think that the surreptitious endgame of the whole climate change movement is about controlling us. Climate activists will deny it but look at what they want to do. They want to control what we eat, what we drink, the kind of car we drive, how our house is built, how much electricity we use, how many kids we have, what kind of straws we use, and on and on. Does that not wreak of trying to control us? My fear is that the movement is opening the back door to socialism and more government control. It appears climate activists are using climate change as an emotional shaming tool and an excuse for taking over and controlling our lives. That might not be their intent, but the ultimate result certainly leads in that exact direction.

The other aspect to consider is that the poor will feel the brunt of the climate change push. If politicians raise taxes on energy, rich people will never even notice. If all houses must be converted to a greener footprint with solar panels or windmills, the rich can afford it. The middle class and the poor will suffer most from these policies and mandates. That really doesn't matter to the rich politicians who want to enact these save-the-planet measures, because they don't consider what impact these policies have on everyone else. Their inevitable and predictable comeback is that they will have to raise taxes in order to help those who can't afford to be "green compliant." Consequently, Jill and Joe Taxpayer in the middle class will be helping fund this "green new deal" – it will be just another tax burden piled on the back of the middle class. I can already hear the climate activists chiming in, saying, "We should not be thinking about money when the fate of our planet is concerned." That's easy for them to say, but a lot harder for the poor and middle class to swallow.

If celebrities like Michael Moore, Al Gore, and all the other rich advocates were so worried about climate change, would it not make sense that they would be spending their fortunes going into poor neighborhoods and making those houses greener? Wouldn't they want to buy electric cars for all the poor people who can't afford them? However, it is foolish to even ask those questions because rich people's money is far more valuable to them than ending climate change. Maybe it's time for them to put up or shut up.

In August of 2019, limousine liberal hypocrisy was on full display in Italy. Former President Barack Obama, Prince Harry, Katie Perry, Leonardo DiCaprio, and numerous other A-listers attended a Google climate change summit that cost Google $20 million. They all arrived via 114 private jets or enormous yachts and were chauffeured around in Maserati SUVs. Just the jets alone were responsible for putting more than 100,000 kilograms of carbon into our atmosphere.

What was to be accomplished? The agenda, according to Google was: "Mornings are filled with 'spirited discussions' on the environment, as well as on human rights, education and how to design cities of the future, while the afternoons are for pure relaxation and lots of food and drink." Now that's an action-packed, highly worthwhile endeavor if I've ever heard of one! Perhaps the summit should be more accurately called "Camp Hypocrite, 2019." I am pretty confident that a holier-than-thou moral authoritarian attitude was on full display in every summit session. I am also sure they solved all the climate change problems.

I think the celebrities and politicians should lead by example by giving up their gas-guzzling SUV's, their private jets, their luxurious yachts, and their enormous mansions. They should not demand that everyone else reduce their carbon footprints until they do it themselves. Trust me, that will never happen because the A-listers would rather degrade the standard of living for us common folk versus degrade their lifestyle and comforts. Real leaders lead by example, while faux leaders simply spew pablum and never do anything. We really should call their bluff to put up or shut up and see how they respond…

Climate change predictions that attempt to peer into the future, years or decades in advance and claim to be able to do that with absolute certainty are ludicrous. Sorry, but anyone with common sense would agree that short-term weather predictions are far more reliable than long-term predictions. Again, ask your local weatherman.

Reasonable climatologists (otherwise known as "deniers") do agree that our planet has warmed slightly. When it's all said and done, the actual global warming number many of the "deniers" agree on shows 0.8 degrees Celsius increase over the past 150 years. Another study found a warming of 0.9 degrees Celsius. The warming trend subsided in 2005, and actually shows a cooling cycle over the following decade.

Our planet's weather is too random to be put on a graph and predicted - not to mention the fact that drawing conclusions from data over a microscopic timescale in the life of Planet Earth is pure conjecture at best. One thing is for sure: when we try and predict what Mother Nature is going to do, it is futile, and She usually makes us look silly as we have seen from the bold and scaremongering predictions outlined earlier.

It's not heresy to question the science. It's not a mortal sin against Mankind as some would have us believe. Are they afraid to be wrong? Will climate change scientists, politicians and activists someday conclude that we can't accurately predict the future? I doubt it. Climate scientists would run out of grant money and be out of a job. Politicians would have one less panic-mongering thing to use to their advantage to get us to vote for them. Also, activists would have to move on to something else to protest and stay up late at night worrying about.

If we don't tap the breaks a bit, we will end up with the proletariat telling us what light bulbs to use (oops, that's already happened), what temperature to set our thermostat (ah yes, they can track that with our wonderful "smart thermostats"), how many plane trips we can take (but, of course the ruling class can take private jets while we schlubs suffer with the chickens in coach), and what kind of car we must drive (yes, some people want to ban SUV's and replace them with battery-operated cars).

Of course, all the important government people and all the sanctimonious actors and actresses are exempt from all that because they NEED them to get around. Is this starting to sound a little bit like the whole climate change push is about the ruling class controlling us? But naturally, it is necessary, and all of us regular people must comply.

Let me just go ahead and say it – this is a big pile of cow manure (which, by the way, according to them gives off toxic gases). If these knuckleheaded politicians, activists and scientists really cared, they would practice what they preach – but they don't, and they won't. They will just keep badgering us until we dutifully shake our heads in agreement, submit, and go on living like THEY say we should live.

We really need to take the emotion out of the discussion, step back, and get real on man-made global cooling (ooops), global warming (ooops), climate change (yes, that's it). We absolutely should be doing what we can to care for Mother Earth. We should be environmentally conscious because it's the right thing to do. However, making outlandish predictions about the world ending in twelve years and saying 97% of ALL scientists agree is demagoguery and alarmism, plain and simple. People aren't stupid, but they can be manipulated and that is exactly what appears to be happening. *"I Know We Are Better Than This."*

Chapter 24

Beautiful CO₂

Some people say that carbon dioxide is a pollutant. It is not. Those that purport that premise are sadly mistaken. Carbon is the sixth most abundant element in the Universe. There are 10 million known carbon compounds roaming around the Universe. There is carbon-14 which is used in dating organic and inorganic materials. There's carbon monoxide which is a poisonous gas. There are diamonds, graphite, and many other forms of carbon that are used in various commercial applications such as providing the fuel to produce electricity with coal.

Carbon dioxide is a wonderful little molecule - two atoms of oxygen, one atom of carbon. Life would not exist without it. Yet I once heard a global warming activist (who shall remain nameless) say that carbon dioxide is poisonous to the atmosphere. He really said that. Maybe he should go ask a tree or a flower how they like carbon dioxide. From my recollection of botany, plants really do like carbon dioxide because it is essential in their survival – the more the merrier. Plant life thrives in high carbon dioxide environments and they so kindly take in the CO_2 and spit out beautiful oxygen so animal life can exist. When plants thrive, they absorb more CO_2 and produce more oxygen. Animals living on land breathe in that oxygen and what they exhale is.........wait for it..................CO_2. It's a beautiful little symbiotic cycle.

Dr. Patrick Michaels, a contrarian climatologist, bucks the trend of believing in the current climate change models and the effect of CO_2. His credentials are considerable. He has been a Research Professor of Environmental Sciences at the University of Virginia for 30 years. He is a past president of the American Association of State Climatologists, along with serving as Program Chairman for the Committee on Applied Climatology at the American Meteorological Society. Further, he is a contributing author and a reviewer of the United Nations Intergovernmental Panel on Climate Change, which was awarded the Nobel Peace Prize in 2007. There are even more credentials, but enough said – he seems like a pretty smart guy.

Dr. Michaels was a guest on Mark Levin's TV show, *Life, Liberty and Levin* in October of 2018 and said that the Earth has warmed around 0.9 degrees in the last 100 or so years. Here's what he stated in the interview:

> "There are two periods of warming, one in the early 20th Century that could not have been caused by human beings because we hadn't put enough CO_2 in the air, and one in the later part of the 20th Century that either slows

down or ends, depending upon whose data you use somewhere in the late 1990s, only to resume with the big El Nino that covered the news the last couple of years.

So that means that probably about half, maybe half of that nine-tenths of the degree might be caused by greenhouse gases because when the planet warmed beginning in 1976, the temperature of the stratosphere started to drop and that's the prediction of greenhouse theory that's not intuitive.

So, the theory [of warming] is right, but the application of it is wrong. It is nowhere near as warm as it's supposed to be. The computer models are making systematic, dramatic errors over the entire tropics which is 40 percent of the earth, and it's where all our moisture comes from or almost all of it.

So, what's happened as it's warmed this half a degree in the late 20th Century and the CO_2 has gone up and up in the atmosphere, well, what we've done is we've created a greener and greener planet and the greening of the planet earth is profound. There's a very recent paper that just came out a couple of months ago, showing tremendous increases in how much green matter there is on the planet.

Prairies that cows either [graze] on or we harvest for hay, the data for 17 years of satellite data show the grassland, green mass, if you will, is growing at 5% per year. That's huge. [In] Another paper, '*Nature*' magazine by Ziaxen Ju two years ago looked at the planetary greening and said what are the causes? He did something called a factor analysis. Seventy percent of it was a simple direct effect of putting more carbon dioxide in the air because it's plant food."

When asked about the cause of the warming trend in the early 20th century, Dr. Michaels said:

"But we just don't really have a good explanation for that, but because we forced the computer models to say, 'Aha, human influence, CO_2 and other stuff.' We made the models too sensitive, and so that's why when you get to the late 20th Century, all of a sudden they're warming up like crazy and the reality is down here [pointing to the floor]. It was guaranteed to happen.

This was revealed in *Science* magazine in late 2016, and there was a paper that was published by a French climate modeler called 'The Art and Science of Climate Model Tuning,' and in it, he speaks of parameterizing -- we could say fudging -- the models to give, in his words, 'an anticipated acceptable range of results.'

So, it's the scientist, not the science that's determining how much it's going to warm. A lot of people don't know this, but it happens to be true."

The whole global warming school of thought was originally fueled by false assumptions based on what many reputable scientists like Dr. Michaels have called flawed data. We all know what happens when we assume something...

As has been discussed in another chapter, there is no proof that 97% of all scientists agree that man-made global warming exists. Truth of the matter is, we simply cannot predict what a short-term change in either warming or cooling may have in a long-term perspective. And if warming is happening and there is a slight CO_2 and a greenhouse gas increase, then Mother Earth is responding by getting greener around her waist (the tropics), and more grass is growing in the plains.

Back in the days of the dinosaur era, it is obvious that plant life and animal life thrived for tens of millions of years. There was a high content of CO_2 and greenhouse gases which allowed life to flourish far beyond what we see today. The Jurassic period had five times more CO_2 than we have today, mostly caused by an extremely active volcanic era that pushed high levels of CO_2 into the atmosphere. It was also warm and humid. Earth has never seen a more abundant amount of life.

It's likely not even possible for Man to produce enough CO_2 to get anywhere near the Jurassic levels. Back then, it took enormous volcanoes erupting all over the world on a constant basis to belch enough CO_2 to create a greenhouse effect. The point is, the greenhouse effect was a result of tens of millions of years of dramatic climate change. How can we humans come anywhere near what CO_2 was put in the atmosphere way back then? We can't. We are fooling ourselves.

We are not killing the planet. The models that predict the world will end in twelve or twenty years and the people that spew out that nonsense are practicing demagoguery. In my humble opinion, it's misguided hysteria.

Come on now, let's all calm down, get real, and stop all the panic-mongering to score political points and stop spreading untruths. At some point, we must stop and say, "*I Know We Are Better Than This.*"

Chapter 25

The Religion of Man-made Climate Change

According to the climate change guru's and activists, I am committing heresy by even writing this. I think climate change believers need to step back and honestly look at themselves and their behaviors. Periodically, we all need to do a sanity check on our beliefs – it's healthy and wise to do that. The believers in man-made climate change have transformed into the equal of a church, complete with a pope, disciples, deacons or elders, a choir, and a congregation.

Al Gore has been selected as the Pope or high priest in the church of climate change. He is the global evangelist. Every member of this religious sect looks to him for guidance and inspiration. He makes movies. He gives fire and brimstone sermons intended to scare the Hell out of everyone.

We are all going to Hell and the planet is going to die at our hands if we do not repent and give up our SUV's and air travel (except for Pope Gore and his followers) because we produce too much carbon dioxide. We must move out of our big, comfortable houses with air conditioning (except for Pope Gore and his followers) because they require too much electricity. We must all turn vegetarian (except for Pope Gore and his followers) because cows and pigs fart too much.

The disciples, otherwise known as scientists, hold conferences and gleefully endorse their fellow brothers' theories and hypotheses regarding climate change and write holy epistles that are blindly accepted as the Gospel. Skepticism need not be brought up because, after all, climate change is "settled science." Don't even bother to challenge because if we do, we are attacked and ridiculed. This is because the true science of climate change has been thrown out the window and replaced in many corners of the scientific community by religious zealotry.

Scientists are not supposed to be zealots who get emotionally involved in a subject - they are supposed to be skeptics who continuously challenge and probe. When scientists get too emotionally attached to a theory, they lose their neutrality. The scientific method must be devoid of emotion.

Scientists who say that man-made climate change is "settled science" and go on tour to start preaching the gospel, relinquish their license to be a scientist while exchanging it for ordination as a disciple in the church of climate change. They preach their gospel of global warming from their pulpits and pass the offering plate among those who are willing to give their money to the cause or fund research grants. They also hold corporations hostage by demanding millions of dollars for their "research".

Politicians, the deacons or elders in the church of climate change, also use scaremongering tactics to garner votes and get their constituents riled up. They seek to use climate change as political currency for their own advantage in order to defeat another candidate who might not accept it as "settled science". Politicians are out of their league when they start claiming to be experts and sling around the "settled science" argument of man-made climate change as is evidenced by the false claim that 97% of all scientists agree on global warming – ooops, sorry, climate change.

Campaign promises of replacing fossil fuels in ten or twelve years should be called for exactly what it is – utter nonsense. Calls for ending air travel and replacing it with high-speed rail transportation should not be taken seriously. Would these politicians be willing to give up their private jets, their power-wasting mansions, and their gas guzzling SUV's? Do people in their right mind think that's really going to happen? They want us to give up our resource-consuming conveniences while they live in luxury. Can one say, hypocrisy?

All the political posturing and proselytizing seems to be empty campaign rhetoric. The deacons and elders are more interested in pontificating about how mankind is doomed unless the congregation votes them into office. They say they can turn the rising tide around and save the planet. Again, I ask, why is it that the congregation must give up all those terrible carbon-producing conveniences, while the Pope, the disciples, and the deacons have no intention of doing the same? Perhaps they have convinced themselves that they are far more important than the congregation. I don't get it. It appears this group in the church might be suffering from a bad case of insincerity, but I could be mistaken. Or could it be a case of "do as I say, not as I do."

The media is the choir that is singing the praises in the church of climate change. They have latched their teeth onto the subject and are like mad dogs ready to attack if we try and take away their bone. They glorify and deify Al Gore, the extreme activists, the celebrities, and the politicians who accept and embrace the "settled science" position. Whatever happened to a media that was supposed to present both sides of the story and remain objective and above the fray? They left all sense of objectivity behind when they converted to believers.

Media members should be like scientists – always questioning, always seeking answers. Perhaps the answer is found in the fact that if media members dare to sing a different tune, they are castigated and banished to write for blogs and websites that no one has ever heard of or ever visits. Everyone in the choir must all sing from the same hymn book or face excommunication by the rest of the choir. To the media, the doctrine of the church of climate change is far more important than free speech and open-mindedness – and truth.

Dissenting opinions on man-made climate change are not tolerated in this choir. Free speech, which the media says is so important, is conveniently forgotten and dissenters are summarily shut down, their voices silenced, and then they are degradingly ridiculed. The heathens are called the "deniers" and labelled with a scarlet "D".

The congregation of the church of climate change is made up of ardent believers who attend the church services or rallies and listen to the sermons. They participate in climate change communion by drinking the Kool-Aid and chewing up the organic, grain-free wafers fed to them by the climate change disciples and deacons.

In order to be member of the church of climate change, individuals must renounce their right to have an independent opinion or ask any questions. They must relinquish their right of free speech. They must also fully commit their mind, body, and soul to the advancement of the crusade against the infidels who are skeptical of the dogma espoused by the Holy Climate Church. To be a member of the congregation, they must also hurl emotionally charged epithets at anyone who doesn't become baptized in the pristine and pious waters in the river of climate change. Finally, they must carry signs in public rallies that say, "We are killing our planet", or "The world is going to end in twelve years", or "Save the penguins and polar bears", or "Global warming is not a hoax", or "Deniers need to die." Yes, that was an actual sign at a rally.

Global cooling fears turned into global warming, which eventually moved to "climate change." I guess if they can't get it right, if they're not really sure what's happening and their predictions were wrong, they just change what they call it and that gives them a better chance of being right on something. It's pretty obvious that our climate does change over time. We have had ice ages, then warming periods. Mother Earth is a living, breathing organism that goes through cycles that are affected by external influences like the sun. Even a very large meteorite can have a sudden and catastrophic impact on our climate (pun intended). There are also internal influences like volcanic eruptions, earthquakes, and storms. Weather patterns are random and unpredictable.

Global warming alarmists will take any chance to say severe weather occurrences are a result of climate change. Extreme weather events have happened throughout the history of our planet. Making this claim weakens the climate change argument when every hurricane, every typhoon, every tornado and every lightning strike is a sign of climate change and the death of us all is imminent. What is the explanation for the lack of a major hurricane not hitting Florida, the gulf coast or the east coast for 11 years from 2006 to 2017? Was the lack of hurricanes a factor created by global warming? Some climate activists would say yes. I think not. A better explanation was that Mother Nature was just taking a nap.

To leap to these conclusions and extrapolate that global disaster is upon us because Mother Nature gets ugly occasionally is short-sighted and does nothing positive to forward the view that man is causing these events. It becomes tiresome to most Pharisees outside of the church of climate change. It seems rather disingenuous when they must stretch so far to prove they are right and say, "See, I told you so!" every time Mother Nature shows her wrath.

Call me in 1,000 years and let me know if fossil fuels and man had any effect on Planet Earth's climate. Until then, let's chill out, and do what we can to find ways to improve the lives of all inhabitants on our planet. Let's keep our own house clean and work to create a lot less trash. Let's find a way to create an endless supply of energy through nuclear technologies and real renewable power sources – not solar panels and windmills. Once this is accomplished, our ancestors can celebrate that we have become good stewards of what Mother Nature has provided us.

One can understand why many early believers like me have become skeptics. Chicken Little got everybody's attention, but soon, everyone just ignored him. It looks like that's what is happening outside of the church of climate change.

Pope Gore might want to climb down off the high and mighty pulpit. The deacons might want to tap the brakes a bit. The choir may want to try some songs out of another hymnal. And the congregation just might want to, at some point, call BS instead of saying "Amen."

It also strikes me as very strange (maybe disingenuous or hypocritical?) for members of the church to do things that don't back up what they espouse. For example, the Obama's purchased a $15 million house on the beach in Martha's Vineyard. Or how about Al Gore himself purchasing an oceanfront property in California for $9 million? Did they forget that both coasts will be under water in a few years? Instead of driving to their beachside homes, they will surely need a submarine, right? Or could it possibly be that they don't actually believe what they are preaching. It certainly makes one wonder, does it not? Perhaps it's another inconvenient truth...

Scientists should more honestly characterize their prognostications as wild guesses and sheer conjecture versus touting them as "settled science." When someone makes incredible claims that don't come true, credibility rapidly erodes, and arguments are weakened rather than strengthened. Let's just be honest. Yes, we must take care of our planet, but it is not necessary for everyone to join the cultic church and worship at the altar of man-made climate change. I keep thinking, "*I Know We Are Better Than This.*"

Chapter 26

Let's Talk Nuclear and Renewable Energy

In speaking about the clean and efficient production of energy, we must focus on what's PRACTICAL, not what makes us feel good. The renewable energy industry is supposed to provide us with a warm and fuzzy feeling that we are reducing the use of fossil fuels, but is what we are doing the right thing? Is our current state-of-the-art in renewable energy technologies the answer?

Our homes and businesses are powered by generating stations primarily using fossil fuels, which is what climate activists and many politicians are up in arms about. The use of carbon-based power generation produces a CO_2 byproduct that is purportedly causing our planet to warm itself – the greenhouse effect. Right now, we don't have any better alternatives to make sure that the lights are on, microwaves can cook, and most importantly, our cell phones and Wi-Fi services are operational. The world would go into melt-down mode if those conveniences were not available.

So, if fossil fuels are nasty sources, where do we turn to make sure we have the electrical power that is critical for our world to function?

One of the big lies perpetrated by politicians and climate change activists is that nuclear energy is just as much, if not more evil than carbon-based fuels. This fallacy is based on fear that nuclear power is closely akin to and potentially as destructive as nuclear bombs. It's absolutely not true – they are totally different technologies.

Yes, there have been nuclear power plant disasters, but in truth, no one died from the Fukishima catastrophe, no one died from Three-mile Island's melt-down, and in the world's worst nuclear disaster, around 200 people died because of Chernobyl. Since 1952 when the first nuclear power incident occurred in Chalk River Canada, there have only been 33 incidences of a nuclear accident, the majority of which were minor and non-destructive in any way.

Nuclear energy does have its downsides, but when compared to burning fossil fuels, creating millions of acres of solar farms or hundreds of thousands of wind turbines, there really is no comparison. By far and away, and at this point in time, nuclear power is our best alternative. Are we really going to clutter up our environment with "renewable energy" eyesores just to make climate change zealots feel good? Renewable energy as we know it today is a bad practical joke that is being played on a gullible group of believers.

Nuclear energy produced by fission has been with us for 80+ years. It is a stable, safe way to produce energy. Yes, it has nasty byproducts, but these issues are far more manageable than the serious environmental problems renewable energy presents.

There was an interesting article on Quilette.com written by Michael Shellenberger titled "Why Renewables Can't Save the Planet." Mr. Shellenberger is an American author, environmental policy writer, and cofounder of Breakthrough Institute and founder of Environmental Progress. He is also an avowed environmentalist and climate change advocate, and he stated, "The reason nuclear is the best energy from an environmental perspective is because it produces so little waste and none enters the environment as pollution."

He added, "We tend to think of solar panels as clean, but the truth is that there is no plan anywhere to deal with solar panels at the end of their 20 to 25-year lifespan."

We are not thinking through the environmental impact of current state-of-the-art renewable power, nor are we investing in the right technologies. We have virtually flushed hundreds of billions of dollars down the toilet – but hey, it's only money – we have plenty of it – we'll just print more!

To Mr. Shellenberger's point, what's going to be left behind is a giant pile of rubbish that cannot be easily or efficiently recycled because of the toxic heavy metals such as lead, cadmium, and chromium contained in solar panels. At the end of their lifecycles, what do we do with the mess that's left? Do we just throw it in a landfill?

Speaking of a giant pile of rubbish – remember Solyndra? In 2009, President Obama decided to hand out 535 million of our taxpayer dollars in loan guarantees as part of his famous economic stimulus plan. He characterized the company as, "The true engines of economic growth will always be companies like Solyndra." Their inexpensive (ha ha), easy to install solar panels were supposed to revolutionize the global renewable solar energy market. Everyone was so excited.

The company was a giant failure, which was certainly an enormous stimulus to their executives who got very rich. We taxpayers were stuck with the bill for $535 million when Solyndra filed for bankruptcy in less than TWO years after the handout was given. The founders of the company should have been brought up on fraud charges, but, of course, they were not. They lied about their technology and their manufacturing capabilities, and the whole ugly incident was just swept under the rug and ignored by the mainstream media and our political leaders. There was no outrage – everyone just shrugged their shoulders and said, "Nice try, thank you for playing, you really were trying to do something great for the planet."

Another boondoggle was the Obama administration's $5 billion program to "retrofit homes and businesses in America so they are energy efficient." After several years, the House of Representatives investigated the program and found a "stunning lack of oversight" of this program. Contractors did shoddy work and ripped off the taxpayer because our government didn't hold these shysters accountable. Oh well, it's only money was the flippant attitude. Yes, but it was OUR money.

And then there's wind turbine technology. Environmentalists and animal lovers should be up in arms about the devastation being wrought on endangered species such as hawks, eagles, owls, and condors – not to mention what it does to disrupt the lives of animals on the ground – plus the effect it has on humans. A while back, I was flying over the vast wind turbine farms in Northern California. I stopped to consider the environmental damage that was done and the huge amount of resources and energy to produce these monstrosities. I also thought what a terrible eye-sore it was for a beautiful landscape. One must stop and ask, "And we do this because?"

According to scientist David Hughes who has researched, published and lectured widely on global energy and sustainability issues, the average 2 megawatt windmill contains 260 tons of steel, requiring 170 tons of coking coal, and 300 tons of iron ore, all of this mined, transported and produced by – you guessed it – hydrocarbon fuel. These white beasts are enormous. I've seen them being transported down the highway. The fins alone are longer than the average 18-wheeler.

Think about it. Wind turbines are also a primitive tool. They have been in use for thousands of years, and they are practical for some things and have come in quite handy for various uses. Harnessing the natural power of the wind is great, but realistically, it can only take us so far without the utter destruction of our beautiful landscape.

Globally, we have invested, or should I say "subsidized" to the tune of $100 billion annually in wind power - and what do we have to show for it? About 1% of our power is generated with wind. Does that kind of investment and cluttering up our countryside really make sense? It's time to fully analyze the effectiveness of these programs and question the sanity of what we are doing.

The push for solar energy and wind turbines continues to drag on, and we have not made a giant leap forward yet. Yes, we should continue to look at energy sources beyond carbon-based fuels, but there are a lot of downsides to solar and wind energy harvesting. There are environmental issues that must be considered as mentioned. I fear that we are not looking in the right direction. At some point, we must stop and think if we are investing billions and billions of dollars into renewable energy sources that will pay dividends down the road. Are we even on the right road? It's essential that we consider the downsides of where current technologies are leading us.

Another thing about renewables. Many politicians, scientists and activists are getting bogged down with the push for renewable energy these days. They don't really consider what it takes to produce a solar panel, a wind turbine, or batteries to store all this energy so it is available on demand. Batteries are nasty little things that require an inordinate amount of energy to produce – not to mention the fact that they are so environmentally unfriendly that one car battery can pollute a small lake for centuries.

Lead-acid, NiCad, and lithium-ion batteries pose a greater threat to the environment than the carbon emissions of our cars. We know by now that lead is dangerously toxic. We know that nickel oxide hydroxide and metallic cadmium (NiCad) batteries are toxic and very bad news for the environment. Lithium-ion batteries are terribly lethal as well. It requires an inordinately large amount of power to recycle many of these toxic metals and the whole process is costly and inefficient – and some are not even recyclable.

Energy stored in carbon-based fuels is far safer and less intrusive than the enormous batteries required to service and store power at the levels we require. We are at the mercy of power and for us to maintain our lifestyles, we need carbon-based fuels right now. The release of energy is there on demand when we plug into an electrical outlet or we turn on the ignition to start our cars. The stored energy is released when we need it.

We have cleverly figured out that gasoline is a very portable means for energy storage and usage; whereas solar and wind-produced energy must be stored in---yes---batteries. These are not your ordinary little batteries that power cell phones or even a car battery. The batteries required for "green energy" storage are made up of massive banks of very toxic and environmentally unfriendly materials as discussed.

Electric cars are a good example of a nice idea whose practicality is dubious at best. They require a bunch of, you guessed it, nasty batteries that must be replaced every few years. They cost a fortune, they require a large amount of energy to produce, and again, they are not environmentally safe nor are they easily recyclable.

Estimates from the Department of Transportation say there are 265 million passenger vehicles and between 6 to 7 million commercial vehicles in operation in the USA. Replacing all those vehicles any time soon is pure fantasy, not to mention a gargantuan environmental disaster in terms of billions of batteries required in the USA alone. Sometimes we need to stop and think about all the unintended consequences of our feel-good efforts to save the planet, all the while destroying it with nonsensical solutions that can bring on even more damage.

This is not to mention the amount of power that is necessary to produce a car. Where does that power come from? It certainly doesn't magically appear at the factories. It requires huge amounts of raw materials and energy to produce the metal, the plastics and all the components that make up a car. And then we must put it all together using assembly machines. Finally, when their usable lifecycle ends, they either must be recycled, parked in our vehicle junk yards, or dumped in a landfill.

One telling example of the impracticality of our current green energy technologies is what Daniel Turner outlined in an article on RealClearEnergy.com. According to data collected from peak usage, New York City requires 11,500 megawatts of power. Let's do some math and see what 4,000 acres of solar panels would provide in terms of power. It's hard to picture 4,000 acres of solar panels, so let's put that into perspective. All of Central Park comprises 800 acres, and those people that have ever seen Central Park know it's a massive park right in the middle of Manhattan. So, it would require five times the acreage, and that many solar panels, according to Mr. Turner, "… will provide enough power to almost run the New York city subway system." Imagine the acreage necessary to power the entire city.

What happens when there's a rainy day and enough power is not produced to run the subway? Commuters would go crazy. We don't even have to do the math to realize that powering New York City would require an inordinate amount of land for solar panels and thousands of wind farms. Where do we store that energy for that cloudy or rainy day when we need it? The number of batteries required to store and serve a city the size of New York would be mind-boggling. Again, as we all know, batteries don't last forever and recycling them would consume a vast amount of energy and leave us with more toxic waste that is not recyclable. Does any of that make sense in terms of practicality? According to activists and politicians, it's the right path for us to go down. If we think that renewable energy will be able to keep up with our demand, and we will be able to manage all the byproducts, we are sadly mistaken. It becomes a ludicrous proposition to think that solar panels and windmills are the answer.

I believe we need to stop fooling ourselves into believing that wind and solar power on a large-scale is practical - and it will never be practical. If we are seeking new forms of energy production, we need to set our sights on technologies that have a much better upside without destroying our landscape and polluting our planet with an enormous pile of toxic waste.

We've got to get real about this. I am by no means an energy expert, but it seems as though we are wasting our time and resources on solutions that may work on a small scale such as powering a house, but delivering enough power to a large city just seems to be an enormous task that solar power and windmills are not remotely capable of accomplishing here in the real world. That's where we need to live – here in the real world.

We need to stop bashing nuclear energy and re-think how we can safely and economically harness the power of the atom. The biggest advantage of nuclear energy is that it emits virtually no carbon pollution into the atmosphere. Now that ought to get the attention of climate change advocates. Other pluses are that it requires a great deal less in terms of materials for production, and it produces far less waste. The energy density of the fuel determines its environmental and health impacts. Nuclear energy is the best solution given our current alternatives.

Two young entrepreneurs from MIT, Leslie Dewan and Mark Massie, are touting the use of a molten-salt reactor that uses a liquid uranium salt as fuel. Their system claims to utilize half the fuel of current fission reactors while producing less than half the waste materials. They also say the containment system in case of an accident is far safer than current fission technologies. These two scientists have resurrected and improved on some early nuclear power designs that can potentially advance nuclear power generation on both small and large scales.

There are other examples of power generation technologies that have been developed that would be beneficial to carbon reduction. NET Power, a start-up venture with a demonstration plant in LaPorte, Texas has developed some interesting technology. As stated in one of their press releases, "The plant is designed to demonstrate NET Power's Allam Cycle technology, which uses a new turbine and combustor developed specifically for the process by Toshiba. Using carbon dioxide (CO_2) as a working fluid to drive a combustion turbine, the Allam Cycle eliminates virtually all emissions from natural gas power generation without requiring expensive, efficiency-reducing carbon capture equipment...NET Power and Toshiba are poised to provide the market with the industry's first natural gas power generation technology that is low-cost, flexible, and carbon-emissions free."

Examining these types of energy technologies is a far more productive activity than bulldozing billions of dollars into the solar and wind power money pit.

Mr. Shellenberger's article also stated, "I thought the solutions were pretty straightforward: solar panels on every roof, electric cars in every driveway, etc. The main obstacles, I believed, were political. And so I helped organize a coalition of America's largest labor unions and environmental groups. Our

Chapter 27

The Pollution Problem

It doesn't take too much digging to realize that we have a global pollution problem that is only going to get worse if we don't do something about it. I can agree with the environmental community on that. Note that I am not talking about carbon emissions, I am referring to pollution on the ground and in our oceans.

After examining climate change, let's look at the damage being done by a few countries and see if we can learn something.

According to a report from the Ocean Conservancy and the McKinsey Center for Business and Environment, there are five major countries that contribute 60% of all plastics that are polluting our oceans: China, Indonesia, the Philippines, Thailand, and Vietnam. Because of the strong economic and population growth of these countries over the past 30 years, inhabitants of these nations are able to afford more stuff. Rather than smartly plan landfills and encourage recycling, these countries dump their trash, including an enormous amount of plastics, straight into the oceans. Every environmentalist should be screaming to the high heavens.

Logic would dictate that the more these countries grow and industrialize, the more trash and plastics will end up in the ocean and on our shores. Why do we let them get away with it? Why is there no outrage? Why doesn't the global community hold these countries accountable? Why aren't environmentalists marching in the streets of Beijing or Shenzhen? Oh, I know why – they would wind up in a concentration camp or quietly and conveniently be executed for crimes against the government. Where are the protesters in Jakarta? Manila? Bangkok? Hanoi?

A recent report in the journal *Nature* revealed that a small island called Cocos that is northwest of Australia and south of India, Thailand and Indonesia showed a shocking amount of debris had washed up onshore and more was buried under the sand on the beaches. Among the rubble was 977,000 shoes, 373,000 toothbrushes, and an estimated 400 million pieces of different types of plastics.

There are ten rivers in the world that carry 90% of the plastics deposited in the ocean. There are two in Africa, the Nile and the Niger rivers. Wonder where the other eight are located? You probably guessed it – India, China, and Eastern Asia. The numbers are startling. Those 8 rivers deposit 2.25 million tons of plastics each year. The Chang Jiang (Yangtze) river alone deposits 1.47 million tons. I had to let those numbers sink in for a few minutes. Those people are rapidly burying us and our oceans in plastics. It's mindboggling that we let them get away with destroying our planet. I wonder if it is caused by laziness, ignorance, or if they just don't really care. It seems like their attitude is to just throw stuff in the river and let the river take it somewhere else. That solves their trash problem and screws things up for everybody else - not to mention what it does to our oceans and wildlife.

Every member of the UN that is concerned about our environment should be fighting this barbarity - and it truly is barbaric. It is grossly gluttonous and should not be tolerated. People in our country are banning the use of straws while an estimated 30 billion pounds of plastics are floating around in our oceans – not from our addiction to straws, but from other countries carelessly dumping plastics into the oceans.

It's a good thing that our oceans are so vast. Otherwise, we would be overcome by the trash and plastics from those countries that don't give a damn about ruining our planet. Who knows, we may get their attention if the global community would put its foot down. The biggest offenders must be held accountable before any progress is made toward cleaning up our oceans.

I have been to Beijing and had the displeasure and bad luck of being there during an air pollution crisis. When we were landing in the middle of the afternoon, it appeared as if the city was fogged in. I didn't think anything of it until I stepped outside. It was not fog - it was air pollution.

I recall getting into my hotel room, opening the curtains, expecting to see a nice view of downtown Beijing. Instead, I literally could not see the buildings that were maybe 2 blocks away. It was truly disgusting and appalling. I kept asking myself how the government and the people would sit idly by and let this kind of thing happen.

Speaking of pollution, let me also hark back to my younger years. Part of my youth was spent in Southern California during the early sixties. I remember the smog alerts that happened. I recall playing outside all day and feeling my lungs ache from the smog. It, too, was disgusting. I give Californians credit because they recognized that we needed to have cars that ran more efficiently, and the catalytic converter was invented along with other techniques to reduce emissions. Californians can be proud that they recognized a problem and did something about it in a fairly short period of time. It was necessary. Far too many cities and countries around the world have not placed a high enough value on clean air and clean water in our oceans, lakes and rivers. Their people will pay the price – and so will we.

There are other pollution problems beyond our air. China and India have enormous populations compared to the USA. They are by far and away the biggest polluters on our planet when it comes to air quality, carbon emissions, and trash. Those two countries combined make up 36% of our planet's population. The USA, the third most populous country, totals 4.3%. The USA has virtually the same land mass, but China has 4.1 times more people, and India has 3.2 times more people than the USA. India is the worst in terms of population density with a land mass that is one third of ours, but a population that is 3.2 times larger. Other statistics include: China has 151 people per square kilometer; India has 460 people per square kilometer; the US has 36 people per square kilometer.

The whole point of bringing these statistics up is two-fold. First: when there is a larger population density as in China and India, one can easily surmise that pollution and environmental damage done will be far more severe and exponentially more concentrated than here in the USA. Pollution concentration directly correlates with population density. Recall that we make up 4.3% of the world's population. The top 5 polluters make up roughly a third of global population. Add in India and we have about half of the world's population producing an inordinately large amount of pollution just by shear population.

It doesn't take a rocket scientist or mathematical genius to understand where our pollution problem lies globally. It seems to me that environmentalists need to focus more of their attention on where the bulk of the problem lies. The problem is not the US – it is the rest of the world. Yet we are constantly berated by environmentalists for being the biggest pollution culprit, but that is FAR from the truth.

Second: When we look at the broad picture, the USA and Western Europe are so far advanced in terms of environmental consciousness than most other countries. Yes, we do need to make a conscious decision to be smarter than we have been about a lot of things having to do with our planet. However, until the rest of the world gets on board in a big way, the efforts from 4.3% of the population will have minimal impact on global pollution.

The good news is that here in the US and Western Europe, we have responded and realized the necessity of pollution reduction. Yes, the environmental movement in the US and Europe has made a positive impact on our countries in reducing pollution and raising our awareness.

Here in the USA, we have changed a lot of our behaviors when it comes to respecting and protecting our planet. Environmental activists will say we have not done enough, and we will not have done enough until all pollution in the

USA has been eliminated. That is a rather lofty and unachievable goal, but we can certainly keep our own back yard clean.

The bad news is that most of the rest of the world that is far more densely populated than the US has not done much to stem pollution. Environmentalists really need to focus more attention on the areas of the world that do the most damage. Until those five countries that produce the most pollution and environmental destruction obtain the same level of awareness and activism as Europe and North America, our global environmental status will continue to deteriorate. It's not our fault. It stems from the lack of attention by people and the leadership of our most populous countries. It baffles me why those countries are not being held accountable by the rest of the world. Perhaps it's a case of thinking ignorance is bliss.

The point of reality here is, if we reduced our pollution to zero, we still would not be able to save the planet from being overrun by plastics and other pollutants that other countries produce. Yes, we can lead the way, but until the rest of the countries doing by far more damage than we are take this matter seriously, whatever we do will be virtually for naught. We cannot save the planet from pollution by ourselves.

Both the global community and the environmental movement need to come down hard on the countries that do the most damage. But the UN, the body that could exert the most pressure, does not seem to really take this matter seriously. Maybe it doesn't want to offend anybody by calling them out. Members are far more worried about a lot less important things than taking action against the major polluters. It appears the UN doesn't want to hurt the feelings of those 5 countries that are the biggest polluters. If it had any guts and truly cared about our planet, the UN would get in their faces and demand some real action.

We don't need any more studies from the UN or anybody else to prove that we have a global pollution problem. If the UN really thinks, as its reports say, that our planet is in danger, then why doesn't it exert more pressure and hold the major polluters accountable? Where is their outrage? Where is OUR outrage? Instead, members of the UN look down their noses at the USA while turning their backs on where the real problem lies. When the feckless UN doesn't hold countries accountable, then it is complicit in these crimes against our beautiful blue planet. Shame on those nations that produce most of the pollution for not educating their people on the damage they are doing. If the rest of the global community does not turn the heat up on these pollution producers, shame on us. As a global community in the 21st century, *"I Know We Are Better Than This."*

Section 8

The Wrap

Chapter 28

The Wrap

So, what does the future look like? A logical outcome of where we are heading does not look promising unless we right the course. At times, our evolutionary journey has been wrought with societal pain, and then we bounce back and regain our balance with some semblance of normalcy and stability. Societies will always experience tension, and sometimes there will be all-out war. Perhaps the good and peaceful times are the end-result of conflict, and the pain and suffering are the only pathways back to that peace. However, common sense dictates that it doesn't have to be that way.

When we look back at our recent world wars, or any war for that matter, we see horrific tragedy, not only for the losers, but the toll is steep even for the winners. Actually, nobody wins in war except those companies that make products to wage war. Outside of that, there are only losers. Both sides merely call an end to the battles, pack up their tents, go home, survey the damage done, and then reflect on what just took place. There is generally a time of peace that follows – perhaps mostly because of the weariness of the fight. Don't misunderstand – there are beneficiaries when people are liberated from oppression, but the cost of war in terms of human capital and money is immense, while the hangover is painful.

I do believe we are at a crossroads. As a country, we began with a solid moral foundation, built up a nation the likes of which had not been seen before through hard work, determination, ingenuity, and perseverance. Unity was a critical factor in our early successes and continues to be critical for our national well-being. Yes, there were differences of opinion within our Founding Fathers. Birthing a nation was an arduous task; the labor was long and exhausting and the delivery was very complicated. However, what held the group together was the desire to form a nation like no other. Despite their differences, they found unity in the ideal of human rights and liberty. That was the bond that linked everything together and it facilitated the compromises necessary to reach agreement.

Yes, we experienced societal tension – even a gut-wrenching civil war (I never understood why we call it "civil" because there is nothing civil about war). However, the sense of unity was the common denominator that helped us through all the challenges we have faced and overcome. There is tremendous power in unity, and there is a vacuum created in disunity. What fills that vacuum is discord, disagreements, and division. Where there is unity of purpose, there is an unspoken bond that holds things together, even when dissention and internal conflicts arise. Societies work best when founded on commonality, and countries become dysfunctional without it.

I liken what is going on in our nation today as similar to what happens when marital strife hits a couple. There are certain external forces that contribute to an erosion of trust and comfort. It produces hurt feelings, emotional disarray, household chaos, and constant turmoil. All marriages experience most, if not all those things. Those marriages that survive when times are tough are usually reconciled when each spouse lays down their differences and goes back to the foundation upon which the marriage was built: mutual admiration, respect, love, and the need to feel "oneness" once again. As marital relationships deteriorate, the road to reconciliation begins when both parties strip away all the rancor and anger and get back to why they were attracted to each other.

The road to recovery will most likely not be totally smooth but rebuilding on the original foundation is necessary. When asked the question of how couples repair a relationship, a counselor once said, "It really is simple – do what love would do. The couple must re-learn and reenact those things that married couples do. They must get back to the basics and what they have in common and what got them together in the first place."

The same is true for our country. We must strip away the disagreements and be willing to get back to what made our country great. The walls that have been erected to divide us must come down. We must lay down our prejudices, and we must put away the weapons of division in order to move toward unity.

When a society comes to a juncture where two differing opinions prevail, civil debate and discussion should take place. When both sides relegate their arguments to name-calling and derogatory accusations, the debate is over. It is truly a sad state of affairs when any kind of debate spirals into chaos and screaming. Yes, we can defend our positions with emotion, but reasonable people should not present false representations and discuss their ideas using hyperbole and hysteria.

Uncivil discourse is a learned behavior. Followers mimic the example set by their leaders. Our country is being let down by leaders that we elected. Far too many political leaders exhibit the abhorrent behavior of insulting and denigrating the opposing viewpoint. Both sides are guilty. Unfortunately, we have not only tolerated it, through our tolerance, we have endorsed it and allowed it to infiltrate deeply into our culture.

Political dialogue is supposed to be an intellectual, reasoned discussion where both sides calmly, sanely, and rationally present cogent arguments for their beliefs, minus over-the-top emotional pontification or scaremongering. If our current leaders were able to do that, our country would be a lot better off than it is now. Tensions would not rear their ugly head, animosity would not rule the day, and our society would be far more peaceful than it is now. A leader intent on ending the polarization and discontent will hopefully emerge at some point – at least that is my hope, and it should be everyone else's as well.

When we are unified, we are an indefatigably powerful force for good in this crazy world of ours. Regrettably, it generally takes a catastrophic event to shake us and bring us back to unity. Recall how we engaged in a united front when the Japanese bombed Pearl Harbor. Remember the feeling during and after the 9-11 attack. We were united. We all felt the outrage, and we all felt the angst of what transpired on those fateful days.

We all witnessed the tragic events, but we all worked together to recover and heal. Afterward, we were the UNITED States of America. Petty disagreements were set aside. The swords of internal strife and discontent were laid down, and we picked up our tools and started to rebuild.

God forbid that another tragedy is the only way to bind us together again. We are smart enough that it shouldn't be that way. However, I fear that with all the modern distractions and influences, and with all the negativity and finger pointing, we will struggle to find unity. We must not sit idly by and simply hope for the best. Yes, we all need hope, but hope will never get us anywhere without action. I am reminded of the old adage, "give a little, get a little." What we need is to find common ground amongst our differences, be open to compromise, come to a reasonable agreement, and then move forward. We need to "do what love would do."

There is no doubt that we need leaders who will inspire us to reach new levels of cooperation. Yes, leaders can have a positive impact, but they can also sow division, which, unfortunately is where we are today. Our recovery must originate as a groundswell that begins at the local level. I believe it all starts in the family, and even more specifically, it begins inside each one of us.

Recall what Rev. Jasper Williams, Jr. said, "Whatever way the home goes, that's the way the world goes. Did you hear me now? As the home goes, so goes the streets. As the streets go, so goes the neighborhood. As the neighborhood goes, so goes the city. As the city goes, so goes the state. As the state goes, so goes the nation. As the nation goes, so goes the world."

The human feeling of attachment to unity emanates from individual interaction. The government bureaucrats and politicians in Washington DC are in their own world and are detached from local neighborhoods. The real action that can move us closer to unity is right where we live – in our homes and in our neighborhoods.

In observing how political discourse has changed and unity has deteriorated over my lifetime, it becomes obvious that it has turned for the worse, not the better. When John F. Kennedy was elected president, the country was not polarized, we were all pulling in the same direction. Yes, there were political disagreements between liberals and conservatives, but nothing near what is occurring today. Back then, politicians were still able to lay down their swords and were willing to seek compromise in order to maintain unity.

I believe the political chasm is widening as a result of us living in a much more complex world today than past generations have faced, which means our challenges and differences are more complicated. Life in our country used to be much simpler. Living a happy life was far easier and far less complicated.

As we have gotten smarter and smarter in terms of our knowledge base, I believe we have become dumbed-down in many ways. It seems as though as we have become smarter, we are less reliant on each other, we are more egocentric, and we don't value that feeling of community like we used to.

Perhaps part of the problem is that we have way too much free time on our hands. After all, "idle hands are the devil's workshop." An 18th century person's primary goals were to work long and hard to put food on the table and make sure their family was safe. Now, a 21st century person is worried about making sure their cell phone doesn't go dead so they can check Facebook and Twitter and deciding such important things as where they want to eat out for dinner.

Most people would agree that we have become more polarized, and the divide between us is getting wider. One must ask, is this a reflection of the culture and the morality we have let deteriorate? I think so. As we have progressed in technology and knowledge, have we degenerated in terms of human interaction and relationships? It seems as though that is the case.

Have our individual egos and self-centeredness clouded our ability to get along with our fellow man? It seems as though that is the case. Thankfully, not everyone has the "me-first, I am the most important person on the planet" attitude, but the trend does not look promising, especially among the younger generations.

We are not as dependent on each other for our well-being as we have been in the past – we have progressed (or regressed) to the point where "community" has lost its importance. I think that is another contributing factor that has led to divisiveness. We are trending toward withdrawal from our feeling of community with each other which is mostly driven by ugly political discourse, the divisive media, and a focus on all our differences versus what commonalities we share. Too often, it appears that the only time we are a community is when disaster strikes. It shouldn't be that way.

Community is defined as "a group of people living in the same place or having a particular characteristic in common." In addition, it can mean a "feeling of fellowship with others, as a result of sharing common attitudes, interests, and goals." Obviously, the word is a combination of "common" and "unity".

People are more comfortable and live happier lives when they feel a "oneness" with their community, whether it is with their family, school, neighborhood, state, or country. We feel safer and more at-ease. Divisiveness and societal tension make us feel uncomfortable, leading to dissatisfaction and unhappiness which causes us to withdraw from the community. I believe that is a major part of the contentious environment we are living in today.

If we ignored all the BS that is going on within DC, we would be a lot better off. If we turned off the TV and other media devices and stopped listening to all those pompous, pious politicians and biased media folks and just started using some common sense when it comes to interacting and settling disagreements, we'd be a lot better off. The constant complaining, bickering and partisanship is inappropriate and unproductive – but the talking heads in the media get paid to sow discontent and focus on victimhood, while the politicians get our votes and then do absolutely nothing to improve relations. Why would they stop doing it? They'd be out of a job if we all got along, so their mission in life is to do what they do – be negative, be divisive and constantly complain about anything and everything. The sad thing is, they think we like it – and we must like it if we keep voting some of these despicable people into office.

We must, however, hold our government leaders accountable. If they choose to mislead us, we need to vote them out of office. If they choose to behave badly, we need to get rid of them. If they choose divisive over unifying rhetoric, they need to go. If they do not listen to their constituency, they need to pack their bags. If they are intent on being uncooperative and uncompromising, they need to find another job.

Our founding fathers did not envision our elected officials to make a lifetime career out of politics. Their vision was for elected officials to come to DC, serve a term or two, and then go back to their community. With the current quagmire in our capital, the case for term limits seems to be a much better option. One has to think that career politicians accumulate too much power, and that a new batch of fresh faces every few years would be a better alternative. The founding fathers certainly did not expect representatives to go to DC, serve multiple terms, and then retire as millionaires, which is what happens to most politicians these days. But I digress.

Calmly listening to and trying to understand other viewpoints will not solve all our problems, but it seems to me it would be a logical place to start. Instead, we are currently mired in mud and slinging it at each other.

The baseline where we must begin is that we are all human and we are all fallible. We all want to live in peace (well at least most of us do). We all want our children to grow up safe and in a healthy environment. We all want to enjoy life – it goes by way too fast for us to waste our lives away on hatred and dissention. It's also wasted energy that could be used in a positive way.

I realize a lot of this book was focused on the many things that ail our society today. My goal was to examine the problems we face and issues we must deal with. I don't purport to have all the answers. However, together we can find the answers. We can choose to take a different pathway, and we must remind ourselves that it is a choice. We can choose to be united, or we can choose to be divided. We can choose to keep yelling at each other, or we can choose to be civil. We can choose to seek common ground, or we can choose to focus on our differences. We can choose inclusion, or we can choose exclusion. We can choose to keep our rights, or we can choose to relinquish them. We can choose to be free, or we can choose enslavement. We will make the choices. I only hope we make the right ones.

I believe that the key is in making the right choices to change our course, and it will require a gradual cultural shift toward higher moral standards. There are two or three generations living now that must be re-educated in terms of morality. This group must be taught the powerful value of individual responsibility to strengthen our society. We must turn our hearts away from selfishness to selflessness. We must listen. We must learn. We must cooperate and compromise. We must give and we must be grateful. We must tap into the wisdom of great teachers and authors. We must cherish our freedoms. We must show respect to people. Yes, that's a pretty long list of "must-do's," and I'm sure we can add to it. And one more. We must reject the notion that creating safe spaces is necessary for our survival as a species.

We must also be ever diligent about defending and maintaining our freedoms. Without them, we will be in an even worse place than where we are now. We don't need government control; we need the people to be in control. The less government intrudes in our lives, the better off we are. The fewer non-elected bureaucrats we have, the better off we will be.

We cannot do anything about the past except learn from it. Dwelling on the past essentially restricts us from living in the here and now, while also darkening and even blinding our outlook for the future. Claiming victimhood is self-defeating and shackles a person with disadvantage.

We are not trying to accomplish the impossible; we merely must do the right things that benefit ourselves and our neighbors – that's where unity starts. Having a successful free society is a lot of hard work that requires a lot of discipline. We'll never see Utopia. Dreaming the impossible dream does not accomplish anything – hard work and determination are what creates success and actuates what enables us to accomplish our dreams. We are certainly more capable of producing a society where we humans can have differing viewpoints yet peacefully coexist. We cannot get there without recognizing that it takes a lot of willingness to have a giving and accepting mindset.

We must admit our faults and frailties, for without that step, we cannot walk forward into the future. We cannot accept the status quo. In order to start our recovery, we must take personal stock in ourselves, look around at our neighbors and countrymen, and we all must come to an agreement that we can solve our problems, and we must do it together. I believe in the following quote whose author is unidentified:

> Tell the truth...even if it costs you something.
> Do what's right...especially when no one is watching.
> Do the right thing because it's the right thing to do.

We better get busy changing who we've become as a society and recalibrating our moral compass. I believe that's where it all must begin.

There are many attributes wrapped up in morality, including honesty, integrity, decency, humility, civility, respect, a giving heart, an accepting attitude, selflessness, accountability, individual responsibility, law-abiding, and tolerance. Most of all, there must be a willingness to live and breathe all those attributes. Doing so will lead us to a more meaningful life, and we will have a more united nation. We must set an example for future generations to learn the importance of a strong moral code and adopting all the beneficial attributes that make a society great.

Yes, there are many challenges ahead for our nation and our world. No one can see into the future and know how we will respond, but we can get a glimpse by looking inward and examining our own attitudes and priorities. Currently, we are not rising up and conquering the challenges we face because we are too busy antagonizing each other.

We are getting distracted by so many things that take our focus away from where it should be – working together to solve problems. We are not communicating well enough. We must stop talking down to each other and throwing verbal hand grenades. Nothing is accomplished in confrontation; everything is accomplished through cooperation.

As pointed out in this book, there are numerous vexing problems that we are faced with both domestically and globally. Finding the solutions will be difficult, but we must relentlessly pursue them with determination and a positive outlook. In this journey toward resolving society's ailments, we must avoid decisions based strictly on an emotional response and let common sense and practicality lead the way. The best course to take is out there ready for us to find, but we cannot be distracted by or ruled by emotion or hostility. We also cannot live in the past, always looking in the rear-view mirror, because our solutions are up ahead. Problems are based on past events, while solutions are out there awaiting our discovery.

John F. Kennedy gave us all some good advice when he said, "Let us not seek the Republican answer or the Democrat answer, but the right answer. Let us not seek to fix the blame for the past. Let us accept our own responsibility for the future."

I do believe we can do far better than our current performance. We are too smart to let things deteriorate further. I hope we can all agree in saying, "*I* **KNOW** *We* **ARE** *Better Than This*." Let's begin the real work.

Acknowledgements

As I have learned, writing a book is as hard as it sounds! A project of this magnitude is time-consuming and tedious, and as it turns out, more rewarding than I ever imagined. This comprehensive piece of work required contributions from numerous people who deserve recognition and my heartfelt thank you. First of all, a special thanks to my wife of forty years for giving me the latitude and the time to accomplish my life-time goal of writing a book. A big thank you goes out to all my great and diverse family members and friends for their encouragement and support, and for being wonderful contributing members of our society. A very special thank you to my editor, Suzanne Berry, for her invaluable contributions in sanity-checking content, her grammar correction skills, her depth of knowledge of the sometimes-enigmatic rules of the English language, along with her overall guidance.

About the Author

B.R. Allen, a retired Vice President of Marketing, is a typical, yet perceptive person who has always had a passion for writing. Mr. Allen is actively tuned into observing and then responding to the numerous cultural fires that are breaking out in various sectors of our society. He was inspired enough to write about what is happening to our culture and the problems that are eroding our foundational principles. In his book, *I Know We Are Better Than This*, he provides his own brand of insights and interpretations, while suggesting how to improve our declining morality, eliminate our combative attitude, clean up our disgraceful public discourse, and alter our divisive behavior.

www.ingramcontent.com/pod-product-compliance
Lightning Source LLC
Chambersburg PA
CBHW060315030426

42336CB00011B/1055